WITH NAPOLEON AT WATERLOO

NAPOLEON

From the marble medallion in the possession of the Editor

WITH NAPOLEON AT WATERLOO

AND OTHER UNPUBLISHED DOCUMENTS OF THE WATERLOO AND PENINSULAR CAMPAIGNS

ALSO PAPERS ON WATERLOO

BY THE LATE

EDWARD BRUCE LOW M.A.

EDITED WITH AN INTRODUCTION BY

MAC KENZIE MAC BRIDE

WITH THIRTY-TWO ILLUSTRATIONS

The Naval & Military Press Ltd

Published by

The Naval & Military Press Ltd

Unit 5 Riverside, Brambleside
Bellbrook Industrial Estate
Uckfield, East Sussex
TN22 1QQ England

Tel: +44 (0)1825 749494

www.naval-military-press.com
www.nmarchive.com

I have to acknowledge my indebtedness for kind help to MRS RYDE-JONES ALEXANDER, MISS FLEMING, MR ROBERT T. ROSE *of Edinburgh,* MR SAMUEL HALES *of Newman's Row, Lincoln's Inn Fields, and to* MR GEORGE PREECE *the courteous chief Librarian of the Borough of Stoke Newington. I believe the late* MR BRUCE LOW *was indebted to* COLONEL GREENHILL-GARDYNE *of Glenforsa for the loan of the diary of* SERGT. ROBERTSON.—*Ed.*

CONTENTS

CONTENTS

CONTENTS

WELLINGTON AND BLUCHER

Facing page xii

LIST OF ILLUSTRATIONS

PORTRAITS

xiii

xiv   LIST OF ILLUSTRATIONS

PICTURES OF WATERLOO

*From the Drawings made by Capt. Jones, R.A., immediately after the
battle was over. By kind permission of Mr George Preece, Librarian
of Stoke Newington*

WITH NAPOLEON AT WATERLOO

LIEUTENANT GENERAL SIR RALPH ABERCROMBIE

Facing page 1

INTRODUCTION

THE manuscripts which make up the present volume are of unique interest and importance. The Journal of Jardin Aîné, Napoleon's Equerry at Waterloo, here translated and published for the first time, was in the library of the late Sir Thomas Phillips, the great collector of manuscripts. On the sale of the library at his death it passed into private hands, and so has escaped notice up to the present. It, and the account of another Waterloo eye-witness which follows, make an interesting chapter in the history of the great battle which altered the fate of the world more than any struggle of modern times has done, indeed, perhaps more than has been done by any battle since the world began.

Next in importance are the extracts from the journal of Daniel Nicol, a soldier of the Gordon Highlanders, who gives an account of the doings of a company of his regiment which was left behind in Spain and served under Wellesley at the Passage of the Douro and at the battle of Talavera. In addition to the fact of it being a singularly vivid human document, the diary adds much to our knowledge of several important events. On this point Colonel Greenhill-Gardyne, the historian of the Gordon Highlanders writes, ' I only wish I had had it (The Diary) before I published *The Life of a Regiment*, although it supports all the information I had it would have added some details of the actions of Egmont op Zee and Alexandria, and particularly the account of the 92nd company at the Passage of the Douro and Talavera, of which there is no other account extant that I know of.'

Sergeant D. Robertson's diary has been long overlooked and forgotten ; from it are taken the account of the Gordon Highlanders in the Retreat to Corunna, at the storming of

A   1

Aray del Molinos and at Waterloo. Robertson, a Perthshire man, joined a volunteer company in 1797 but, desiring a more active life, enlisted later in the Caithness Highlanders (Fencibles) commanded by Sir John Sinclair, and was sent with the regiment to Ireland in 1798. An invitation was sent to the Fencible regiments then in Ireland to join the Egyptian expedition under Sir Ralph Abercrombie and Robertson joined the 92nd Highlanders. In addition to the Waterloo campaign described in the following pages he served in Egypt, Walcheren, Denmark, Sweden, Portugal, and Spain, leaving the army in 1818.

Besides their historical value these diaries throw an interesting light on the character and education of the men who then formed the Highland regiments; for example, the following incident, related by Nicol when in Portugal— 'About this time I was on picquet duty and was planted sentinel on a bridge over a river that runs in the valley, at daybreak I commenced to read a book, Butler's *Hudibras*, when in a moment a lusty friar made his appearance at the end of the bridge. This rather startled me, he saluted me, and was very friendly, looking at the frontispiece of my book, he exclaimed "Oh Hudibras ! you are a bon Christian," and, pointing upwards and clapping me heartily on the shoulders, told me I was sure to go to Heaven. He gave me five reas, a copper coin of less value than a halfpenny, which I put in my pocket and carried for many a day as I did not wish to offend one who had so high an opinion of my being a Christian. But I had doubts of him, for a few minutes after, I saw him taking particular observation of a newly made battery on the road leading up to the heights.'

Nicol, in fact, always seems to have had a book about him, though to-day it would astonish us to find a private soldier reading a book like *Hudibras*, but in those days education in Scotland was a solid thing. Further proof of this is afforded later where he tells how in the cathedral of Alcobace, the priests 'who offered great civility to our troops,' showed them two brass chains hanging from the roof from which they said two gold chandeliers had been carried away by the French. The parish schoolmaster had done his duty so well by Nicol that he was able to tell the priest 'in the best Latin he could muster,' which was so good that the Padre 'readily understood,' that he did not think the priests such fools as to allow gold or silver utensils to remain in their churches after they knew an enemy to be in their country.

At Coimbra the men visited the Royal Library in which the interpreter told them were books in every language in the universe. On this Sergeant MacBean, a sturdy old Highlander of the Gordons, began to speak in Gaelic to the professor and students who formed a ring round them. They were completely baffled, and afterwards MacBean made a boast that he had beaten the learned professors of the most learned town in Portugal. Nicol seems also to have been strongly possessed of the 'historic sense' as is shown in his remarks on entering Egypt. 'We were now upon Scripture ground,' he says, 'we had come from a distant island of the sea to the country of the proud Pharaohs to carry on war where Nebuchadnezzar and Alexander the Great, Cæsar and the other warriors had put armies in motion.'

Sergeant Robertson when left to himself is also a clear and intelligent writer, occasionally he is indeed, very graphic and poignant, as when he describes with so much interesting detail the retreat to Corunna and the scene on the battlefield the day after the terrible night attack at Alexandria in which Abercrombie was killed. 'After the action was over,' he says, 'we were ordered to go and take all the wounded of both armies, and carry them to the boats. . . . It was truly a horrible sight to see French and British writhing in the agonies of death and making friendship who had only a few minutes before been filled with rage and hatred at one another —all their fierce passions stilled, and like a hushed child, taking one another into their dying arms.'

It has been the invariable custom in teaching history to centre the story round the few great men who acted as leaders in our wars; the imagination of the British citizen is filled with this picture of the General on his horse directing his troops. Of the horrors of the stricken field he has little idea, or of the extraordinary exertions, privations, discomforts, which are suffered chiefly by the common soldier in the ranks. Of the real warfare no accounts with which we are acquainted give a picture anything like so graphic as the words of the actual soldiers themselves, such as are here given, and such as Mr Forbes Mitchell's graphic story of the doings of the Sutherland Highlanders in the Indian Mutiny.

If the lot of the common soldier in Mitchell's day was

not a happy one that of the soldier of the Napoleonic wars was at least a hundred times more miserable. He was badly paid, his pension when he got one at all was small, he suffered from all kinds of petty tyranny from officers often possessing half his own experience ; and rain and frost and snow, hunger and thirst and weariness, were his familiar friends. Amongst the officers were many fine and kindhearted men like Abercrombie, Moore, Rowland Hill, Doyle, Napier of Blackstone, and Macdonell of Hougoumont fame, who were loved by their followers, but others there were who at times had the same absolute power, but seemed to have been entirely heartless and indifferent to the comfort of the men.

Promotion from the ranks though of everyday occurrence in the French army was almost unknown in ours, and in reading these diaries one cannot but be impressed at the unfairness and the foolishness of a system which made it possible for men of the high stamp of Nicol and Robertson to go unrewarded by a commission. Robertson was orderly-sergeant all through the terrible retreat to Corunna, was frequently then and at other times placed in command of a company and in charge of the colours ; at Waterloo he commanded two companies, and on many occasions showed great capacity and initiative. If ever a man deserved a commission he did, yet he was allowed to leave the army entirely unrewarded for most distinguished services.

In view of all these things, and especially of the fact that, while honours were showered upon the officers which must have in many single instances cost the nation far more than the paltry rewards meted out to entire regiments of rank and file, one cannot help being impressed with the great debt we owe these intrepid soldiers of Egypt and the Peninsula, without whose steadiness and splendid instinct for giving to their leaders the best that was in them, Britain must inevitably have become a province attached to a great Napoleonic Empire.

By an accident it happens that the writers of the two diaries from which extracts are here given, belonged to one of those regiments of Highlanders whose doings in the wars of this period read like a chapter out of Froissart or some old romance. The grandfathers of these men had been out in the ' Forty-five,' and had learnt in long centuries of clanship that noble virtue of loyalty. They wrought with a thoroughness that knew no stint, and raised the dignity of the British soldier of the line by their superior education, manners, and conduct, but above all by this habit of romantic devotion to a leader or a cause which they had made their own. How badly we have rewarded them may be seen from the depopulated state of the Highland counties to-day.

One word more : in the Journal of Napoleon's Aide-de-camp a translation of which is given on page 190 an attempt is made to belittle Bonaparte by suggesting that he showed cowardice during the last few.hours at Waterloo. It is as absurd as the attempt to make light of the great success of Wellington. At the last the rats leave the sinking ship, and even the members of the fine staff of Napoleon could not all be as heroic as Ney or the constant and indomitable Soult, but fortunately we have the account of Napoleon's last stand given by a witness whose interest was opposed to the French and who had been forced into an unpleasant and dangerous service. This was the Belgian Lacoste who says : 'He was perfectly calm, and showed great *sang froid* during the action, and that on one occasion, seeing a battery close to his own position was not working well, he dismounted, ascended the height of the road, advanced to the piece and rectified the error, whilst the bullets were flying around him.'

Equally unfair is the attempt to minimise the generalship of Wellington. This point is dealt with late in the present volume by Mr Bruce Low in his ' New Legend of Waterloo.' Napoleon had done well in many lands in fighting with his splendid armies against nations which in modern times, had never before put great forces into the field and had therefore none of the experience acquired by the troops of France in a hundred battles. It was not surprising that the French were uniformly successful. Where all are blind the one eyed is king and Napoleon with his wonderful ambition and con-structive policy was then able to enslave half Europe. When he came to meet born soldiers like Moore, Wellington and Abercrombie, it was different ; the British had been obliged to fight for very existence for centuries and had a great military tradition behind them. Napoleon's conventional methods of warfare were good enough for the Russian peasant or the Portuguese and Spaniards, but his best generals like Soult and Ney, Victor and Foy were beaten by Wellington's captains and were hopelessly outshone by Wellington himself. In an interesting paper on 'The Evolution of the Thin Red Line,' * the late Mr Bruce Low has pointed out that Wellington had realised a new truth in warfare and instead of meeting Napoleon with Napoleon's own antiquated methods he opposed to his vast columns of infantry the British 'Thin Red Line.' As Wellington himself said of Waterloo—'Napoleon did not manoeuvre at all. He just moved forward in the old style in columns and was driven off in the old style. The only difference was that he mixed cavalry with his infantry, and supported both with an enormous quantity of artillery.' Napoleon was obviously outclassed.

MacKenzie   MacBride

---

* Published since going to press in *Chambers's Journal*.

I

WITH ABERCROMBIE AND MOORE IN EGYPT

FROM THE UNPUBLISHED DIARY
OF SERGEANT DANIEL NICOL

DANIEL NICOL

THE soldier to whom we are indebted for the graphic details which follow was Daniel Nicol, a native of Crossford in Lanarkshire, his grandfather being tenant of the farm of Nemphlar under Lockhart of Lee. Young Nicol was caught by Lord Douglas's gamekeeper while poaching in the Clyde, and was to have been brought before the sheriff at Lanark. To avoid this exposure he made his way to Edinburgh and enlisted on the 12th March 1784, in the regiment of Highlanders then being raised by the Marquis of Huntly. He mentions that, after being taken to the Council Chambers and passed by a surgeon, he received a red jacket turned up with yellow facings, white trousers, and three ostrich feathers stuck in his hat.

It was not till he reached Aberdeen that he received his full uniform, a short jacket faced with yellow, a kilt and bonnet, in time for King George's birthday on the 4th June ; and shortly afterwards the whole town was en fête when the news arrived of Lord Howe's great victory gained on the 1st June over the French fleet off Ushant. A treat was given to the soldiers in town, who paraded over the links 'where a bullock was roasted and twelve hogsheads of porter set abroach. Dancing and sports were kept up to a late hour, while the Freemasons, with the trades in town, walked in procession with their emblems, etc.' He adds : 'Some fine looking men were brought for our regiment by Captain Cameron of Fassifern, and on Tuesday, 24th June, the regiment was embodied by General Sir Hector Munro. The test of fitness set by the General was that each man should run past him for fifty paces, when only one man was rejected being too old.' The Gordons then numbered seven hundred and sixty men, of whom seven hundred and fifteen were Scotch, chiefly from the northern counties, many speaking only the Gælic language ; there were

9

also thirty-two Scoto-Irish, twelve English, and one was a Welshman.

Nicol saw service of a most interesting kind in the suppression of the rebellion in Ireland ; and after engaging in the expedition to Holland, where he took part in the battle of Egmont op Zee, he passed through the whole campaign in Egypt from Aboukir to Cairo.   After a spell of garrison-work in Ireland and in Glasgow, the corps was sent to Denmark and Sweden in 1807 and in the following year on its return to England, was despatched to Portugal.

E. B. I.

CHAPTER I

CAPTAIN LIVINGSTONE

WE sailed on the 24th of June 1801 under sealed orders, leaving the ships of the Channel fleet behind us. We had a very quick and pleasant passage to the Straits of Gibraltar, where our ship ran foul of an American merchant vessel and damaged her much. Our commodore informed us that our destination was Minorca, there to join an expedition that was forming under our old friend Sir Ralph Abercrombie to assist the Austrians in Italy. We passed through the Straits but did not touch at Gibraltar and on the 17th July fell in with the *Bulldog* gunbrig on her way home with despatches; they told us that Malta had surrendered. We had very light winds off the coast of Spain in passing Yvica and Majorca, and arrived at Minorca on the 21st of July. We then learned that Sir Ralph Abercrombie and Lord Keith had been at Genoa and had offered to land 6000 troops, which offer had been refused by General Melas. On 14th June the battle of Marengo was fought, which sealed the fate of Italy and the French got possession of the country. Many of the inhabitants of Genoa were actually on the point of starvation and supplies of provisions were sent to them from the British fleet. Lord Keith arrived on the *Foudroyant* 80, and Sir Ralph in the *Kent*, 74.

Disputes arose betwixt our officers and the captain of the ship about having the regiment inspected on deck. One day he bawled out, 'There is but one God in heaven, and only one commander on board his Majesty's ship *Diadem*; and I am he—Thomas Livingstone.' This his crew knew well for he was a tyrant.

The regiment was ordered out to bathe and swim and a number of us swam ashore. I took my canteen and a comrade had a Spanish dollar so we sent for wine and were sitting on the beach enjoying ourselves when unfortunately General

Foxe and his suite came riding past.   He ordered us all to be
taken to the main guard.   In a moment we jumped into the
sea and, by diving among some small vessels lying near the
shore, got all clear off except Corporal John MacDonald of
our company, who was caught by an aide-de-camp and taken
naked as he was to the main guard.   All the others got on
board safely except myself who, having a canteen slung round
my neck was nearly drowned when one of the ships' boats
came to my aid.   An oar was put under me and I was raised
up and taken on board insensible.   A shocking thing it would
have been if I had been drowned in this condition, but the
Lord has ever been merciful to me.   Next morning the
swimmers ashore were put in irons and we lay at the wardroom
door for thee days.   One of my comrades had secured my
canteenfull of wine, which had been searched for by the
master at arms.   On the third day all hands were piped up to
see the swimmers flogged for going on shore without leave ;
but being all men of the very best character, it was decided
that one should suffer for the whole.   Lots were drawn and
the lot fell on James Gardner, who took his punishment very
contentedly.

Corporal MacDonald was tried by garrison court-martial,
and our company having given most of the offenders was sent
ashore to see the sentence carried out at the back of the
quarantine island.   This was a mess we had got into innocently
enough ; it was the first offence with most of us and nearly all
the squad rose to be useful non-commissioned officers.

The troops were landed for refreshment and exercise and the
vessels cleaned out.   Our regiment landed at Georgetown where
lay the 42nd and 90th regiments.   Wine was very cheap here,
about 3d. the bottle and rum and brandy sold for about 5d. the
bottle, so many a gallon was drunk with our old acquaintances
in these regiments whom we had not seen since we left the
Rock.   Bread was dear.   On the 7th of August Colonel
Erskine ordered us all to get sober as it was our turn to take
duty to-morrow.   I was made corporal on the 12th of
August 1800, and mounted Little Bay guard at the back of the
fort.   Our regiment was inspected on the glacis by Sir Ralph
and General Foxe and we were paid up on to the 24th of July.
I got liberty to go to Port Mahon, one of the chief towns in
the island ; it has some good streets and buildings.   In the
dockyard undergoing repairs was the French ship *Genereux*,
eighty guns, taken while trying to escape at the battle of the

Nile and the *Guillaume Tell*, taken at Malta. I returned to Georgetown by water on 30th March 1806. We got blue pantaloons and black gaiters served out. Lieutenants George Fraser and Gordon's wounds broke out afresh and both officers were sent back to England.

Minorca is of great service to Britain, it having a large harbour with water so deep that war vessels can come within a few feet of the shore. It is well sheltered by hill and there is plenty of fresh water which makes it very serviceable to our fleets in the Mediterranean ; but now that Malta is in our possession it is not likely we will retain them both. The harbour is well defended by batteries on one side and by Fort St George formerly St Philip on the other. The chief town is Crudadella about 30 miles from Port Mahon ; it is very strong, with batteries cut out of the solid rock and mounted with heavy guns ; four regiments were doing duty here. The island has a barren appearance and most of the articles here are brought from other ports of the Mediterranean. The inhabitants appeared to me to be smaller than the generality of Spaniards.

We embarked on the 30th and sailed on the 31st. Colonel Erskine got the regiment transferred from the *Diadem* where we had been very uncomfortable to the *Stately*, 64, Captain Scott, who was quite a different character from Captain Livingstone ; it was a pleasure to be on board his ship. We had very light winds and came close on the small island of Alberan, half-way between Spain and Barbary. On the 14th September we anchored in Tetuan Bay to the south east of Gibraltar belonging to Morocco. Here the fleet completed its stores of provisions and water and on the 29th sailed with a light breeze ; passed the Spanish garrison of Ceuta on the north point of Africa opposite Gibraltar which is, I believe, very strong ; some gunboats are stationed there ready to take an advantage when it offers. We thought we were to attack this place, so that we might command both sides of the straits. In this we were mistaken, but the garrison gave some of our vessels that came within range a salute of round shot, which our men of war were not slack in returning.

CHAPTER II

WHY THE BRITISH DID NOT TAKE CADIZ

On Wednesday the first of October we anchored in Cadiz bay alongside our blockading fleet. On the 3rd the fleet and troops under command of Sir James Pulteney arrived. They had sailed from home in July and had attempted in August to cut out the Spanish fleet at Ferrol but did not accomplish it. They then put in at Vigo Bay where they lost the *Stag* frigate. They had just kept the enemy's coast in alarm, as we had been doing.

The *London*, 98, arrived and anchored close to us. Four days' provisions were served out on the 6th and we got sixty rounds of ammunition and everything was made ready for the landing which was to be near the town of St Mary's. The war vessels had taken up their position and the 1st division of the troops were in the boats and were moving off for the shore, when a flag of truce was sent out from Cadiz to the Admiral's ship. Some of our gunbrigs were fired on by the batteries and we could see the Spanish troops running along the beach to oppose our landing. Meanwhile the flat-bottomed boats continued to move towards the shore when a gun was fired from the Admiral's ship and a signal hoisted for the boats to return and put the troops on board their respective ships. We were struck with the suddenness of the change, which was received with discontent by the whole army.

A report was spread that the place had been ransomed by money. Be that as it may some agreement was come to the terms of which will probably never be known to us. There was one thing however, and perhaps it was the only reason, that prevented our landing; Yellow fever was raging in Cadiz at the time. The troops were very anxious to land as they had been a long time afloat, and we thought that with an army of 30,000 and a large navy, we could easily have taken the place, especially as we had come unexpectedly upon them and they had few troops to make resistance. But doubtless our chiefs knew their orders and they also knew that it is a Briton's right to grumble.

Cadiz has a fine appearance from the sea studded with fine white houses round the bay to St Mary's. We left the bay of Cadiz on the 7th returning to Tetuan Bay and part of the fleet put into Gibraltar. We anchored in a semicircle, the war vessels outside the transports to prevent the Spanish gunboats from molesting them. One of them had tried to surprise one of our storeships in the night time but was chased under their own fortifications by our guard boats.

On the 15th the north-east wind rose to so great a height that our boats which had gone with empty casks to get water, were obliged to return to the ship and leave the casks, after being filled on shore, and the storm kept increasing as the night came on. There was much rain, lightning and thunder. All was bustle among the shipping. Our cable slipped and we began to drift; we then let go our best bower cable and anchor; the vessel caught fire by the cable running over the bitts and was only extinguished after great exertions by the seamen. We still kept dragging, so we were obliged to slip and put to sea. This was done at great risk, for we were in the midst of a large fleet, and were in danger of running foul of one or other of the ships. Although the night was very dark and the vessels were crashing against each other, yet by the goodness of God we steered clear and got up our staysails. All our boats were on board except a large flat-bottomed one which was dragging at our stern; in the morning nothing of it remained but the keel and the ring bolts by which it was fastened. On the 16th we were close on the coast of Spain and out of our large fleet saw only a storeship. We took her in tow with a hawser but were nearly pulling her under water so she had to throw off. In the afternoon we put right before the wind and made for Gibraltar; got round Europe Point and went down the bay under shelter of the Rock, thinking we were safe out of storm but, as we passed the *Foudroyant*, the Admiral ordered our Captain to lay about his ship and pass through the Straits round Cape Spartel to No. 7 on the west coast of Barbary, the rendezvous for all vessels leaving Tetuan. Our captain said that he had lost his anchors, was in want of provisions, etc. To this the Admiral replied, 'I don't care a d—; you must go where you are ordered.' At this we were not at all pleased, as it had the appearance of being a dismal night and I recollected the fate of the *Courageux* which was dashed to pieces while getting out of the bay.

We put about accordingly and passed through the Straits before the wind, going about eight miles an hour under bare poles. On the 17th it still blew very hard; we set the foretopsail and tried to bear up to No. 7 but it would not do. A gun got loose on the lower deck and cleared all before it and some men were hurt before it could be secured. Shortly after this the foretopmast yard broke and came down, the sails flying like ribbons; two seamen were hurt, one had his thighbone broken. We ran along the coast of Africa, keeping the land in sight and the weather becoming moderate we came to anchor about four miles from the shore off the town of Sallee. A boat was sent ashore with one of the lieutenants to inform the Governor, who sent us a bullock which was very acceptable as our rations of late had been flour and salt pork; the Governor got some gunpowder in exchange for his bullock.

On the 20th the wind changed and we steered back again and joined the fleet at the appointed place, got our damages repaired, and received an anchor from the *Ajax*; we then set sail and anchored in Tetuan Bay for the third time, on the 26th. The ships No. 7 arrived and our regiment sent a picquet ashore to the watering place which is situated very conveniently; deep water with a fine sandy bottom and plenty of good fresh water near the shore. The Moors claim a big-gun cartridge from every ship getting water. We formed a chain of sentries to keep them back, which was not easily done, for they crowded around us selling figs and grapes and other fruits. These natives were of a stout make but were poor and miserably clad. One of them ran off with a bayonet which he took from the muzzle of one of the sentries' muskets. Complaint was made to one of their sultauns or officers. The man was pursued and brought back, laid on his back and bastinadoed on the soles of his feet with a pole about six feet long; he was afterwards carried away. This cleared the crowd and we had no more trouble with them. We got a supply of provisions, bullocks etc. from Tangier. This town I am told looks best at a distance. Their soldiers

THE MARQUIS OF HUNTLY

Who raised the Gordon Highlanders

Facing page 16

wear a long robe of coarse cloth of a dirty white colour, turbans on the head and sandals on the feet. They carry large clumsy firelocks and a cartouch box strapped round the waist. The country so far as I saw it had a wild uncultivated appearance.

On the 8th of November the fleet sailed in three divisions; the first two for Malta direct and the third, in which was the 92nd for Minorca, to get our provisions and stores completed. We reached that island on the 21st and found everything in a bustle with ships preparing for a long voyage. We now learned that we were bound for Egypt, to drive the French out of that country. Egypt was the word on every tongue; it had a novelty for us and we were all on the *qui vive.* Our ship was repainted, our rigging overhauled, and all our stores got in, which kept all hands at work. We escaped some very squally weather while lying here. Two Danish frigates came in from the Gulf of Venice sounding brass trumpets; these were the first armed vessels I saw of that nation.

We set sail again on the 27th, passed some high land belonging to Sardinia; came close to the Isle of Sicily at a place where the beach was gravelly. In passing the small isle of Gozo to the west of Malta, one of the ship's boys while getting in a foretop studdingsail, fell into the sea and was drowned. As Malta was a place of note on various accounts and amongst others as being the place where the apostle Paul suffered shipwreck, I did not quit the deck from the time we came in sight of it till we anchored in the harbour. The day was very fine with a steady breeze as we passed St Paul's Bay. We anchored on the 6th of December.

The entrance to the harbour is narrow; the water so deep that vessels can ride within a few feet of the shore; it opens out to the left towards the town of Cottaneo. On the Valetta side are storehouses for the shipping. Round this place batteries and cannon are placed in all directions, tier above tier, with forts etc., fit, if manned with stout hearts and willing hands to blow all the navies of Europe out of the water. In the middle of the harbour is the Grand Mason Lodge, a fort mounting four tiers of guns. The troops landed in brigades by turns, for air and exercise. Our regiment landed and marched to the glacis and formed there and had a full view of the defences of the town on

B

the land side—very strong, with walls, towers and trenches. We marched into the country about five miles and piled arms in some stubble fields, then walked about till evening when we returned by another road. We passed some fields of cotton ; the bushes were about 3 feet high and some women were gathering what was ripe. The ground is rocky with very little soil to be seen and we were surprised to see gardens and vineyards where one would think scarcely anything could come to maturity, the ground being so dry and stony. The market is well supplied with fruits and garden stuffs from Sicily. We had to wait some time at the naval yard for boats to take us on board ; the Maltese came among us selling wine, which is very cheap.

On the 20th a fleet arrived from home and brought our regiment about 200 volunteers, chiefly from the Caithness and Inverness Fencibles, with Lieutenant Brodie Grant and Ensign Baillie. They came in the *Resource*, 32, frigate. Some very strong regiments were left in Malta as they had been filled up from the militias, and their agreement was not to serve out of Europe, but the 9th regiment, 35th, 2nd battalion 36th, 2nd battalion 40th, 52nd, 2nd battalion 82nd, and the 40th flank companies, volunteered to serve anywhere.

We left Malta on the 21st and sailed for Marmorice Bay in Asia. We passed many of the Greek islands on our left about the Dardanelles entrance, on the way to Constantinople. Coasted along the south side of Candia the ancient Crete ; the land lies but rises high in the interior ; it is inhabited chiefly by Greeks, who are subject to Turkey as are most of the islands in the Levant. Off the island of Rhodes we came up to Sir Sydney Smith's squadron which had come to meet us to be our guide on this coast. Our fleet lay to off the east end of Rhodes. The hospital ships were here with some of the medical staff to form a general hospital for the army. Rhodes has a fine fertile appearance from the sea with gardens and white houses but some of our men who were ashore told me that the walls and town were ruinous. Over the harbour which is now much choked up, once stood the famous Colossus, being a lighthouse in the figure of a man with a leg on each side of the entrance. This figure was regarded as one of the seven wonders of the world. The island was the residence of the Christian knights after their retreat from the Holy Land, and many sieges they stood and battles they fought before they were expelled from it. I felt a more than usual interest in looking at those places, from what I had read of them in history and Scripture ; I stopped aloft on the foremast crosstrees until I could discern the objects no longer.

CHAPTER III

A TURKISH GOVERNOR

FROM Rhodes we stood direct for the mainland, Sir Sydney Smith in the *Nigre*, eighty gun-ship, leading the van, and entering a passage between two hills we wondered where we were going, for the inlet was very narrow and the ships ahead of us were going out of sight. When we got a little further we found a passage which turned round a very perpendicular hill as suddenly as if it had been the corner of a street. Into this passage we sailed and in a few minutes we were in one of the finest and largest bays, it is said, in the world. It is surrounded with hills except on the south-east side ; these hills are covered with wood from the summit to the water edge. There are great numbers of wild beasts in the woods. On the east side of the bay stand the Turkish village and castle of Marmorice, in the province of Natolia, in Lesser Asia. Our Admiral saluted the castle with seventeen guns and the salute was returned. The war vessels anchored at the mouth of the bay. The Turkish Governor accompanied by Sir Sydney Smith, visited most of the ships. On coming on board the *Stately*, this long bearded Turk, who was between seventy and eighty years old, seeing some of our men on sentry on the gangway accosted them in Gaelic, which surprised them much. It turned out that he was a Scotchman from Argyleshire, of the name of Campbell aud had been obliged to leave his country twenty years before for some misdemeanour. Some said it was he who had shot Lord Eglinton. Others held that he had killed a schoolfellow in a quarrel and fled the country to escape punishment. He had lost his nose in the late war between Russia and Turkey and had a silver one painted flesh colour. He dined on board with our officers and claimed relationship with Paymaster Campbell.

We pitched our tents on 2nd February 1801 on a pleasant plain by a little brook and our volunteers were landed from

MAJOR GENERAL SIR C. W. DOYLE K.C.B.

Facing page 21

the *Resource* frigate.   All the sick were likewise landed.
Some vessels were despatched to Macri bay for bullocks and
others to Smyrna and Aleppo for bread which was furnished
us by the Turks, a kind of hard dried husk.   We were glad
to get this as we were then put on full rations and our biscuits
were bad and full of worms ; many of our men

COULD ONLY EAT THEM IN THE DARK !

A company of bakers arrived from England, hired at five
shillings a day when at work and three shillings at other
times with rations ; these were the best paid men on the
expedition.   They erected a field bakery and the sick men
were supplied with fresh bread.   A market was erected on
shore which was well supplied by the Greeks who came in
boats from all parts of the Levant with the produce of their
country.

On the 8th of February a storm came on from the south-
east, with showers of hail or lumps of ice, the largest seen by
any of us.   The tents on shore were beaten down and riddled
as if by musket balls.   Trees were broken down and rooted
up.   When night came on it was dismal to hear the wild
beasts yelling and howling in the woods ; they came down
to the plain so near that our sentries fired and killed some,
though fires were kept burning in the rear of the tents to
keep them at a proper distance.

Some sailors strayed from their party, stole a bullock
and abused and struck the owners.   They were detected
bringing it on board.   A complaint was made to the Admiral
who had them tried by court-martial when two were sentenced
to be hanged and the others condemned to be flogged.   A
gallows was erected in the market-place, the yellow flag hoisted
on their ship, and the culprits sent ashore with halters round
their necks.   But the Governor and other Turkish officers
begged their lives from Lord Keith, which were granted.
We thought much of the Turks for this.   The army was
exercised by brigades in landing in flat bottomed boats, with
regiments keeping in line and advancing or retreating on
signals from the naval officers stationed in the boats.   The
men-of-war launches had field pieces fastened on the prow,
with slides for the wheels ; when the lashings were cut, the
guns were run on to the beach ready to act with the troops :
this was an excellent plan which we had felt the want of in
Holland.

Parties were sent ashore from each ship to cut wood and many fine myrtle and box trees were felled for fuel, dragging the wood down the hillsides to the beach was fine exercise for us. Our regiment was employed for three days in the engineer department making fascines and palisades. We were frequently landed for exercise and were brigaded with the 1st Royal Scots and the 54th, under command of Sir Eyre Coote, a good man and brave soldier.

A French polacre from Marseilles on her way to Alexandria was captured and brought here ; she was laden with brandy, hats, shoes, fans and trinkets for the French army.

An infectious slow fever broke out in our regiment. Few of us escaped it and those who were longest in catching the infection were the worst. Our condition on board the *Stately* contributed towards it for we had no hammocks or beds but only our camp blankets to sleep in. We lay on the under deck and when the weather was stormy so much water leaked in by the edges of the ports as made the lee side of the ship very wet. When she tacked, the water that was lying on the lee side would run across the whole deck and so we had to lie in the damp. This made us very uncomfortable and caused us to feel stiff and our bones sore. On this account our regiment was landed in Egypt very weak, when all its strength was needed.

Some vessels arrived from Britain with detachments for various regiments. Lord Keith was promoted from being Vice-Admiral of the Red to be Admiral of the Blue and Sir Richard Bickerton to be Vice-Admiral of the Red. A Turkish line of battleship, a frigate and some heavy gunboats arrived from Constantinople. One of their great men accompanied by Sir Sydney Smith was rowed round the fleet in a thirty oared barge, with a silk flag at the stern.

Arrangements being now complete, the troops were ordered on board, and the worst of the sick were sent to the General Hospital at Rhodes. The men of our regiment formerly on the *Resource* were put on board the *Niger*, 32, frigate, a clean vessel, the captain of which was a pious man and seldom was duty more pleasantly done than on board his ship. A number of Greek vessels were hired to carry horses and stores ; and general orders were issued concerning our duty and our conduct towards the inhabitants of the country we were going to ; we were especially cautioned not to interfere with them in the matter of their religion.

On Monday the 23rd of February the fleet weighed anchor and we were out of the bay before sunset. I took up my station with a few others on the foretop. As the fleet consisted of about 200 ships, many of which were large and elegant vessels, it had a grand and interesting appearance. The island of Rhodes lay on our right and the coast of Asia Minor on our left ; and to see the last golden beams of the sun glancing on the wide spreading white sails with the wind beginning to blow fresh, brought to my mind what has happened on this very coast, of people being driven from their country going to found a new settlement under some adventurous chief. Little did I think while reading of these countries when a boy, that I should one day see them or that I should do the duty of a soldier on these coasts.

A MOTLEY CROWD

The nations on board our fleet were many, Turks, Greeks, Albanians, Scotch, English, Irish, Corsicans, Maltese and a brigade of soldiers in our service composed of men from various parts of Germany. The wind got rather high and the Turkish and Greek vessels left us and took shelter in the nearest ports, although the weather was not what any British seaman would call bad, only squally. Their departure was a serious loss to the army for we were in want of the horses on board of them.

On the 26th we passed the island of Cyprus on the right ; what we saw of it lay low, with trees to the water's edge. On the 28th we fell in with our squadron that was blockading Alexandria and on the 1st of March saw the low sandy beach of Egypt between Damietta and Aboukir bay, which is formed by the main branch of the river Nile, that flows past the town of Rossetta and forms the main entrance to the lakes.

We anchored in Aboukir bay on the 2nd of March. The night before the wind freshened and there were some heavy showers of rain. This made us remark that if there was no rain in Egypt there was rain very near it, contrary to the account given by the Bible ; but this conversation was dropped on one observing that the Bible did not say that there never was any rain in Egypt but that when it spoke of there being no rain there, it meant that the land did not depend upon rain like other countries for raising the crops, but on the annual inundations of the Nile. We all agreed after we had marched through the country that the Scripture account of it was perfectly correct ; and the universal remark was that a remnant of the plagues of Moses still existed in it.

Some of our men began to complain of the want of their ordinary sight. The wind continued high and the sea stormy and rough and any of our vessels getting near the shore were fired upon from the enemy's works ; the shore seemed to be well fortified from Alexandria to the entrance of the lakes. A boat set off to reconnoitre on 28th February with General Moore and an Engineer officer. The French allowed it to come close in, but the instant it began to return a well aimed shot from the castle killed Lieutenant-Colonel MacKerris of the Engineers and wounded some others. So the French drew the first blood. Some guns were fired from a low sandy island at the mouth of the bay, (where the *Culloden*, 74, ran ashore in Nelson's engagement) this forced some of our ships to change their position. The *Foudroyant* fished up an anchor of the *L'Orient*, the French Admiral's ship that blew up at the battle of the Nile.

On the 7th the wind moderated and our gunbrigs, cutters, and the Turkish gunboats, anchored as near the shore as they could, the water being very shallow ; these with the armed launches were to clear the beach while the troops made good their landing in Egypt.

CHAPTER IV

A HARD FOUGHT LANDING

THE troops first to land in Egypt were about 5500, called the
Reserve, under command of Generals Moore, Ludlow and
Coote ; the boats were under the conduct of Sir Sidney Smith,
Captains Cochrane and Stephenson, R.N.   These troops
were in the boats by daybreak and at three o'clock were
ordered to row for their rendezvous in rear of the light-armed
vessels which were to protect the landing.   This was a very
fatiguing duty for the seamen, for the fleet was so widely
anchored, and the large vessels so far from the shore, that it
was nearly nine o'clock before the boats were collected and
arranged.

The enemy could see all our movements and the delays
which took place gave them a fair opportunity to collect their
forces and provide for their defence, for they knew the only
point at which we could land.   Several regiments were put on
board light vessels which went as near the shore as they could,
that support might be quickly given on the return of the boats
to those who landed first.   Our regiment was in the 2nd division
and we were spectators of the 1st's landing ; and though we
felt thankful we were not in the boats, yet our anxiety for those
that were was as painful, I believe, as if we had been in them.

At nine o'clock the signal was given for the boats to
advance and the whole line advanced very regularly, giving
three loud cheers.   The French were posted on the top of
the sandhills, forming the concave of a circle of about a mile,
60 yards in the centre of which was a very steep height ; their
left extended to the blockhouse at the entrance to lake Maadie.
To the right the shore was flat and covered with thick bushes,
such as form the date or palm tree, which were favourable for
concealing the enemy ; while on the extreme right stood the
castle of Aboukir which commanded the whole shore.

As soon as the boats set out for the beach, our bomb ketches and war vessels began to throw their shot and shells upon the shore, and the light vessels with their carronades, moving in a line with the boats began to fire. The enemy had twelve pieces of artillery on the heights and the beach and heavy guns on the tower in Aboukir castle. As soon as the boats got within reach of their shot they opened fire on them. The scene now became dreadful, the vessels pouring whole broad-sides, the bomb ketches throwing shells and the gun-boats and cutters exerting themselves to the utmost. All eyes were directed towards the boats and every flash of the enemy's guns was noticed to see whether the shot struck the water or the boats, and when there was any confusion among them we wondered how many might be killed or wounded. But still the boats pressed on towards the shore and persevered in keeping good order. The firing from our war vessels over their heads did not for a moment interrupt the enemy's fire or silence a single gun.

We soon observed the right flank of the boats get nigh the shore, while the enemy from their elevated position began to pour volleys of musketry among them, our brave tars and soldiers giving them cheers for their shot and shell. In a few seconds after the 40th flank companies and the 23rd regiment were in line and without firing a shot cleared all that opposed them at the point of the bayonet, pushing them over the heights. This movement was clearly seen by all the fleet. The 42nd regiment was next seen ascending the heights ; they charged the enemy opposed to them, who fled and disappeared. The left of the boats was the last to reach the shore, and the troops there were roughly handled before they got formed, and sustained a charge of cavalry ; but they maintained their ground and in less than half an hour nothing was to be seen from the ships but the empty boats coming back for the 2nd division. Some of them soon reached the ship I was in and we lost no time in getting to the shore. On the way we saw some boats that had been struck with grape shot and swamped ; the men in them had been picked up by the small boats in the rear which followed for that purpose.

We reached the shore in peace and quietness. The beach was strewed with dead and wounded men, and horses and cannon taken from the enemy. We formed in a hollow to the left of the centre height where many of the 42nd lay dead and wounded, and then advanced through the first range of sandhills and found the 1st division formed with their artillery which had been landed with them and were drawn by seamen. Our bringing our guns on shore along with the troops was what the enemy did not expect and it contributed much to their speedy retreat.

Eight pieces of cannon were taken from the enemy ; their loss of men we could not learn exactly. Our loss was great, as was to be expected in front of an enemy posted to so much advantage ; it was between 700 and 800 men of all ranks, the greater part of whom were killed or wounded in the boats previous to the landing.

We took up a position with our right to the sea and our left to the lake. Strong picquets were sent to the front, and we had likewise to watch the castle in the rear, which kept firing at anything that came near. Our first care was to learn whether water could be obtained in this sandy desert, and we were glad to find it could be got in the hollows by digging with our bayonets in the sand about 3 feet below the surface. All the troops were landed in the course of the day and the wounded were sent on board the fleet.

On the 9th, our regiment with a party of Corsican riflemen advanced along the peninsula to a place where it was contracted to about half a mile broad. The enemy had a redoubt here and a flagstaff for communicating signals between Aboukir Castle and Alexandria. We thought a stand would have been made here as the position was a good one ; but the enemy had left it and thrown a large gun into the ditch.

In the course of the day the 42nd regiment relieved us and we went back to our former position, where we remained till the morning of the 12th. We made ourselves booths of the branches of the date tree to shelter us from the heavy dew which fell at night, and we had some showers of hail and rain which made it cold after sundown. Many of our men complained of blindness after sunset ; this continued for days after we landed. By this time our ammunition and stores had been brought ashore and then began the landing of guns and the making of batteries and entrenchments across the neck of land so that we might attack the castle. This business was chiefly left to the naval officers and seamen of the fleet. The army got out three days' provisions and all was ready for a movement to the front.

But I must here give an account as well as I can of the troops landed ; they were as follows : The first Division consisted of the 1st Royals, 2nd regiment, 8th, 13th, 18th, 30th, 44th, 50th, 54th (two battalions), 79th, 89th, 90th, 92nd, the Guards, De Rolle's regiment, Minorcans, Dillon's regiment. The Reserve consisted of the 23rd, 28th, 40th flank companies, 42nd, 58th regiments, a troop of the 11th Dragoons ditto of Hompesch regiment, the Corsican Rangers, and 12th and 26th Light Dragoons. About 300 seamen were landed with the guns as also a battalion of Marines.

The total force landed was about 15,000 men commanded by the following general officers : Hutchinson, Hope, Ludlow, Coote, Craddock, Stuart, Doyle, the Earl of Cavan, Moore, Oakes, Finch, Colonel Spencer, etc. The Engineers and Artillery were under Brigadier Lawson, Physician-General Dr Young, Sir Ralph Abercrombie, Commander-in-chief.

MARSHAL BERESFORD

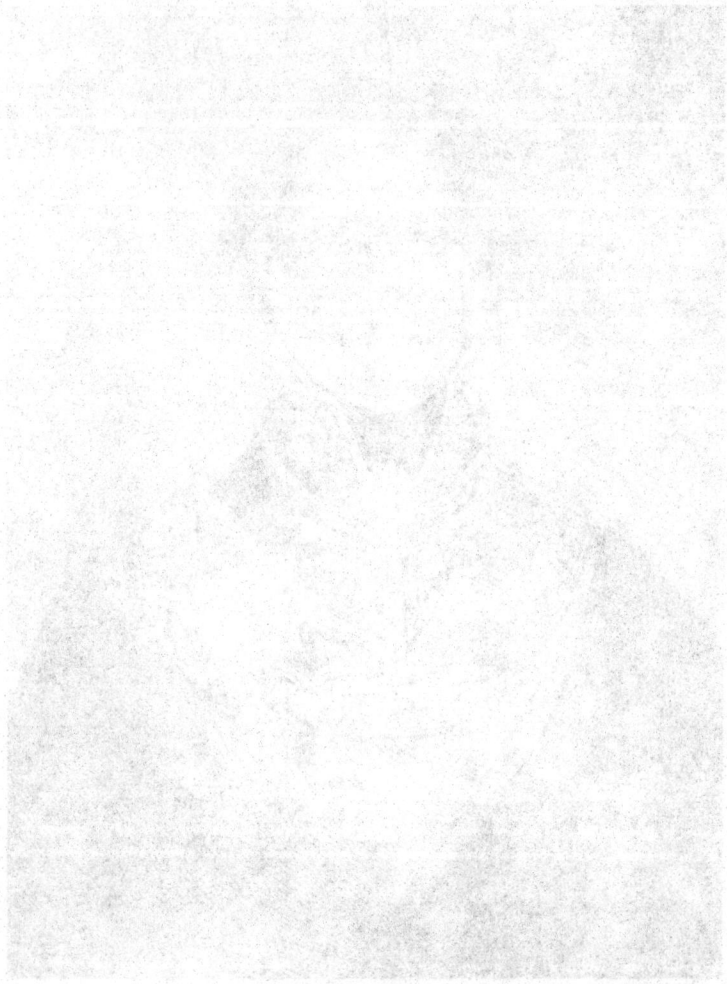

CHAPTER V

THE GALLANT STAND OF THE 90TH AT MANDORAH

On the 12th we advanced after filling our canteens with water ;
for in this dry sand, with a burning sun overhead and living
on salt provisions, water is a precious article indeed. Having
proceeded a little beyond the narrow neck of the peninsula the
enemy's cavalry began to dispute the ground with us. Our
march was slow and often interrupted ; the ground being un-
even and the sand very deep, parties were frequently sent to
assist the seamen with the guns. Before night, we came in
sight of the French army posted on a height. Their strength
was about 6000, with cavalry, and from 20 to 30 field pieces.
We halted and began to dig for water, which was greatly in
demand ; each company dug a well and we were out of patience
till the water made its appearance but before we were half
satisfied the regiment was ordered to picquet in front of the
army. There was no help for it. We formed a chain of
sentries ; a half blind man and one that could see were put
together ; those that were quite blind were left in groups here
and there in rear of their companies.

On the morning of the 13th our regiment formed the
advanced guard on the left, and the 90th on the right. We
got a little rum served out and began our march, leaving our
knapsacks with a guard. Before we had gone far our light
company which was in front fell in with the enemy's picquets
and a skirmishing began. The light company was reinforced
several times and drove in the enemy's outposts. The ground
over which we marched was covered with thick bushes until
we approached a rising ground on which the French were drawn
up in order of battle. Our regiment kept to the side of the
lake, the 90th was on our right, and the army followed us in
two lines. The armed boats from the fleet had kept pace on
the lake with the left of the army, but the water was now so

shallow they could proceed with us no farther. We had a
nine pounder field piece and a howitzer along with us ; but
very little ammunition for them.

As soon as the 90th had cleared the broken ground and
began to ascend the height, a heavy body of cavalry advanced
to charge them. The 90th formed in line, but before their
line could get formed on the left the cavalry was close on them.
We thought it was all over with the 90th but they stood
firm, and when the cavalry were about to strike at them they
opened their fire ; it ran from right to left like a rattling peal
of thunder. By this well-timed volley they saved themselves
most gallantly, and the cavalry being so near, not more than
20 yards distant, it proved most destructive to them. Of
those that wheeled past the left of the 90th few returned, and
many horses were seen galloping with empty saddles.

During this transaction which was all over in a few
seconds, our regiment made a pause, but on the retreat of
the cavalry we again advanced. The enemy then began
to open their artillery upon us from the heights but we
still pressed on and they, seeing we were considerably in
front of the army, formed the resolution of cutting us off
before we could obtain assistance from the main body.
When we saw their intention we halted, formed five companies
in line and extended the other companies in rear of the
bushes on the left towards the lake. We kept at them
with our two guns until the last shot of ammunition was
fired when they were drawn off to the rear.

Our situation was one of great danger. The enemy
in front was advancing in a line formed like the blade of
a scythe, the curved point towards the lake and that part
was cavalry, said to be the dromedary corps. It seemed
as if they meant to turn our left and get into our rear, while
they attacked us in front, and, getting round our right,
they would thus have surrounded us and made us prisoners
or have destroyed us at once as we were not above 500
strong and every minute were getting fewer. The enemy
had some fieldpieces in front which were making sad havoc
among us, every shot sweeping down some of our men.
Our commanding officer ordered us not to fire but to
stand firm until we could see their feet as they advanced
from the hollow in front of us. When the order to fire
was given, like magic it dispelled the gloom from our
countenances and everyone did his duty manfully. We

encouraged one another, firing and at the same time praying, for soldiers do pray and that very fervently on occasions of this kind and, I believe, serious thoughts were with most of us, even the most profligate.

Our first fire caused the enemy in front of us to halt ; and they kept firing on us ; this we were not slow in returning, the smoke soon making us almost invisible to each other.

Our men on the left posted among the bushes did their duty admirably and maintained their ground. But our ranks were getting very thin in this unequal combat. To our great joy a party of the Marine battalion doing duty on shore arrived on our right and Dillon's regiment on our left. On the first fire of these troops the enemy retreated in a hurry. We pursued them to some distance and Dillon's regiment coming up with a party of them charged and took two pieces of cannon. The enemy was so closely pressed that he divided his forces ; part of them retreated through a shallow part of the canal and the other part retired upon Alexandria. Had our cavalry been mounted and we had ammunition for our few guns we would certainly have taken all the enemy's artillery and Alexandria into the bargain, for we were nearer to it than that part of the enemy's force which retreated to the left. *

Our army formed in line on the heights the French had occupied in the morning. They kept cannonading us through the day and annoyed us much with their sharp-shooters as we kept shifting about taking up different positions, making room for the troops coming up from the rear. This day was very warm and we suffered much from thirst ; I have seen a Spanish dollar offered for a draught of water and in some instances refused.

The enemy now concentrated his forces on the heights of Alexandria. Our division advanced to possess the high ground on the left in rear of the canal over which was a bridge defended by a party of cavalry and infantry with two guns which played upon us as we formed in close column of companies ready to descend into the hollow. The 44th regiment was sent to the front and at the point of the bayonet captured the bridge ; the party which defended it retired into their own lines. The enemy then began to move some

* The 90th lost about 400 and the 92nd about 200 in this action.

heavy columns on the plain and opened on us with his artillery, thinking I suppose, to draw us under the guns of his fortifications ; but our troops were ordered to screen themselves by the heights.   Those who had no shelter sat or lay down on the ground so as not to be so much exposed to the enemy's shot, but still were ready to be up and at them if they offered to come nearer.   Our regiment retired to the rear and sent out parties in search of water, which had been in great demand during the early part of the day. They were fortunate in finding it ; and the eagerness with which each man grasped his canteen and the pleasure it gave can only be imagined by those who have been in similar circumstances.   We remained in the same position till near sunset, the enemy still cannonading us and cutting down a file here and there.   Major Napier had a narrow escape from one of these shots.

By sunset the enemy took up the position in which it remained during the siege of Alexandria ; our right to the sea and our left to the canal that separates Lake Maadie from the bed of the Lake Mareotis.   We soldiers thought we had nothing to do but take the town whenever our heavy battering guns and ammunition arrived : but alas, much had to be done before the surrender of Alexandria.

As soon as our position was adjusted and we had piled arms, the cry was for more water and parties were sent out who brought it to us as thick as puddle, as men and horses had been promiscuously knee-deep amongst it trying, as it were, who could drink the fastest.   After getting our water, being much fatigued we sat down among the sand and began to examine our haversacks.   I observed some holes in mine ; and taking out some biscuits found a grape shot in the centre of a bit of pork.   I might well return thanks to God for the protection afforded me this day.   Many miraculous escapes some of my comrades made ; but our loss was great.   Colonel Erskine was severly wounded in the thigh by grape shot ; Captain Ramsay, Archibald MacDonald, Cameron and Palton wounded ; Lieutenants Norman MacLeod, Ranald MacDonald and Donald MacDonald, C. Dowie, Tomline Campbell, Alexander Cameron and Foreman wounded ; Ensign Wilkie wounded ; John Mackintosh, sergeant-major wounded in the right arm. In all our regiment lost about 150 in killed and wounded ; but our wonder was how so many had escaped.   The loss

MAJOR GENERAL SIR ARTHUR WELLESLEY

Facing page 33

sustained by the army was about 1500 in killed and wounded of all ranks. Four field pieces were taken from the enemy ; their loss otherwise I never learned.

Colonel Erskine was taken on board one of the ships of the fleet when, after having one of his legs amputated he died on the 23rd. His remains with those of some other officers who had died on board were buried in the sand in front of the regiment. Lieutenant Dowie died on the 16th and Norman MacLeod about a month after. Tomline Campbell died on the 17th May.*

On the 11th the commander-in-chief in general orders bestowed great praise on the 90th, 92nd, and Dillon's regiment for the bravery and steady conduct manifested by them while on the advanced guard yesterday ; for maintaining their ground against a superior force of the enemy and baffling the enemy's attack until the line was closed up and formed. This day parties were sent to bury the dead and assist the wounded to the boats. I buried John Nicol from Banff, the only namesake I had in the regiment. He had been struck in the centre of the body by a large shot which had doubled him up ; he lay a shocking sight, but his death must have been in a moment.

We got our tents on shore and pitched and were employed in landing heavy guns which had to be dragged to the heights through the sand. The fatigues of the army were very great, building batteries, raising redoubts and making entrenchments ; the men affected with night blindness had to take their turn of night duty. The sentries on the outposts were all doubled, a blind man and a seeing man were put together, the former to hearken and the other to look out ; and a blind man and one that could see were set to work together, to carry two handed baskets filled with earth to raise the breast works, the one that had sight leading the blind. Every place that could be fortified from the sea to the lake was made as strong as it could be in so short a time. On the large central height was what might be called our Grand Battery where proudly floated the British flag. From this place we had a view of all the plain to the fortifications of Alexandria.

When the working parties were digging among the ruins and turning up fine pillars and blocks of marble and placing

---

* The skeleton of Colonel Erskine was discovered by some workmen while digging a foundation in 1894. It was recognised by its having only one leg and by a locket or love token found lying on the breastbone.

in the breastworks and redoubts these ornaments of ancient palaces, it made me and many others reflect on the ancient glory of Egypt of which there are so many evidences even in the barren peninsula of Aboukir. I saw in these ruins the fulfilment of Scripture and from the description which I read on board ship after I knew we were bound for this place, I supposed such a city might have stood in this vicinity.

These reflections gave great interest to our operations. We were now upon Scripture ground ; we had come from a distant island of the sea to the country of the proud Pharaohs to carry on war where Nebuchadnezzar and Alexander the Great, Cæsar, and other great warriors had put armies in motion.

Our camp stretched from the sea to the lake on which were numerous boats bringing provisions and military stores from the fleet, while parties of seamen and soldiers were dragging them through the deep sand from the depot about two miles in rear of the army. This fatiguing work was cheerfully done notwithstanding the hardship that attended it. On the 17th Colonel Bryce of the Guards while visiting the picquets at night got among the French outposts ; he was wounded and taken prisoner ; he died a short time after. On the 18th our cavalry on the plain disputed a round hill with some French cavalry and on charging the French were fired upon by some infantry posted in rear of the hill ; on this our cavalry turned and took some prisoners.

CHAPTER VI

THE NIGHT ATTACK AT ALEXANDRIA

ABOUT 400 of our men were left on board the fleet ill of fever when we landed ; on the 20th our regiment being so much reduced, having scarcely 300 fit for duty ; was ordered to march next morning to Aboukir to do duty there until our strength was recruited. We marched long before daybreak, and left our tents standing for a regiment that was to come from the second line to take our place. We had gone but two miles on our road, when we heard the discharge of musketry on our left. On this we halted and immediately could see more firing, even the flash of every pan was visible from where we stood ; then we heard a fieldpiece and after that a roar of musketry. We knew there was a strong guard with the working party about that spot, and that a gun was with them. As the firing ceased we thought it was a false alarm and began to proceed on our journey but had not gone many steps when we heard the discharge of some muskets on the right of the army. This produced a voluntary halt with out any word of command. Some more discharges were heard in the same direction. We were then ordered to the right about and we went as quickly as possible to the tent of the commander-in-chief. By this time the firing on the right was going on briskly among the picquets. We were now ordered to take up the position we had left. It being still very dark our artillery began to play with the help of lighted lanterns, to let the men see to load. By the time we got to our position the action was close and heavy on the right of the line, and in the darkness not one regiment knew what the others were doing, or what was opposed to them, so they had to stand in awful suspense till the firing came in front of them. There could be no doubt of a powerful and determined attack by the enemy.

35

When we arrived at our post we found the ground unoccupied, the regiment which was to take our place not having arrived. This would have been a fine passage for the enemy to have entered had they only known of it; and we just arrived in the very nick of time when the enemy had gained the brow of the hill in our front, and a column was advancing towards the opening in the line where we should have been. We filled up the opening and fired on the enemy's column whenever we came up. And if this column had resolutely pushed forward, it might have done great mischief in the rear before it could have been overpowered; but on receiving our fire it retreated under the brow of the hill out of our sight, but left a line of sharp-shooters which annoyed us very much. Thank God, daylight began to appear and we could see what we were doing and where the danger was, as before this the only order that could be given was : 'Stand fast, and defend yourselves to the last, if attacked.' At this time the battle was raging on the right with terrible fury, and the brigade of Guards next to us on the right was closely engaged. The roar of the artillery was dreadful, and little could be seen through the smoke but the red flashes.

The action was short and severe and great injury was sustained by the right wing of our army, while the left was only partially engaged. The object of the enemy was to dislodge our troops on the right and then drive the army into the lake. He expected to gain the heights before daybreak and being well acquainted with the ground and the way we were posted, he could easily attack us in the dark. But we were not to be taken by surprise, as it was our practice to stand under arms an hour before daybreak. So instead of the enemy driving us into the lake, we drove them back out of our lines into the plain with great loss. Here they formed into columns, and a shell, the last one that did execution, was fired from the flagstaff battery, which fell in the centre of their columns and blew up an ammunition waggon and made a great scatter among them. About eleven o'clock the enemy retired under the protection of their own batteries.

General Menou, the French commander-in-chief, who had posted from Cairo to drive us into the sea, and who said that it was only Turks who had landed and that he did not believe a British army was in Egypt, found out this morning that his old stubborn enemy had landed, and was not to be chased or drowned at his pleasure. It was reported that a copy of his orders was found in the pocket of General Roiz who was killed in our lines, that no quarter was to be given but that we were all to be put to the sword or driven into Lake Maadie. The plan of attack was first to, draw our attention to the left, while the coup de main was to be on the right, by the hollow between the flagstaff and the ruins of Ptolemy's palace, where the 28th regiment was posted and where it did good service. The French fought desperately aud got among the tents of our first line, their cavalry charging through the hollow was stoutly opposed by the 42nd, which suffered severely, as did also the right wing of the guards ; the foreign brigade from the second line was sent to their assistance under General Stewart. About this time and place our worthy commander-in-chief, Sir Ralph Abercrombie, was mortally wounded ; he died on the 28th, and was deeply regretted by the whole army ; General Moore was again wounded.

Our army by its losses in former actions, by parties absent at Aboukir on duty, and by sickness, had been reduced to about 10,000 before this action commenced, with about 40 pieces of cannon. The enemy's force was about the same number with the addition of cavalry. When he retreated he left 1700 men dead and wounded on the field of whom above 1,000 were buried the first two days ; he lost also 400 horses. Including the wounded who made their escape or had been removed, the enemy had lost one-third of the number he brought into action. The total loss of the British was about 1500. The loss of our regiment was 50 men, Captain John Cameron and Lieutenant MacPherson wounded. We were now a small regiment indeed. This day I had a friend wounded in the left ankle ; the wound never thoroughly healed. He was a pious lad, a very rare character indeed in the army in those days, and was a spiritual guide to me and many others. He was invalided and got a small pension ; he now resides in Glasgow where he has been an example of goodness and uprightness. He has corresponded with me ever since. *

Among those wounded was Corporal MacKinnon whom we thought to be dead when Sergeant MacLean saw some signs

* George Bellanie mentioned later. After his discharge he interested himself in the establishment of Sabbath Schools ; he wrote several pamphlets on religious subjects.

of life just in time to save him from being buried alive.*

The result of this day was that we kept our ground and as a trophy took one of the *Invincible* standards belonging to the 32 demi-brigade. It was lettered in the centre in gold 'PASSAGE DE SERVIA,' 'PONT DE LODI,' 'DE PAVIA,' 'ET CASTEL NUOVO,' etc., on a blue ground with laurels fringed with white. This flag was said to have been taken by Sergeant Sinclair of the 42nd, but got into the possession of Anthony Lutz of the Minorcan regiment after Sinclair was wounded. An investigation was ordered : Lutz got 20 dollars and a medal and a pension for life and Sinclair got a commission some time after. The standard after being exhibited to the army was sent to Sir Ralph, then lying on board the *Foudroyant*.

On the 23rd our regiment marched and reached Aboukir about nine in the morning before the day got excessively hot ; we encamped beside a good well of water, the first I have seen in this country. Things were in a very different state from what they were when we were last here ; then there was nothing but blood and carnage along the beach and the French Artillery from the top of the castle dealt death and destruction among us. Our people here had not been idle. Intrenchments and batteries had been made and the castle bombarded till the central tower was in a tottering condition and it was ready to fall before the enemy surrendered ; 300 were sent prisoners on board the fleet. Marquees were pitched for the sick and wounded who were brought ashore. Many of the sick belonging to our regiment were put under the charge of Dr Hamilton, our own regimental surgeon, Dr William Findlay, being promoted to be physican to the forces.

A market was formed at the commissary's near the block house and the produce of the country was brought in by the Arabs who found a ready-money market for their goods, sheep, fish, vegetables and fruits ; sometimes a kind of brandy was brought in in boats by the Greeks ; but woe betide them if caught by the Turks selling liquor ; they were at once seized and bastinadoed on the spot and their goods taken from them.

* Alexander MacKinnon, a native of Arisaig and the author of several pieces of Gaelic poetry. His descriptions of the battles of Egmont and Alexandria are considered by those competent to judge as among the most spirited of modern Gaelic poems.

On my first visit to the market I bought a sheep for a Spanish dollar and a cheese about 10 lbs. for 60 paras and a bunch of young onions. This was the first fresh provisions our mess had in Egypt and we could obtain for 3 paras as much fine bread as a man could eat. As the produce of the country was so plentiful our salt beef and pork were not used, but the casks stood at the quartermaster's for any one to take what he pleased, and it was no uncommon thing to see one piece of pork cut up to boil another with some green date branches, the only fuel we could get. This was extravagant enough. Our salt provisions ran up in the hands of the commissary to the value of £150, this sum was proposed to be given to the widows and orphans of the regiment.

The French barracks called the Hutts erected by them for their troops stationed at Aboukir, were converted into a general hospital ; and at this place that dreadful calamity the plague first made its appearance. I was sent with a party there and we buried a surgeon and two women in one hole in the sand and seven men in another ; all had fallen victims to it.

The wounded men seemed to be comfortable in the Hutts but were much tormented with flies and other vermin. I visited the castle which had annoyed us so much in landing, it surrendered on March 17th after a siege of five days. It stands on the point of the bay about 13 miles from Alexandria. Our dismounted dragoons were doing duty here. There is a ditch and drawbridge on the landside and it is nearly surrounded by the sea. The ramparts are mounted with mortars and cannon. In the centre stands the great tower on the top of which are two brass 32-pounders but the place is sorely battered by our shot and is in a tumble down condition. The view from the top of the tower is excellent ; the east as far as the eye can reach is low and sandy, with date or palm trees which have a fine appearance at a distance ; on the west stands Alexandria, which has a formidable appearance, with its towers and newly-raised fortifications ; closer to us is a large plain, where the Turkish army landed and was defeated by the French. Many bodies lie here unburied and uncorrupted : the hot sun has dried all the moisture out of them and their skin was quite fresh like parchment. Near the castle once stood the town of Aboukir, now deserted and in ruins. This place had been under

cultivation at some time, for we could trace where gardens
had been and saw the remains of a few stunted fig trees, vines,
etc. John Key of our company and Richardson of the 6th
company were severely punished for going straight on to
Aboukir on the morning of the 21st March when the
regiment returned to the lines and giving the alarm that the
French were driving us before them, and so causing great
consternation among the sick and wounded.

A Turkish fleet sailed into the bay, and landed about
5,000 troops, 3 regiments of which had got British arms and
accoutrements. They wore scarlet jackets, wide blue trousers
tucked in at the knees, turbans and sandals on their feet ;
they had a number of flags of different colours. They were
stout men, chiefly Albanians. These were the finest and best
disciplined troops I had seen belonging to the Turkish army.
April 2nd at twelve o'clock all the troops were under arms
to receive the Turkish commander. He rode along the
line with Lord Hutchinson. The Turkish flag was hoisted
alongside the British on the castle.

The Hompesch cavalry, commanding officer Sir Robert
Wilson, was sent here and dismounted, on account of some
of them deserting to the enemy ; their horses were given to
the 12th Light Dragoons.

It was reported that a French fleet under Admiral
Ganteaume was at sea on its way to relieve Alexandria. On
this the seamen and the battalion of Marines were sent on
board and Admiral Keith sailed in search of the enemy.

On the 13th of April openings were made in the banks
of the canal leading from the Nile to Alexandria ; and the
water from Lake Maadie rushed into the bed of Lake
Mareotis, which was nearly dry and passable in many parts
both for horse and foot. The water continued to flow for
about a month, having at first a fall of above 6 feet, when it
nearly found its level ; but there continued always a fall of
above a foot owing to the sand absorbing the water. By
this means a large extent of country was inundated. This
contracted our position in front and protected our left from
assault and armed boats and large germs could come up to
the left of the line with stores and provisions.

With the strong batteries and entrenchments our men had
raised since the action of the 21st March the army was secure,
and Lord Hutchinson who had succeeded Sir Ralph Abercrombie as commander-in-chief, had a disposable force to march

to the banks of the Nile while General Coote was left with the remainder to blockade Alexandria. Before this some of our troops had marched from the lines and with about 4,000 Turks had driven the French from the caravansery and taken Rosetta. Fort St Julian was bombarded by our gunboats ; we heard the cannonading across the bay at Aboukir on the 17th and 18th. This fort surrendered on the 19th ; it stands on the left bank of the Nile and commands the main branch of the river.

Our regiment was ordered to get ready for the march and every one that was able to march was ordered to join. I went round to the hospital sheds and took leave of some of my wounded comrades ; the plague was stealing in amongst them, and few that had limbs taken off recovered. This day I shook hands with many a one I never saw again. About this time our surgeon William Findlay who had been promoted to be Physician of the Forces, died.

CHAPTER VII

A HOT MARCH

On the 23rd of April we marched and crossed the lake Maadie
near the blockhouse which with some guns defends the entrance ;
there is a stockade and battery on the other side. We crossed
on a large raft drawn from one side to the other with ropes
fixed on supports of wood and pulled hand over hand by
about twenty sturdy Arabs nearly naked and making a great
noise in their own language. When we got over we travelled
on a causeway composed of large blocks of stone built as a
dyke to keep the sea back and answer the purposes of a road.
We soon left this hard road and marched through the sand,
sinking every step to the calf of the leg, until we came to the
entrance of lake Elko. By this time it was dark. We got
into flat bottomed boats belonging to the fleet and landed on
the other side, at the caravansery, a kind of Turkish inn for
travellers which the French had converted into a fort for the
protection of this passage. We stuck our bayonets into the
ground and slept sound after the fatiguing hot day's march.
24th to Etko a fine village but very dirty ; here we made
ourselves booths of the date trees, as their long branches made
a good shelter from the sun and dew. The inhabitants came
among us in a friendly manner selling bread, fried fish, eggs,
fruit, etc. We found good water here and the Arabs came
round with it in skins selling it to us. Lord Hutchinson left
for El Hamet.

This being the first town I was in in this country I was
curious in examining it. It stands very high, and has had a
line wall round it which is now tumbling into decay. The
lake is close by the south and east of it ; the bay about four
or five miles to the north ; and nothing is to be seen growing
but date trees, the only thriving article I have seen in this
country. With others I visited a school and looked attentively
at some boys receiving instruction from one of the lower mufti

or clergy, a fine fatherly looking man. He showed us the books they were using, but we could make nothing of them, we supposed they might be some parts of the Koran. In writing, this was unaccountable to us, they began the line to the right and wrote towards the left to the end of the line, then began at the right again and so on ; they used small reed or cane pens. The teacher was at great pains to explain things to us, and in return for his civility I showed him as I best could how we wrote and our method of teaching from a book I had in my pocket. He seemed to understand me and we parted good friends.

We then visited the mosque or place of worship. It contained no furniture except some stone benches round the walls. The pulpit which was not unlike those used at home, stood in the centre ; on it lay a large book which we took to be the Alcoran. In the passage were some large stone baths filled with water, as we thought for the Turks washing before going into prayers. This place of worship was small with a lofty spire or minaret shaped on the top like a turban, but with no clock or bell, indeed I saw none of these in the country.* These minarets have balustrades round them in which men are posted night and day ; their duty is to call the people to prayers, proclaim the hours, and give notice of any accident that may occur. We next visited a weaver's shop ; the weaver was weaving linen but not the fine linen of Egypt, for it was coarse enough. We then left this dirty village and its swarms of flies which had been buzzing about us all the time we were in it. We noticed that many of the people had sore eyes.

On Monday, 25th, we marched by the side of the lake on which some of our armed boats were sailing. Many Arabs came with pitchers of water selling a drink for a para. Some stout fellows among them would carry eight or ten men's knapsacks a whole day's march for ten or twelve paras. We now began to get clear of the sand and glad we were to get our feet on cultivated ground once more.

We got among fields of grass and corn and encamped at El Hamet where we joined the brigade under Sir John Doyle, which consisted of the 1st Royals, 30th, 50th, and 92nd regiments. General Doyle was a true, hearty Irishman, and well fitted to have command of men. He had none of that pride and sullenness which too often attend those in authority.

* The Mohammedan religion prohibits the use of bells.

He was ever attentive to our wants and his affability and kindness can never be forgotten by any soldier in the brigade. And it was the same wherever he had the command. The men that mounted his guard seldom went without a glass of rum in the morning from his own hand. General Craddock's brigade consisted of 2nd or Queen's, 8th, 18th Royal Irish, and 58th regiments. The four flank companies of the 40th and the Corsican Rangers were under Colonel Spencer. The cavalry were the 11th, 12th, and 26th regiments, General Finch. There were three brigades of artillery. The cavalry got all mounted on good horses and some of our artillery was drawn by bullocks, and other pieces were carried on camel's backs and covered with tarpaulin to prevent the heat of the sun from rendering the wheels and carriages unfit for service.

A bridge of boats was formed across the Nile and the 89th regiment, Colonel Lord Blaney with other troops chiefly Turks, crossed over to advance on the Delta side of the river. The Grand Bashaw arrived with the Turkish armed flotilla ; he acted as Admiral and General and had his flag hoisted on one of the largest of his vessels. Captain Stephenson, R.N., had command of the British armed boats and was a more useful man for the service than the Great Turk.

This camp was about a mile and a half from Rosetta which is the chief trading town on this branch of the Nile. It has some good brick houses whitewashed over with latticed windows without glass, streets narrow and dusty and swarming with flies. The Greeks had followed us in their boats and were the chief retailers here also. A great trade seemed to be carried on in grain, and many germs or country boats are here loaded with it. The entrance into the mouth of the river below the town is difficult on account of the Boghaz or bar and the sand shifting from one side of the river to the other, and in a strong westerly wind it is nearly choked up ; some of our armed launches had to wait some days before they could pass. The river at this place is about 200 yards broad with a steep bank and a blue clay bottom, runs smooth, and is very muddy, yet it is the only good water in the country, is very wholesome, and is even said to be nourishing for the body. I have known some of our men drink from ten to twelve quarts of it in the course of a day's march, just as it was lifted out of the river and never heard that it hurt any one.

The heat was very oppressive and I have seen us while on

the march during a halt, wringing our clothes and buff belts, they being as wet with sweat as if they had been soaked in water ; they soon dried in the sun and we were never a whit the worse. This part of the country is intersected with deep canals with high banks ; they were all dry at this season of the year, but when the Nile rises to its height the water flows in ; the mouths of the canals are closed up and the water retained and this serves for watering the fields. No tillage is required for the first crop ; when the river retires within its banks the seed is thrown among the mud and slime left behind and little else is done to produce a plentiful crop. When a second or third crop is required the land is tilled with the plough, drawn by oxen. Wheat is the chief grain raised, but I have seen plenty of barley and all other grain except oats ; and at this season, standing on one of the raised banks and looking east over the river across the Delta which is level as far as the eye can reach, to see the fields bringing forth their yellow treasure is a very pleasant sight it being nigh harvest ; this made us repeat the saying 'There is corn in Egypt.' We enjoyed the sight all the more from having seen little but sea and sand for a long time back.

The villages on the banks of the Nile are numerous and well inhabited ; they are generally built on mounds of earth and are surrounded with a high bank to prevent the river, as we thought, from sweeping them away in the flood when it overflows. Most of the towns have a wall of bricks or mud built round to protect the inhabitants from the Bedouin Arabs, who sometimes make a rush from the desert and carry off the people and property of the village. There are no houses outside of these walls for want of security, yet their grain lies outside in heaps in the open air beside their threshing floors, where it is trodden out by oxen and other animals, and winnowed much the same as I have seen in Scotland. The heaps are divided from each other by a row of bricks or a piece of wood ; they lie till a merchant is found, when the grain is carried in baskets to the boats on the river. I have taken great pleasure in sitting by the river side and seeing these mountains of corn disappearing ; most of the people of the villages seemed to be employed in their embarkation ; they looked poor but happy. There are many hungry looking dogs about these small towns which are turned out at night, when they make a great noise barking and howling. The Turks here do little but sit and smoke and

drink coffee.   The Copts, the ancient Egyptians, and the
Arabs do all the servile work.   The Mamelukes are gentlemen soldiers commanded by their own officers who rule the
country as tyrants under the Turkish Governor who resides
at Cairo.

CHAPTER VIII

THE ENEMY RETIRE

On the 5th of May the army marched by the side of the Nile : the bank was covered with reeds and thick bushes. As there was no regular road we marched in companies or half-companies in a straight line through fine cornfields, treading down the ripe grain. Passed some large town and villages. On our approach men, women, and children got on the top of their flat-roofed houses and shouted for joy. The Turkish Bashaw's vessel was received with marks of great joy, beating of kettledrums, clashing of cymbals, and playing pipe organs, while a multitude followed on the river bank crying at the top of their voice 'O ! Allah Humbo, O ! Allah Humbo.'

We saw some of the enemy's picquets who retired quietly on our advance. We encamped this day in two lines with the armed flotilla in the rear of our left. Our tents were brought from the baggage boats and pitched at night and put on board before we marched in the morning. 6th, this day the Turks took up a position in our rear next to the river ; they have a great number of camels, horses and asses all in disorder. 7th, to Deirout, where some of the French had been in huts ; they retreated after having set fire to the huts, which were composed of the materials of a village they had wrecked. Here we got provisions served out, and some buffaloes were killed for the use of the regiment. The flesh of this animal is coarse and soon gets black if exposed to the sun, but it eats well with a piece of salt pork, and makes excellent soup.

On the 9th we resumed our march to Rhamanieh and heard some popping of musketry on the right of our front, by the French outposts and our advanced guard. The artillery and cavalry moved to the front with Colonel Spencer's brigade and drove in the enemy's outposts to the bank of the great canal which runs through the country from the river to Alexandria, the same canal that we cut in front of our lines in order to fill the lake Mareotis. This was a fine place of defence for the enemy, as they could move their columns and artillery from right to left unobserved by us as there was no rising ground in the neighbourhood. We closed to quarter distance, threw off our knapsacks and left them with a guard, formed line among some large fields of wheat while firing was going on briskly to our right. Captain King had a leg carried off by a cannon shot, and Sergeant Clark of our light company was wounded in the jaw. The Turks formed in three lines on the left of our regiment and brought up some clumsy pieces of artillery. On them in particular the French directed their fire from Fort Rhamanieh, throwing shot and shell, which set the fields of ripe wheat on fire, this being very dry burnt with fury ; the fire ran like lightning among us so we were obliged to shift our position. Our dragoons dismounted and cut lanes with their swords between the burning and the standing corn ; when the flame reached these openings it generally went out.

We halted until most of the fires were extinguished and then advanced : the enemy retired behind the canal bank, raising their heads above the level and giving us a few shots as they were closing in their force to the right. Meanwhile the Turks were advancing briskly on our left, their officers or standard-bearers running to the front with the flags and holding them up, their front line formed upon them and discharged their muskets, then the flags started to the front again, and so on. This did very well till some of them got within a few yards of the canal bank, when a tremendous fire opened upon them from the fort and the French artillery and the infantry rising from behind the canal bank poured a volley among the Turks, and with a shout rushed upon them at the charge. The Turks ran like a drove of sheep, and I could see that those who carried the standards were amongst their best runners. They fell back on their 2nd and 3rd lines when they all got into confusion. The French ran after them hallooing and firing until they were checked by the fire of the gunboats on the river, and General Doyle formed an oblique line with the 30th and our regiment which fired on them as we got into the alignment facing the river. On this they ran as fast from us as they had done after the Turks. Our good and faithful allies began to entrench themselves by the river side and came back and picked up some of their wounded men ; they made

ROWLAND HILL, BARON HILL

Facing page 48

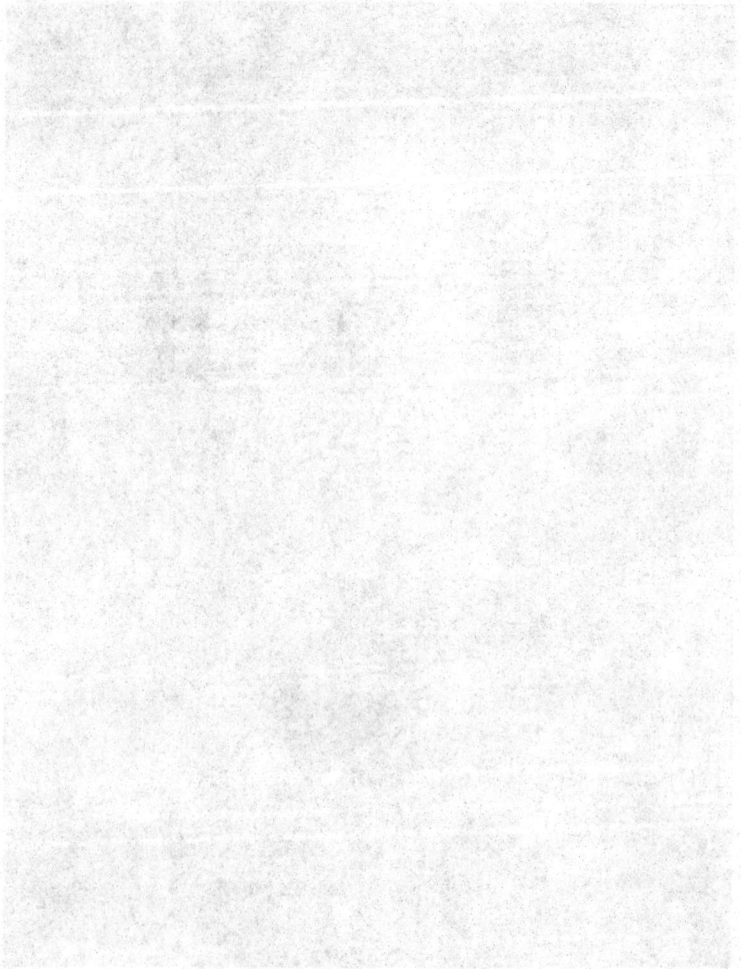

a great lamentation over some great personage whom they carried on board one of their vessels.

At night we lay down in our positions in the ranks, and a chain of sentinels was posted a few yards to the front. When placing them I was challenged and fired upon by some of the French vedettes. I returned no answer but drew back nearer the regiment. After it was dark the troops on the other side of the river contested a rising ground which commanded the turn of the river above the fort. After taking this all was still till about one o'clock in the morning when a gun was fired from the fort and there was a running fire from the sentinels opposite us. We jumped up in the ranks, thinking we were to be attacked, and stood to our arms but heard nothing more. When daylight appeared we saw the white flag flying on the fort and an officer with a drummer beating a parley came to our lines. They were conducted to General Hutchinson. The officer offered to surrender the fort, which contained 300 men, most of them wounded; he said their army in the field had marched off on the road for Cairo.

On the officer mentioning that the French army had escaped and that there were only 300 men in the fort, General Hutchinson got into a violent passion and it is said was only prevented by General Craddock from knocking the officer down. We halted on the 10th and the French were put on board some country germs and escorted to Aboukir by some of our armed boats. The Turks got possession of the fort and some of their numerous standards were placed on the walls. They kept firing off their muskets all day as was their practice on entering towns or villages.

The result of this day's work I never heard; but I saw two of the Turkish gunboats sunk in the river, and many Turks were killed and wounded by the river side. Our own wounded were put into boats and taken down to the General Hospital formed at Rosetta. The Grand Bashaw came on shore and pitched his tent, which for grandeur surpassed anything of the kind I ever saw. The marque was covered with red velvet lined with blue, gold tassels and fringes. The Bashaw sat in state on velvet cushions distributing rewards in money to every Turk who brought a Frenchman's head, and they were scattered through the fields in search of heads and were not very nice as to how or where they obtained them; it was said that some of our soldiers' heads were among them. I went to view the

D

horrid spectacle of a pile of heads, and beheld with detestation
the exulting manner in which they brought them in and the
way they kicked them about—heads of the very men who were
a terror to them yesterday. He also gave money to some
British women who were washing at the river.

Fort Rhamaniah is well calculated to defend the river and
the entrance to the canal to Alexandria. There has been a
fenced city here ; the walls are built of brick with a ditch and
drawbridge. There are some large brick buildings called by
us granaries. Some of our people would have it that they were
built by the Israelites and they look very old indeed. The
French had collected a great number of boats in a creek of the
river ; when they retreated of course the boats fell to be
divided among us. Our regiment got five of these germs
to carry the tents and the men's knapsacks ; this enabled us
to march lighter and make longer stages. Reached a town
called Nickle. Being a namesake of my own I paid more
attention to it than I did to most of the towns. Indeed I
seldom went into them for they are nearly all alike, dirty and
full of vermin, with brick and mud walls ; and many a
farmer at home would not keep pigs in the styes in which
I have seen families huddled together in the villages on
the fertile banks of the Nile. Some of them no doubt
contained better houses than others, with more mosques
and minarets and palm trees anything beyond these had no
enticement for us.

The Arabs were continually going amongst us selling bread,
as much as a man could eat for two paras, three boiled eggs
sold for the same money ; water, butter or oil, and honey were
carried about in skins for sale ; onions, cucumbers, etc., all very
cheap. Yet notwithstanding this and that our men had plenty
of money some of the baser sort could not refrain from taking
the goods for nothing and even beating and abusing the
Arabs. When so used they made a great outcry beating their
breasts and tearing their beards, and throwing dust on their
heads calling out ' O ! Allah Allah, Sultan Sultan a how '. I
have often had pity on the poor creatures when I could not
assist them.

11th Shibnaghie, twelve miles from Rhamaniah. 14th
Benoufar. We halted a day here to get our knapsacks ashore
and wash our linen ; this was quickly done as one shirt was
dry before the other was washed, the heat of the sun was so
great. This day I swam across the river to the Delta and

bought two melons. I was much fatigued in coming back and was carried far down the stream, yet kept a firm hold of my goods. Melons became very cheap a few days after, selling for five or six paras : when ripe they are delightful and refreshing to a thirsty person.

CHAPTER IX

IN THE DESERT

W E encamped on the 16th at Algam where the cultivated land is narrow, and the sandy desert is gradually making it less, for the sand is continually gaining towards the river. On the morning of the next day the 17th, as we were going to the boats for our rations an Arab was seen riding into the camp at full gallop with his turban flying at the end of his lance. He was directed to the commander-in-chief's tent, where he gave intelligence that the French were in the desert to our right and rear. On this alarm the dragoons and light artillery and our brigade got under arms. General Doyle rode along the ranks and told us he would get us bread and rum before we started, and he rode off at full gallop to the commissary's for that purpose but, just as he and the rations came in sight the order to march was given, and we entered the desert very ill-prepared indeed. We followed our guide as quickly as we could and at length, after marching seven miles, we came in sight of the enemy, who fired upon our advanced guard and retreated but after a few shots being fired from our artillery they surrendered. We found them to be a party of 600 men with 550 camels, on their way from Alexandria to Cairo for provisions. They had a large sum of money with them but before they surrendered their commissary caused it to be divided among his own men. This was the worst day's march we had in the country. Very few men had had time to get water in their canteens, at every step we sank over the ankle in light sand, and for three paces to the front we slid one back. The sun was very hot and not a breath of wind. Hundreds of our people dropped down and had to be taken up by the camels and I am sorry to say that some of the men of our brigade while in this helpless condition were killed by the Bedouin Arabs for the sake of their arms and accoutrements. On our return we met some Turks

WELLINGTON

Facing page 53

coming to our assistance with many camels and horses bearing skins of water. This was a blessed relief ; we all drank greedily ; our throats being so parched it was long before we were satisfied, and in the hurry much of the precious water was spilt. No tree nor bush nor any herbage grows here ; sand, nothing but sand and sunshine. Sometimes you think you see water before you at a distance. ' A lake, a lake ! ' cry some of our people, in a short time it is gone, but it appears again and again ; it is a strange illusion.

We got out of the sand about 6 o'clock in the evening. On the plain we fell in with some sort of fig-trees, the fruit having a notch on one side ; we devoured everyone we could reach. We escorted our prisoners to the river where they were embarked in boats, then returned to our tents and found that the men who went for the rations had done their duty ; every camp kettle was full of water and our rum and provisions ready. When the roll was called of our company one half was absent : they all joined during the night.

A camel park was formed under charge of Captain John MacLean of our regiment and Sergeants James Clark and Alexander MacLean went as assistants to him. Each regiment got camels to carry the tents in lieu of the boats which were sent down the river with the prisoners. Our officers got some good horses and asses, and the soldiers' wives were provided with these latter animals which are very large and superior to any we had ever seen. But they caused a great noise in the camp in the night time, for when one began to bray they all got on the same tune and disturbed our sleep much. At Algam were the greatest flocks of pigeons I ever saw or ever will see I believe. The town is surrounded with dovecotes built round from top to bottom with earthen pots ; in these pots they breed and hatch their young. The Turks kept firing at them most of the time we were here—no sparing of ammunition with the Turk. We had to wait three days here for bread and when we got it we found it coarse rusks, as hard as bricks which had to be steeped in water before we could use them.

We had one day's hot wind from the south (23rd May) which will ever be remarkable to the Egyptian army. The morning was lowering and the sun was of a blood red colour. It began to blow about 9 o'clock : and woe be to him that is far from shelter, as neither man nor beast can survive in it three days ! It came from the desert as hot as the opening of an oven door, bringing small sand like mist along with it. All our sentinels were called in and the cattle crept close to the ground and groaned for fear. The buffaloes took to the river, covering themselves all but the nose in the water ; flesh putrified ; any metal substance could not be touched with the naked hand ; and no man was able to stir out of his tent until the evening when happily the wind changed to the north-west.

We crossed a neck of sand and passed a deserted village which had been overflowed with this shifting sand. On this march we heard that a Turkish army had marched from Syria into Egypt by way of Salehieh and Belbeis. We encamped on the 28th at Manouff a large town where the French had a garrison. It stands on the left bank of the river, near where it divides, one branch flowing to Damietta, the other to Rosetta, and enclosing what is called the Delta, the most fertile part of the country. A canal here unites the two branches. This day we took a prize of five boats laden with stores, shoes, and money ; they had got on the wrong branch of the river, and missed the French who were retiring before us. General Menou's lady was in one of these boats ; she was a native of this country and lately married to the French commander-in-chief : she was sent to him at Alexandria. We were not permitted to take any article from the boats, though shoes were in great demand among us ; but when our faithful allies the Turks arrived they took whatever they wanted.

THE PLAGUES OF EGYPT

This part of the country so abounded with frogs that it was impossible to get at the water in the river without treading upon them, and from their slimy nature many a tumble some of our men got : after dark they croaked so as to be heard at a considerable distance from the river. So some of the plagues of Moses exist here yet. The flies are in swarms about the towns ; you must keep your hands in motion to prevent them going down your throat or into your eyes. In some places the ground was black with fleas, especially in places where the French had been in camp. As for sand lice, when the date trees were split at Aboukir for making the general hospital, I have seen so many in the hearts of them that they might have been gathered in handfuls.

One day locusts passed from west to east in such numbers

as to darken the air ; while as to boils, few of the army that marched to Cairo escaped them. I myself suffered from this trouble and also from prickly heat but was forced to do my duty with them the best way I could, and some days that was bad enough.

Marched forward to Mishlee and encamped. On 1st June we were joined here by Mamelukes under command of Ibrahim Bey, fine looking soldiers indeed. Many of them were mounted on those running camels or dromedaries, with all the luxury the country can afford, dressed in fine silk robes, fitter for a court than a camp, with red velvet saddles and silver rings in the noses of their camels and with silk cords to guide them. At a distance they looked like a lot of women ; yet they are said to be brave in the field. Each of them has an Arab or two running in the rear on foot carrying lances which they throw with great dexterity from their camels or dromedaries, and are sure of their object at 30 or 40 yards distance ; I have often seen them at practice at their camp at Cairo.

Our army marched past in open columns of companies with drums beating and I am certain they could think no less of us than we of them as they sat on their camels smoking. This day while marching in companies some men on the right of our company fell in to a slime pit ; the sun dried the clay upon their clothes and they were droll figures.

4th June to Lochmas ; 5th, Ouardan ; 7th, Gatta ; 8th Burlos ; 14th Saael ; 16th to a place almost within reach of the enemy's guns. Here we were joined by the 28th and 42nd regiments, which had marched from Alexandria in twelve days. 18th, came in sight of the Pyramids, the two large ones : this cheered us on.

On the 21st we halted within two miles of Gizeh and encamped with the enemy to our front ; threw a bridge of boats across the Nile and raised batteries on each side for its protection. A line of dried buffalo skins was stretched on stakes, musket proof at 30 yards distance. All stores and baggage were halted below the bridge.

The Grand Vizier's army arrived on the other side of the Nile, nearly opposite to us, and a great multitude they appeared to be. With tents and marquees pitched without order, camels, horses, asses, Arabs, they covered a great extent of ground. There was little subordination or regularity among them. Some of our artillerymen who had been at Constantinople instructing the Turks appeared here like gentlemen. I went over to the Turkish camp with Corporals Sinclair and Innes of our company, drank some very strong coffee, and got two whiffs of an opium pipe, which some of the Turks smoke until they are intoxicated.   As the bridge of boats was a ready means of communication between the two camps many of the Turks came over to look at the people who could beat the French.

The whole army advanced and drove in the French outposts.   They disputed the ground on the east bank of the river with the Turks and kept up a heavy cannonade upon them from a battery at a windmill ; this kept them at bay. We marched on and took up our position with our left opposite the centre of Gizeh and at a great distance from the river, for the French had fortified the banks as well as Rodda Island in the middle of the river.   Some heavy guns were brought up from our flotilla.   We were joined by the 42nd, 79th, and 90th regiments under command of General Oakes.   It was reported that the Indian army under General Baird had sailed up the Red Sea and landed at Cosseir and Suez, marched across the desert, and was driving the French down the river.

Thus being fairly hemmed in on all sides the enemy offered on the 22nd to capitulate to the British generals *only*. This was agreed to, and a large marquee was pitched between Gizeh or what was called the Horse Barracks, and our front line.   The staff of both armies met accompanied by a guard of twelve men from each, who were very friendly with one another.   The capitulation being signed and hostages exchanged the French were to march to the seaside and embark with their arms and ammunition, bag and baggage, and to be taken to the nearest port in France in our ships at the expense of the British Government.   I believe they were very glad to return to their country.   This was done 27th June 1801.   On the 29th General Moore joined us, having now recovered from his wound received on 21st March.

CHAPTER X

ON THE BANKS OF NILE

ON the 6th of July the British troops were reviewed by the
Grand Vizier, a fresh looking middle-aged man, with a great
retinue of Bashaws, Agas, etc. He was escorted by a squadron
of the 12th Light Dragoons. We received him with presented
arms. He rode along the line and looked very attentively at
us. We then marched past with drums beating and music
playing. From his gestures he seemed to be well pleased
notwithstanding our ragged condition. Our chief guide and
interpreter dressed in scarlet and with a regulation feather in
his cap rode between Lord Hutchinson and the Grand Vizier.
We received the thanks of the Commander-in-chief for turning
out in such good order and having so cleanly an appearance
before the Turkish commander. This day the French removed
the remains of General Kleber their late Commander-in-chief
who had been assassinated by a fanatic Turk ; minute guns
were fired by them as he was borne along.

The thanks of both Houses of Parliament were read to us
on 8th July for our meritorious conduct in landing in Egypt
and for our conduct on the 13th and 21st of March. A
general promotion took place among the officers ; General
Hutchinson was raised to the peerage and many of the Generals
were made Knights of the Bath, etc.

With some others I obtained a pass to view the Pyramids.
We started at reveille in the morning, and reached a small
village called Haurige where we hired an Arab for five paras
each, there might be about twenty of us, to guide us over and
into the Pyramid. We soon reached this stupendous second
wonder of the world, but as every Gazetter gives an account
of these Pyramids I need say little. They stand about 9 miles
from the bed of the river and about 5 from the right of our
camp, but the ground being so level it appears to the eye to be

not more than 2 miles. We resolved to have an outside view first. The Great Pyramid is built of very large stones from 12 to 18 feet long and 4 feet and upwards thick ; these form irregular steps to the summit, which is level and may be about 36 feet square. A great many names are here cut out by different visitors ; I wrought very hard and got D. NICOL, 92 REGT carved, and broke my knife while finishing the job ; this is on the south-east corner, and is likely to stand some time.

The greater part of the French army marched and encamped along the great plain, with their left to the Pyramids, and the 79th's grenadier company did duty on the bridge of boats built by the French between Gizeh and Cairo. The Turks entered the city, hallooing and firing their muskets, and making all the noise a disorderly mob was fit to do. Sir David Baird's army occupied Rodda Island and some barracks opposite our left on the other side of the river. It consisted of some troops of the 8th Light Dragoons, 10th, 19th, 61st and 88th regiments, with some of the East India Company Artillery and a few battalions of Sepoys, the first I ever saw. They were fine stout-looking men, and when off duty wore nothing but a very short pair of drawers, which gave them an odd appearance to us.

July 11th, I mounted Sir John Doyle's guard with six men. We had to strike his marquee and pack his baggage on two camels to go into Cairo as he had that morning obtained leave to return to Europe on account of sickness. I crossed the bridge of boats built by the French and entered into a mass of confusion, the French with their baggage marching out and the Turks marching in.

The streets in Cairo are narrow and we were like to be choked with the dust or squeezed against the brick houses. At length the street got quite blocked up ; there were so many animals, camels, mules, and asses, that no movement could be made one way or other, but a party of Turkish cavalry going my way cleared a passage by blows on every poor Arab who had charge of a beast, whether in fault or not. I got our camels into the wake of the cavalry and in a little time after saw Sir John's aide-de-camp his nephew, looking out for us. He kept by us until we reached an open square with some large brick buildings ; into one of these we entered and found ourselves in a fine courtyard planted with trees and a fountain in the centre. I asked permission to visit the castle, as we

were not far from it.   This the aide-de-camp granted but said
we must be in our camp by sunset.   Off we set for the castle
or citadel which is very large, standing on a height in a fine
commanding situation, but I think it could be commanded by
the hill to the south of it.

At the west side stand some fine buildings with trees, the
principal magazines and stores.   The French had a mint and
a printing office here.   Saw many piles of shells made of a bluish
kind of marble which must have been hollowed out with great
labour, and many large mortars for discharging them.   Also
piles of new made shot of brass and copper.   I should not
wonder if the Turks have them carried off for gold, as they
have done the brass works of a gun which the French con-
structed, and which fired every day at 12 o'clock by the heat
of the sun through a burning glass just over the touch hole.

Most of the shops were shut, the merchants preferring to
take their goods to the British bazaar rather than trust the
Turks who at almost every open door were to be seen drinking
sherbet and smoking.   We were right glad when we got out
of the confusion and gained the end of the bridge where we
turned our backs on Grand Cairo, with its narrow streets,
brick and mud buildings, and its poor half-naked inhabitants.

15th July, all the arrangements for the march down the
country were now completed.   The French that surrendered
and marched out of Cairo on 9th July amounted to about
13,000 under command of General Belliard.   Some Greeks
and Copts in their service got liberty to go to France if they
chose.   The British took up their position in front, the French
were placed in the centre and the Indian army in the rear.
The boats belonging to each division kept the same order on
the river.   The Mamelukes kept on the left and the Turkish
Albanian regiments marched regularly on the other side of the
river.   A party of French dragoons with some of ours and our
quartermaster general took up the alignment of the camp.

At daybreak on the 15th a gun was fired and we all got on
the move.   A strict eye was kept on the French, for we were
not sure of them although the treaty was signed.   No
accident occurred.   When we came within seven miles of
Rosetta on the 28th we took up a strong position on the plain
with a high canal bank on our right and left.   Our cannon
were pointed and matches burning and strong guards sent to
the front.   The French then marched past, between us and
the river, in open order of companies with about sixty pieces

of cannon, all the cannoniers fine looking men well clothed, mounted on asses. Their 14th and 22nd regiments of dragoons were allowed to be the finest cavalry we had ever seen, and I have no doubt they showed themselves to the best advantage while passing the British army. They all marched on to the sea-side to embark. It was feared by some of our people that they would start off across the country to Alexandria, but I never believed they had any such intention, as they seemed very glad to get home to their own country.

On the 29th, General Hutchinson, who had been left behind at Cairo, arrived. We encamped about 2 miles above Rosetta where the ground was covered with black beetles, which annoyed us very much. The Nile had swollen greatly since we commenced our march down the country. Most of the canals began to fill and those drawn between the river and the lake began to run like mill-courses, and the water was very thick and muddy for drinking. The river so gained on us that we were forced to remove our camp to the edge of the sandhills below Rosetta among some date trees, where we were in no danger of being carried away by the flood.

On the 31st the French began to embark and the embarkation continued for ten days. A great number of women, natives of the country accompanied the French to the seaside, but they were not allowed to embark except a very few who could show that they were lawfully married ; the rest were left to find their way home as they best could.

General Lawson, R.A., took two guns from the French which had been taken from our army in the retreat from Dunkirk ; he claimed them as British property. Our cavalry were all fresh mounted by the horses of the French dragoons, which were far superior to any we had. Our artillery horses were replaced, and Donald MacIntosh of our company went as an artillery driver, one man was sent from each company. At this time Sergeant Symon of our company died, also Strong-ale Rab and Robert Cameron, Earl of Alkmaar, all great personages in the regiment. The Arabs who had attended the French army began to flock about our camp and also some of their women who had been turned back on their embarking.

As we passed along the inhabitants of the villages seemed to rejoice that the war in their country was at an end. They would call out 'Tieb tieb Anglo, Francois, Turk, soa, soa.' This as far as we could understand means, 'Good good English, French and Turks the same and the same.' But if

SIR JAMES MACDONELL

Who commanded at Hougoumont   'The bravest soldier at Waterloo'

Facing page 60

you asked them for a drink of water they would hold out their hand and say 'Had fluce a para,' and if you said 'Ma fish fluce,' they would say 'Ma fish moy,' and point to the river. If you said 'No money,' they said 'No water,' or 'You may go to the river.'

Our brigade was inspected by Lord Hutchinson who ordered us camels to carry our packs to Alexandria but Colonel Spencer said there was no need for it. This officer had had command of the brigade since General Doyle left and what different treatment we received, the one always looking out for the comfort of the soldiers, the other harassing us as far as he thought we would bear it. Marched, and the lake being much overflowed by the rising of the Nile we were obliged to march among the sand, whereas if we had started early in the morning this might have been avoided. Many of our men fell behind, for water was scarce. We encamped at Etko and surrounded the wells. I sat by one of them and drank water more than I had done since I came to the country. I thought I was never to be satisfied, and my eyes were getting dim for want of it. On August we came upon the great causeway leading from Rosetta; it is about 12 feet broad: thought it must have been the main road to Alexandria. Came to the seaside once more and thought ourselves refreshed by the air from it. Crossed at the caravansery on a bridge of boats, halted an hour and had a scramble for some brackish water. Reached the block-house where we offered some Turks money for water, half a dollar for a canteenful. A rush was made upon the Turks, they were knocked over and their water taken from them. This day some men of our brigade dropped down dead while marching in the ranks. I happened to have good luck: being on the right of the company my feet were kept moist all day with the salt water. We met the 22nd Light Dragoons just landed from Britain; they were mounted on French horses, having arrived just in time to receive them. We crossed on the raft at the mouth of the lake and halted by the wells we dug before the battle of the 13th March. Next day, August 9th, we marched into the lines and took up our station on the left of the Grand Fort. Great alterations had been made since we were here; deep trenches were cut, breastworks raised, pits dug in front to prevent an attack from cavalry, redoubts well finished and mounted with heavy cannon from the fleet from the sea to the lake. Wells had been built by new troops from Britain,

20th, 24th, 26th, 27th, and the Loyal Irish Fencibles. Detachments had arrived for all the regiments ; we got sixty men for ours. Everything appeared in a state of security ; officers' marquees were screened by date branches and gravel walks made round them—very comfortable indeed. Here was an excellent market formed on the left of the line, in which all the produce of the country was exposed for sale ; it was under the superintendence of Sergeant-major Miles of the 28th regiment who was made provost-marshal. A wine store was erected and on a pass signed by an officer four canteens were filled for a Spanish dollar. Bridges were made across the cuts made in the canal for joining the two lakes.

CHAPTER XI

THE SIEGE OF ALEXANDRIA

On the 16th of August in the evening, the armed launches and flat-bottomed boats were assembled to the left of the line. The greater part of the troops last arrived from Britain and the Guards, with some artillery, embarked under command of Sir Eyre Coote, and sailed after dark up the lake Mareotis, and got quietly landed to the west of Alexandria about daybreak, while we made a diversion in their favour in front. About two hours before daybreak we marched into the plain in three divisions, one by the seaside, one in the centre of the plain, and one on the left by the lake side under General Doyle who had again joined us. After passing our advanced posts in silence the enemy fired into us. We formed in line in rear of what we called the Green Hill and brought up our artillery and stood under arms till daylight when the French marched in columns in front of their batteries to oppose our division in the centre of the plain. The 30th regiment advanced to check a party of the enemy advancing from the bridge towards the hill when a smart firing commenced. General Doyle desired us to lie close to the ground until ordered to rise, telling us in an Irish whisper to level low, for said he, one bullet in a Frenchman's shin bone this day is as good as two in his head some other time. The enemy drove in the 30th regiment. We were ordered to advance and when we began to move received the fire of all their guns that could bear upon us, as well as a volley of small arms from the division coming towards us. This we returned in good earnest. On this the enemy retreated under shelter of their guns and we were ordered back to screen ourselves as much as possible from the fire of their heavy cannon, which kept playing most of the day. A shot knocked away Colonel Napier's horse's hind leg, and threw the Colonel on his back

63

among the sand. The Colonel sat up on the sand, and called out to get the saddle and bridle and he would get another horse. A cannon shot struck a white stone in front of me, which flew in pieces and hurt some of the right of our company about the neck and face, while a tooth was knocked right down my throat with a bit of it. I had good reason to thank God things were no worse with me.

The division on the right kept disputing a round hill nearly opposite us most of the day; it remained in our possession at night. The centre division having no shelter on the plain was drawn back to our lines. We lost between thirty and forty men of our brigade in this affair; working parties with entrenching tools were ordered out to us in the afternoon, to throw up breastworks and entrenchments along the brow of the hill. The enemy kept up a constant fire upon them until they reached us, doing them much damage. This party consisted of the Irish Fencible regiment and they never having seen anything of the kind before, were rather amazed poor lads. About this time some Arabs ventured out amongst us to sell bread, which they carried in baskets. It was soon bought and they sat down on a bank of sand exposed to the French lines to count their gains, when a 24-lb. shot struck the bank and almost buried the Arabs in the sand. None of them were seriously hurt. After shaking themselves they ran off leaving baskets, turbans, and money behind, crying out 'O Allah, Francois,' etc. ; our division never got such a hearty laugh together since we came to the country. No more Arabs appeared this day.

After dark we were relieved by the centre division. On the 18th, our regiment struck their tents and moved into the plain in rear of the Green Hill. At this place the ground was covered with fine salt about 6 inches deep incrusted by the sun. On the 19th, all our troops were drawn across the plain. We thought we were to storm the town, and I am certain the French thought the same. As we advanced their sentinels fired and retreated. We fired none, as we were ordered not to fire on any account. The alarm being given, the enemy opened a tremendous fire of shot and shell ; from the seaside to the lake seemed in a blaze, and the air was full of shells ; they dropped them so as to clear their own works, for they certainly thought we were upon them. But not a shot was returned by us, except by some of our skirmishers in front who were close on their works. This was a false attack on our part,

GENERAL SIR DE LACY EVANS

Facing page 65

made to enable Sir Eyre Coote's troops to take possession of a
height which commands the western harbour of Alexandria.
This they did and threw up a blue light as a signal ; on
this we marched back to our tents about daybreak.

We did duty by brigades at the advanced posts.   A
road was made on the left by the side of the lake, and heavy
cannon were mounted on two batteries erected on the hill,
and on two by the seaside.   It was a fatiguing job getting the
heavy guns to the batteries through the deep sand, and this
had to be done in the night time.   We got everything ready
to commence firing on the 1st of September, which we did
powerfully from every gun that could be brought to bear.
Our war vessels stood as close in to the harbour as they could ;
some very heavy metal was opened on them from Pharaoh's
Castle.   Our gunboats on the lake kept up a constant fire on
the right of the enemy's lines, while General Coote's batteries
joined in from the western side of the town.   All this made
the place hot enough for them.   One of our twenty-four
pounders on the left battery burst and killed and wounded
some of the artillery.

On the 27th, in the evening an officer came from General
Menou with a letter asking a cessation of hostilities for three
days that he might draw up articles of capitulation.   This was
agreed to.   On the 29th an extension of time for thirty-six
hours was asked.   General Hutchinson sent back word that
if the articles of capitulation were not sent in by twelve o'clock
that night, our batteries would open and the place be stormed.
About 10 o'clock a message was sent by the French General
that the articles would be ready the next day.   After some
delay the articles were signed by Lord Hutchinson,
and on 2nd September by Lord Keith who came ashore for
that purpose.   It was stipulated that our army should take
possession of the outworks, and the French be drawn within
the walls of the town till they were ready to embark.   At
twelve o'clock the grenadiers of our different regiments, Sir
John Hope riding in front, began to cross the plain with bands
playing the Grenadier March, while the troops of both armies
stood looking on, they had such a noble, majestic appearance
on entering the French lines.   The four flags hoisted at the
main entrance into the enemy's lines, the French, the Dutch,
the Spanish, and one for Egypt, said to be Coptic, were struck,
to be hoisted no more and the white flag displayed.   In the
evening the Grenadiers were relieved by the following

E

regiments :—2nd or Queen's, 79th, and our regiment, extending from the little Pharos tower to the main entrance ; a
brigade of heavy artillery pointed to the Rosetta gate, on one
of the guns was hoisted the British flag ; on the height in rear
of the wells was General Stewart's foreign brigade. The
evening gun was fired before our regiment sent out their
watering parties ; they were turned back by Sir John Hope
when within 300 yards of the wells : this kept us badly off
for water during the night. We did duty here along with
the French, they in the inside of the gates, and we without
and we were very familiar together. The French officers and
a proportion of men had liberty to go to our market and make
purchases, as they had been on low diet for some time back.
They came among us disposing of watches and gold rings
very cheap, some of their Italian plunder I have no doubt.
Some of our men taken prisoners in the month of March
were sent in to our lines ; they looked as if they had been
badly kept, were like skeletons, dirty and ragged. While
digging in the sand some of our men discovered a canvas hose
charged with gunpower leading to a 13 inch shell, from that
to another, and so on extending on both sides of the main
entrance into the enemy's works, on the very ground where
our tents stood. As this was thought to be some piece of
French treachery it was inquired into, and it was explained
that it was laid there in case the British had stormed the place.
The shells were dug up and collected in one place in case of
any accident.

The French had very strong fortifications here. On the
heights from the sea to the lake was one entire battery with a
deep ditch about 18 feet broad, and palisadoes, and in the
hollow between the walls of the town and this fortification the
French lay in huts. If we had stormed these outworks we
would have been exposed to the fire of the citadel and forts
Cretain and Caffarelli as well as from the walls of Alexandria,
which are about 30 feet high and flanked with towers, which
in some places are falling into decay.

On the 11th of September the French marched out at
twelve o'clock at night. We stood under arms until they
passed, about 11,000 of all descriptions, on their way to
embark at Aboukir. This put a finish to our labour in this
country, and we had now some time to look about us—for
we had lain every night fully accoutred and with our firelocks
by our side since we came up here. We were ordered to take

down the French huts in our rear and build two huts for each company, but with these materials were brought such a quantity of fleas that we could not get peace to sleep quietly afterwards. We now got plenty of firewood, an article we had been very scarce of in this country : villages have often been unroofed to supply fuel for the army. Flour was served out in place of bread, which was much against us as we had no way to keep it clear of sand, our method was to make dumplings of it and boil them in the camp kettles. On the 27th it was my turn to draw the company's rum. Corporal MacBean went for me, and coming back at full speed one of the cords of Mr Mackay's tent took his feet, he fell and all the liqour was sunk in the sand in a moment. He generously offered to purchase two dollars' worth of date brandy : this we all rejected.

On the 4th of October, Lieutenant Ranald MacDonald, who was our acting adjutant, ordered me to get six men and four camels to take the officers' baggage to the commissary depôt, where I was to get a boat to take it on board. When I reached there I found Adjutant Campbell, and all the sick of the brigade, and learned that the regiment was to be embarked on board the *Renommee*, forty-four, and *Modeste* frigates, five companies in each. I delivered over the camels and got a boat on the 5th. We wrought very hard all morning putting the baggage into the boat, keeping each ship's baggage as much by itself as we could. We had very poor assistance. The boat was overloaded and could not get off, so we had to strip naked and push her out into the lake where deep water was : she got on several shoals and we had to again push her off until we got into the bay. I got a very severe headache and pain in the brow by over-exertion in the heat of the sun ; this terminated in sore eyes. I regretted much that I was taking this disease the very last day I was in the country, for I had been exceedingly healthy since we landed in March, but I was not permitted to pass out of the house of bondage without affliction.

We reached the *Renommee* frigate after dark, and got part of the baggage on board. Early next morning we went to the *Modeste* frigate, where I delivered over my charge to Mr Donald MacBarnet, formerly quartermaster sergeant, but who has now got a commission, while poor John MacIntosh, Sergeant-Major, who was wounded and present with the regiment during the campaign was entirely overlooked. On the 6th of October the five companies came on board commanded by Major Gordon.   They were much fatigued with a long march through the sand, but as it was the first step on the road home they stood it with the greater fortitude.

II

CORUNNA—THE STORY OF
A TERRIBLE RETREAT

FROM THE FORGOTTEN JOURNAL
OF SERGEANT D. ROBERTSON

CHAPTER I

THE MARCH TO BURGOS

WE continued our march towards Burgos, says Sergt. Robertson in his narrative, and when we came to Toro, we met with a party of dragoons belonging to the army under the command of Sir David Baird, that had landed at Corunna. They had, in a skirmish with the French, taken four waggons laden with cotton which were proceeding under a strong escort. We proceeded on our route till we reached Villada. On a party of sergeants of which I made one entering the place to draw billets for the men, we found that it was occupied by a patrole of French dragoons. There being about half-a-dozen of us, and not a single firelock amongst us we felt rather nonplussed. We proceeded somewhat warily, however, and discovered the French regaling themselves in a wine-house, having their horses tied at the door. A thought immediately struck us, that if we could make a seizure of the horses we could easily secure the men. Being market-day in the town there were a great many people in it ; but the Spaniards, not knowing whether we were French or not, all was quiet on their part. All went on smoothly till we reached the tavern door and had the bridles in our hands. The dragoons when too late discharged a few shots at us, but without effect when we rushed in and disarmed them and made them prisoners. The French patrole consisted of a corporal and five privates. When the Spaniards saw what we had done they seemed frantic with joy, and would have given us anything in the market. One of them, on seeing that I had no gloves, and that my hands were cold went to a merchant and bought me a pair.

The army at length came up to us, very much fatigued on account of the state of the roads, which were very heavy and deeply covered with snow. We were ordered to clean ourselves as we were to halt here for some time ; but all of a sudden, on the evening of the same day 24th December, we were ordered to fall in for marching. By eight o'clock we were all outside the town and formed in columns expecting to be engaged by morning. It was a beautiful moonlight night, but the cold was so severe that we could not sit down so we kept walking about till daybreak. Every heart beat high with the thought that we were to measure arms with the great Napoleon. The notion entertained by the British army was, that the great victories gained by him had been over raw and undisciplined troops ; and we ardently wished to see how a British force would act when opposed to a French one under his command. Every man felt confident of his own prowess when compared with a French soldier's, and nothing was more earnestly wished than an opportunity of engaging, and an order for battle. But judge of our surprise and disappointment when, about twelve o'clock at night, a staff officer delivered an order from Sir John Moore that we were to go into cantonment and prepare to proceed to England. And now the horrors of retreat were depicted before our mind's eye in all their dark colouring ;—the weather extremely cold, the roads broken and heavy, and the men badly off for shoes, with a distance of some hundred miles from the nearest place where we could find shipping. All ranks called out to stop and fight and not to run away (as we termed it), which would be a disgrace to the British army.

We commenced our retreat on Christmas forenoon at eleven o'clock, and arrived at Mayerga after nightfall. To add to our mortification the inhabitants had barricaded the doors and windows and would not let any of us in. At this season of the year, and the ground being covered with snow, we thought this treatment very bad. We then had recourse to another method of effecting an ingress, by breaking down everything that opposed our entrance, and from this circumstance arose all the disasters that subsequently befel us on our retreat ; for the news was at the next village before us, and so on all the way. We came to Valdross, the town appeared to be deserted. We were put into a convent for the night, and sentinels were posted at the entrances to keep the men from going out.

On coming to Bounevento, we were all put into a convent where we had to lie on the stair or any place where we could find room. The following day the army continued their retreat. I was left behind to try and procure some blankets and shoes for the men; but scarcely had our army cleared the town, when the French appeared on the other side of the river. Our rear and baggage guards turned out and marched to a plain outside the town to receive them. When they came on, our dragoons showed that, though retreating, it was not from fear.

Having got a supply of shoes, I proceeded after the division and came up to it at the end of the stage. This night we were quartered in a miserable little village and had very bad weather. Through accident, or from a spirit of wanton mischief on the part of some of our grenadier company a house was set on fire, the flames of which communicating with the other houses, the whole village was burned down not leaving a single building with a roof on it in the place. As the French were close upon us there was not time to discover the perpetrators of the mischief and bring them to punishment. The road during this day's march was in a very bad state; and on coming up to some of the divisions that preceded us, we found that they had been obliged to destroy a quantity of the stores among which was a cask of rum, the head having been stove in. A young man of the name of Bruce belonging to the 92nd, was drowned in it; in consequence of his inebriated state he had fallen in headlong, and before he could be extricated was quite dead.

We arrived this night at a large village of the name of Benbevera and were put into quarters. In almost every house we found some of the Spanish soldiers either dying or dead. The house in which I was lodged contained four dead bodies which had to be removed to the street before we could get accommodation for sleeping. There were two of our men who died here next morning of a fever; their remains were buried by their comrades in the ruins of an old house.

Upon the first of January 1809, we proceeded towards Villafranca. While on the road, a few Spanish peasants stole some ammunition from the cartridge-boxes of several of the 52nd. When captured they were severely flogged by orders of Marshal Beresford, and made to pay a dollar for every round of cartridge amissing. When we came to Villafranca, all the spare ammunition was thrown into the river and every thing that could be wanted was destroyed. This was truly the most disagreeable new-year's day that I ever spent. At this time we were enduring all the miseries of retreat;—our clothes were falling off our backs and our shoes worn to the welts. From the officer down to the private, we were overrun with vermin, bearing alike the extremities of hunger and cold, and forming altogether a combination of sufferings sufficient to appal the stoutest heart and break down the strongest constitution. As we had a good position, we wished to make a stand here ; but Sir John Moore did not think it proper to risk an engagement with such a superior enemy. Here we were put into a large inn, and it was the lot of the 92nd to get the stables, which turned out to be the most comfortable lodgings we had during the campaign, although we had nothing but the soil of the stables for our beds. Indeed, so comfortably did we find ourselves quartered, that next morning, when called upon to march, it required all the authority of the officers to get the men to move. After all, we were forced to leave two of them behind, who were unable to proceed from fatigue and privation.

This morning our real unmitigated hardships may be said to have begun in earnest, compared with which every thing before was but child's play. The army had now commenced to ascend the Gallican mountains. Here there had once been a good road but it was so destroyed by the heavy rains, and cut up with the carriages that had gone over it, that we could not go a step without sinking to the knees in mud. The first who stuck on the road was the Paymaster-General of the army. He had brought his lady with him out to Spain, and had got for her convenience a four-wheeled carriage, which was drawn by two fine English horses. We often envied them when we saw how easily they moved along ; and they were at times somewhat troublesome to us, as we had to open out to the right and left to let them pass—not a pleasant matter for poor fellows worn out with the want of food and clothing. Here at last, the vehicle stuck fast, all the efforts made to extricate it proving abortive, and it had to be left where it was. This circumstance may give the readers of this narrative some idea of the state of the roads over which we had to make our way ; of it those who have not seen any but the smooth macadamised highways of Britain can form no adequate conception.

The snow was now falling very thick and the cold was intense. Having progressed a little farther, we came up to a brigade of artillery which had to be destroyed and the horses shot, it not having been able to proceed owing to the impassable state of the road. The next part of the wreck of the army were the carts containing the money which we had to make away with, rather than let them fall into the hands of the enemy. The horses were shot and the casks with the money rolled down the side of the hill, which is very steep and high, having at the bottom a deep and woody ravine.

CHAPTER II

HOW THEY CAPTURED A FRENCH PICQUET

On the 4th January we arrived at Lugo, and were put into a convent for the night where we expected to remain for a few days and give the French an offer of battle ; but on the evening of the 5th an alarm was sounded that the enemy had approached within a league of the town. Having got flour served out instead of bread and the issue being made at a late hour, we had not time to cook it before we were obliged to turn out and form up in a field to the left of the main road in front of Lugo, where we remained all night without being disturbed. In the morning, everyone was happy that we had got the French in line, and that an end might be put to our hardships one way or another ; we longed very much to fight, and abhorred the thought of running away in the manner we had been doing for some time past. About ten o'clock, as the rain was beginning to fall in torrents, the French began to extend their line, and beat the charge. They occupied a ploughed field, and we were posted on a heath, with a small river running in the hollow of a valley which separated us. A farmhouse lay at the foot of the rising ground having a few stacks of corn about it. As it stood at a little distance from both lines but nearer to the British than the French, General Hope thought fit to take occupation of it. Accordingly the company to which I belonged was ordered to advance and take possession of the farm-yard and when going down for that purpose, General Hope accompanied us. While moving along the French fired one of their cannon, the ball from which fell close beside us but did no hurt ; on seeing this the General good humouredly took off his hat and saluted the gunner.

As I was the only sergeant with the company and there being only one subaltern officer, I got the command of a section, to act under the orders of the captain. When we came to the house we found a party of the French there before us and a strong reinforcement coming to their assistance. However, they did not think fit to wait and receive us for after firing a few rounds on both sides, they fell back on the reinforcement, and we occupied the farm-yard. Though we had thus accomplished our object, we were not allowed to remain long in quiet possession, but were obliged to quit our position, as the enemy came upon us in overpowering numbers. We fell back the breadth of a field in our rear and posted ourselves behind a stone wall that enclosed it whence we opened a fire upon the enemy. The French attempted to charge us but in this they failed. On the left of this field there was a cart-road that ran between two deep hedges. At the time the French in our front were keeping us in play, a party of about forty went up this road and unperceived by us, got in our rear, while those in our front made a feint of giving way with the intention of decoying us, and so getting us between the fire of both parties. But fortunately I happened to look round in expectation of some assistance, and judge what was my surprise when I saw a party of the enemy forming at the head of the field we were in, not above forty yards from us. The thought struck me at the moment to go into the lane and prevent them from getting into their own line ; upon which the section under my command jumped into the road and prepared to charge them. When the French saw this, they endeavoured to get on to the lane at the other end of the field, and then ran down to us calling out 'Prisoners.'

By this time I had got my section regularly formed, and answered them with a volley that left eighteen of them dead and wounded. On seeing the fate of their comrades, twenty-two of them laid down their arms and were taken prisoners, whom I sent along with our corporal to the commanding officer of the regiment. When the French saw how roughly this party had been handled, they sent another detachment with a sergeant at its head who immediately commenced firing upon us. The French sergeant got hold of one of our men to take him prisoner, when I leaped back and drove my pike through his body. Upon seeing their leader fall the remainder of the men ran off and we were not able to follow them. About the same time there were a good many of the 91st taken prisoners. We were now thoroughly drenched with the rain which had fallen heavily all day ; and when night came on, we were relieved by an equal number of the regiment, that we might have an opportunity of resting ourselves for a little.

CHAPTER III

THE TERRIBLE SUFFERINGS OF THE ARMY

HAVING had nothing to eat for two days, we were now very weak. Some of the men having found a quantity of apples in the farm-house, we devoured them very greedily although a more substantial sort of food would have been more acceptable to our craving appetites. In the evening we got our beef served out ; but having neither bread nor salt, it made rather an unsavoury morsel. Although the weather was frosty and very cold we slept very comfortably by the side of several large fires, which we had kindled in the open air.

We remained in this position till the evening of the 8th, and about seven o'clock we made great fires and left small picquets at them, in order to deceive the French, while the main body of the army formed on the highway leading through Lugo. We marched all night along a very bad road, and next morning about daybreak it came on a dreadful storm of wind and rain. It fell to my lot, along with other three sergeants to be entrusted with the care of the colours that day, but scarcely any of us were able to carry them, being so exhausted and fatigued from hunger and cold. With very great difficulty we managed to keep up with the rest of the army, until we came to the end of the stage, where we arrived about noon the following day and formed line on a black heath. Soaked to the skin with rain, we lay down cold and comfortless ; for having nothing to cook, we did not light any fires. I offered a good price to any of the soldiers who would give me the least crumb of bread, but all in vain, as there was not a morsel among the whole of us. Evening at length came on and we resumed our dreary march. I was ordered forward to take up quarters somewhere on the main road. The men had now become so unmanageable from fatigue and hunger, that neither promises nor threats could induce them to go on. Some of the men, breaking through all restraint, went off to the fields and lay down and slept till daybreak, when the French came up and made them prisoners. Those that did come on had their feet so sore blistered and swollen, that they must have marched under excruciating pain.

By daylight I reached Botanson, and so ravenously hungry was I, that I ate the frosted turnips by the roadside. When I came to the end of my journey I procured some bread and wine which I devoured with a very craving appetite. Having secured the quarters for the regiment I went out to meet it ; and while on the way met with a number of the officers, some of whom were riding fast asleep, and when I asked at them about the regiment they could not tell anything of it, not having seen it since twelve o'clock at night. At last, about two in the afternoon the stragglers began to come in.

What might now be called the regiment consisted of the Commanding Officer, the colours, and about twenty men to act as a guard. As an encouragement to those who came in along with the colours they were ordered a double allowance of rations and liquor ; but the difficulty was to get men to distribute them when issued. The worn-out soldiers had lain down and fallen asleep, and could not be roused up, till at length by a strange contrivance, we mustered as many as were required to carry the provisions from the store, which we soon got cooked in the houses where we lodged for the night. Our shoes being now literally worn off our feet we were obligated to take pieces from the hides of the cavalry horses which had been shot, and tie them on like sandals.

Next morning we continued our retreat and were not so closely pressed, as we had stolen a march on the enemy during the preceding day. When we left Botanson the men were so lame that they could scarcely creep along the road. There were several of the non-commissioned officers placed in the rear of each company carrying knives in their hands ; and when any of the men fell behind their knapacks were cut off and thrown away and the men were left with nothing to carry but firelock, pouch, and bayonet. On account of depredations having been committed some days before, the Commander-in-chief was under the disagreeable necessity of making an example of some of the perpetrators. One of the 50th was hanged on a tree by the roadside, and all the army marched past the place of execution ; but even this severe punishment had but little effect in deterring others from committing like crimes. Shortly after this, the sergeant-major of the 92nd was detected in the act of plundering a house on the highway, and was taken up and ordered to be shot ; but General Hope, on account of his wife and family, interceded for him and his sentence was commuted to eight hundred lashes. A number of the guards were also punished at the same time for a similar offence. In fact, a part of every regiment in the army was guilty of the same outrages and suffered a like infliction of punishment.

After enduring all sorts of hardships, we at length reached a village within a mile of Corunna, where we took up our quarters for the night. No ships had arrived to take us on board, and this vexed us very much, being in such a deplorable and broken-down condition that we did not think ourselves capable of fighting, even although we should be attacked. When the 92nd were mustered, it was found that there were no less than 197 deficient of the roll that turned out on Christmas day. Of this great number a few afterwards came up and joined us as we were going on board ; but with the exception of a few that made their way into Portugal, and attached themselves to the army under Sir Arthur Wellesley, the majority either fell by the shot of the enemy, or being exhausted and overcome by the severity of the weather and other hardships during our march, lagged behind and were taken prisoners by the French as they came up.

SIR THOMAS PICTON

CHAPTER IV

THE BATTLE OF CORUNNA

HAVING rested ourselves here for two days, and being now plentifully supplied with victuals and provided with shoes and ammunition, we could not brook the thought of being driven into the sea (for the prisoners whom we had taken told us that such were Napoleon's instructions to his generals) without making an effort to retain our ground. We had scarcely taken up our line before Corunna, when the French formed upon a hill in our front apparently with the intention of coming into immediate action. At this time the shipping made its appearance, the welcome sight of which so inspirited us that we gave a loud cheer of defiance to the French on the opposite height. As there was no way of carrying off the spare ammunition the whole of it was conveyed to the top of a rising ground and a match applied to it. The explosion was so tremendous and unexpected that it astonished the French, who thought it was some infernal machine, and made them run off in terror leaving their arms behind. Had we been on the alert and taken advantage of the opportunity their flight afforded us, we might easily have secured their arms and ammunition. Not being aware, however, that such an effect would be produced upon them, we contented ourselves with merely looking on and laughing at the panic into which they were thrown ; but as soon as they saw that their apprehensions were groundless, they returned to their position as before. About mid-day they sent out skirmishers and discharged a few shots from their batteries to try if our line was in range of their guns. This was the prelude to what was to happen next day. The 92nd now took up its position on the left near the sea, having in its front a steep hill, which protected it from any attempt that might be made upon it in

F

that quarter. All the divisions under the command of General Hope were at or near the same place.

On the morning of the following day (the 16th) the picquets were relieved before daybreak. Being the commanding officer's orderly sergeant, it was my duty to take charge of the picquets, and see that they kept their posts. Lieutenant-Colonel Napier of the 92nd, who was field officer for the outposts that day, desired me to look after his horses and get them safely embarked on board the ships. I was on my way to Corunna to execute this message when the firing commenced, and I immediately turned back and joined the picquet, which was now hotly engaged with the French riflemen at a few houses in front of the line. Colonel Napier was at the time giving orders to carry the village by storm when he received a shot in the groin from one of the French riflemen, which almost immediately deprived him of existence. One of the men immediately took off his shirt, bound up the wound with it, and carried him to the rear. In consequence of this lamentable affair the command devolved upon Colonel Lamont. Although we were twice driven from the post, we returned to the attack with redoubled fury, and at last retained it in defiance of all the efforts of the enemy to dislodge us. Exasperated at being thus repulsed, the French sent down a strong reinforcement upon us to drive all before it. In this however, they were disappointed; for General Hope, on perceiving the movement ordered two companies of the 14th to our assistance. Then came the tug of war—such bayonet work I never saw before. There was little or no firing on either side, but fair hand-to-hand fighting. Night at length came on and put an end to the contest—the French withdrawing from the village, while we remained masters of it.

Shortly after this, Colonel Lamont was sent for by the Commander-in-chief and, as it was dusky, I accompanied him. When we arrived we received an order requesting us to keep our post till five o'clock in the morning to deceive the enemy, as it was intended that the army should embark that night, and then we were to make the best of our way to the ships. We now heard for the first time that Sir John Moore was no more, and that Sir David Baird was severely wounded. But what added most to our grief was the death of Colonel Napier of the 92nd, whom every man in the regiment adored, and to whom he was more like an affectionate father than a commanding officer. On our return Colonel Lamont and

I lost our way and before we were aware found ourselves among a French picquet. They were busy at work killing a bullock ; but as we did not think proper to wait and partake of it, we made the best of our way to where our own picquet was stationed. We remained here until five o'clock when we started off for the beach as fast as we could. We had not proceeded far before we were observed by the French dragoons who gave the alarm that the whole army was off and none remained but the picquets, who had been left to cover the movement. On giving this intelligence, they were ordered to pursue us with all their might ; but having only about a mile and a half to go over, we managed to keep out of their reach. Just as we arrived at the beach the last boat was pushing off; but after jumping from a height of twelve feet, we got into it, and were taken on board the transport, where we thought we were safe from all further danger. In this, however, we were disappointed for the French incensed at being outwitted in this way, and to have a parting shot at us, brought down two field pieces, and commenced firing at us with great fury. The sailors not having been accustomed to that sort of work, would not come on deck to work the vessels, but left the management of them to the soldiers who could not be supposed to be very proficient in nautical affairs. The consequence was that a number of the transports ran foul of one another, while some got on the rocks and became wrecks. During all this confusion the French still kept firing upon us, till the *Victory* of 98 guns brought her broadside to bear upon them and quickly silenced their noise. Such was the hurry and confusion attending the embarkation of the troops that no less than part of seventeen regiments were on board one transport.

The condition in which we were now with regard to clothing and cleanliness, beggars all description. From the length of time we had been without getting our clothes shifted or cleaned, we had become overrun with vermin, while our dress was so encrusted with mud, as to baffle all attempts even to discover what colour they originally were. In addition to this, a violent flux broke out among the men, which made the ships in a most loathsome state, while the effluvia it occasioned brought on a severe sickness from which few escaped.

At last however, we came in sight of England, and landed at Portsmouth. When we arrived here, I had neither shoes nor stockings on my feet, but had to walk along the streets barefooted. When we came to our billets, about six miles from Portsmouth, the inhabitants would not allow us to sleep in their beds, nor sit by the fireside, on account of the vermin that infested us ;—cleaning ourselves was out of the question without a complete change of clothing.

When we reached Warley barracks, where our heavy luggage was lying, and among which I had a trunk containing a suit of clothes that I had left before we embarked for Spain, I soon divested myself of my filthy raiment and reduced it to ashes, with the exception of the Highland bonnet and feathers, which I preserved.

After such a disastrous result some will be anxious to know the cause of such a relaxation of discipline as there appears to have been in the course of this memorable retreat ; and to enquire why we were worse off than the French army when we were going over the ground first, they pursuing in the same tract. It is well known that a finer body of men (to appearance at least) never left the British shore, nor better equipped for service than this army. No expense was withheld to complete them with every requisite necessary for the expedition. We were not as yet enured to this sort of warfare, and, of course, did not understand how to conduct ourselves. The British soldier, when at home, has every thing provided for him and of course does not know how to live without all the conveniences to which he has been accustomed. There is thus so much method in the army, that any deviation from the line laid down is considered a gross misdemeanor ; and the consequence was, that when the army was reduced to live upon scanty allowance and to suffer privations to which it had not been accustomed, it went into disorder. There is no doubt that had we been brought into action with the French on equal terms, we would have maintained our ground against them, or any army of like numbers in Europe ; but not one of ten amongst us was used to campaigning, whereas the French had been long on the war establishment, and had lately come from Germany where they had been enured to hardships for some years, which gave them a decided advantage over us. Another thing greatly in favour of the French arose from the relative condition of the two armies. The French entered Spain as invaders—we as allies. Plunder was not only tolerated among the former, but even encouraged ; hence, if provisions

LORD UXBRIDGE

Afterwards Marquis of Anglesey

Facing page 8₅

were to be got in any way, they were not deterred by the fear of punishment from taking them ; while if any act of a similar kind was detected in the British army, the perpetrator was in most instances punished with death. The French commissary department was also under better regulations than that of the British, which circumstance told greatly in favour of the French ; and above all, they had all the advantage which a pursuing army has over a retreating one, being inspired and emboldened by the thought that retreat is an acknowledgemt of inferiority.

Soon after our arrival at Warley barracks in Essex, the most of our regiment, along with the other regiments that had been in Spain, were seized with typhus fever, which carried off a great number of us. Indeed, so great was the prevalence of that contagious and fatal malady, that an order came from the War Office to the effect, that we should be relieved from doing any duty till further orders were given, that every article of clothing be burnt and that we be supplied with every thing new. There was also £2 given to each of us to provide necessaries in lieu of those destroyed. The Lords of the Treasury ordered another £2 to each man who was sickly, with which to purchase any cordial that the doctor thought proper.

III

THE GORDON HIGHLANDERS IN SPAIN

A FORGOTTEN PAGE IN THEIR HISTORY FROM
THE PUBLISHED DIARY OF SERGEANT NICOL

CHAPTER I

THE INVALID DETACHMENT

From mountain side to rocky glen,
They hear, they answer Huntly's call,
The gallant Gordons well beloved,
Prepared to fight or fall.
Regimental Song of the Gordons.

IT was in 1808 that Napoleon, roused to frenzy by the news of the advance of Sir John Moore, declared that he would chase the British armies from the Peninsula. At that moment he commanded two hundred thousand veteran troops, while Moore could only gather from his scattered garrisons a fighting force of twenty-three thousand men. With these he struck vigorously at the armies commanded by Soult and Ney. In consequence Napoleon changed his plans, and when his generals reported to him that the passes were blocked with snow, he answered that if the British troops could face the rigours of the winter march in the mountains, the men under his command must do likewise, and so, with the loss of many men and animals, the passes were traversed.

Meanwhile the Spanish armies, upon whose support General Moore had relied rapidly dwindled away, and Moore having by his attack upon Bonaparte's communications succeeded for the time in saving southern Spain, recalled his advance guard and prepared to retreat. The story of what followed is too well known to need repetition here. In the trying marches and continuous fighting of the next four weeks the newly raised regiment—the 92nd or Gordon Highlanders bore their part nobly, and in the battle of Corunna held the post of honour on the left wing. Their losses on that occasion were heavy and included their leader the popular Colonel Napier of Blackstone, an excellent officer.

Previous to the attack of Moore on Napoleon's communications, the British army had been quartered in all the principal towns in the south and west of Spain and of Portugal and in Lisbon large numbers of invalids and convalescents had been assembled. When the news of Napoleon's advance reached Lisbon, these parties and detachments were formed into two battalions of about eleven hundred men each ; one company of the first battalion was composed solely of men from the 92nd regiment, the other companies were made up of men belonging to the 42nd, 79th, and 91st Highlanders, besides some Rifles.

Colonel Greenhill-Gardyne the latest historian of the Gordons, in his most interesting and elaborate work, completed in 1903, has omitted to refer to this company, although in a footnote he mentions the fact that some of the invalids of the regiment had joined what were called the 'Corps of detachments.' The work done by the detached company has however, fortunately been preserved for us in the hitherto unpublished journal of an ex-sergeant of the regiment, who was with it during the time it formed part of the army commanded by Sir Arthur Wellesley, who had just landed at Mondego Bay.

The crisis in the history of Europe at that moment was intense, for the Germans and Austrians had risen in arms against their French conquerors ; and if the British Government had only sent an adequate force into Spain to support the rising of their Spanish and Portuguese allies, there is little doubt that five years' fighting in the Peninsula would have been prevented. Instead however, of providing an adequate force, the Ministers resolved to subdivide their magnificent army of ninety thousand men. This force the Duke of York had collected so that it might be immediately available to strike at whichever point should prove to be the most vulnerable in the armour of the French Colossus, but the Government dispatched a portion of it on the hapless expedition to Walcheren and Antwerp, and sent a second corps to Sicily. Wellesley was thus compelled to accept the command of a force of only twenty thousand men, with which to secure the liberties of twelve millions of Spaniards and to overcome the combined armies of France, at that moment ten times more numerous than his own.

Nicol entered upon his experiences in the Peninsula, which are detailed with so much graphic power in his very interesting manuscript, shortly after the ignominious convention of Cintra, which for a time liberated Portugal. Incidentally it also saved the French armies at a moment when they might have fallen an easy prey as prisoners into the hands of the newly arrived and highly organised British forces.

While in Lisbon he saw the departure of the Russian fleet, consisting of seven large vessels of the line and a frigate, which had been blockaded in the river by the British fleet, under Sir Charles Cotton, and which in terms of the Convention were allowed to set sail with the Russian colours flying; all to the intense indignation of the soldiers and sailors, who regarded the fleet as a lawful prize stolen from them in the moment of victory.

From August till October 1808, the regiment lay in the neighbourhood of Lisbon; and it was on the 1st October, that while on picquet-duty in a ploughed field, Nicol was forced to remain all night exposed to the rain and wind, which produced a fever and invalided him for two months. Meantime the regiment marched into Spain and in the following month began the retreat to Corunna. From the regiment Nicol received the letter of an old comrade telling of his arrival at the Escurial near Madrid, and reporting the approach of the French, who were now advancing under Napoleon, by way of Valladolid. 'We will defeat them,' said the letter-writer, 'with the help of the Spanish army, and return to England by way of France.' This prophetic utterance, which was realised in 1814, was the last communication that Nicol had with his regiment for many years.

E. B. L.

CHAPTER II

THE PASSAGE OF THE DOURO

THE invalids of the 92nd left in Portugal formed a company of the first battalion of detachments, which was commanded by Lieutenant-Colonel Bunbury and Major Ross. The company of Gordons consisted of Captain Logie, Lieutenant Cattanach, Lieutenant Durie, Surgeon Beattie, eight sergeants, a piper, and seventy-six rank and file.

Sir Arthur Wellesley who landed on the 22nd April 1809, marched on the main road direct to Oporto, and came up on several occasions, with the enemy under Soult. The Portuguese troops under Marshal Beresford joined in the march, and a battalion of these under British officers, was added to each brigade of the British army.

The company of Gordons was associated with a battalion commanded by Colonel Doyle, formerly a lieutenant of the Gordons when in Egypt, and he found that nearly a dozen of the men in the company had already served with him there. Nicol tells us that the old comrades gladly drank the health of their colonel and that of his uncle Sir John Doyle, with whom they had also seen service. On 12th May 1809, at about three in the morning, an explosion was heard which made the company stand to its arms, and this proved to be caused by the blowing up of the bridge across the Douro by the French army, which had entered Oporto and sought to cover its retreat.

Wellesley determined to force the passage of the river at all costs, and having then got the enemy 'on the retreat' to keep at them. He accordingly at once prepared to cross the great river. The Gordons marched into Villa Nova and joined General Sherbrooke's brigade which had landed in boats from Ovar.

So close was the pursuit of the French that Nicol tells us

MARSHAL NEY

Facing page 92

that 'if our artillery horses had been able to drag forward the guns, they would have taken many prisoners and have entered Oporto pell-mell with the French.' The enemy, however, had taken possession of all the boats they could discover, and the British fleet moved accordingly close into the mouth of the river and provided boats for the crossing. The Gordons' detachment, with two regiments, marched in double-quick time to the Sera convent, which the French had fortified and mounted with cannon, but which had been abandoned. 'We trailed arms and ran up the riverside through a firwood to a creek, where we found some large boats manned by Portuguese.' In them they crossed the river, when the French came fiercely upon them in two large columns with cannon. The enemy were driven from the top of the bank, which was held by the Gordons till the Guards and the Third Buffs had almost crossed the river, when Nicol's battalion charged the French columns and the 14th Dragoons attacked the French left and put them to rout with great slaughter. The inhabitants of Braga cheered the British troops as they approached, and took the opportunity of killing all the wounded Frenchmen they came upon, and stripping them.

After following the retreating Frenchmen for about a league, the British troops were recalled to Oporto. In the fighting the battalion had lost sixty men ; and when they had got to quarters Sir Arthur addressed them and expressed how thankful he was to them for the way in which they had crossed the river, and enabled the other regiments to follow so easily.

Nicol makes this remark in passing, that ' Marshal Soult was neither prepared to defend Oporto nor to retreat out of it, but seemed as if taken by surprise or confounded at our impudence in crossing the river in the face of the whole French army.'

At night the city was illuminated, and the men-of-war boats formed a bridge of boats by which on the following day all the cannon and cavalry were transferred to the north side.

When the regiment marched from Oporto Lieutenant John Durie was left behind sick, and the following day the same fate befell 'the good Captain Logie, which every man in the company was sorry for, the more so as no officer of the 92nd was left with them, and they soon felt the want of him.'

The French army succeeded in escaping over the mountains, to the extreme annoyance of Sir Arthur and the British troops, who blamed Marshal Beresford and the Portuguese, who had been posted in the passes to prevent this. 'But for this,' Nicol says, 'Soult's whole army would have been taken, as well as their guns and baggage. Negligence or mismanagement there was somewhere ; but these things are not easily proved when committed by the higher powers. Beresford was challenged, and we heard no more of it ; but General Toilson was sent back to England.' This, however, is only a soldier's surmise, as we know that it was the advance of Marshal Victor which compelled Sir Arthur to turn from the pursuit of Soult and join the Spanish General Cuesta, who had now reformed his force after being heavily defeated by Victor.

By the end of the month the troops had again marched 'over the bridge of boats across the broad and rapid Douro, and bade adieu to Oporto for ever, with its churches, convents, and port wine. To the last the British troops paid more devotion than to the first.'

The Gordons had an unpleasant experience in crossing the broad, navigable lake between Ovar and Aveiro, for when they had embarked in boats which were crowded, they were very uncomfortable, and the rain came on, with a high wind, so that many of the boats were blown ashore, and the rest did not reach Aveiro till the forenoon of the following day. On landing, Sir Arthur Wellesley at their head, they were joyfully received by the inhabitants with a salute of twenty-one guns. After marching through Coimbra, they reached the river Mondego on the 4th June, when the King's Birthday was celebrated by a bathe in the river and the distribution of a pint of wine to each of the men. Now began the famous march which ended in the victory at Talavera, fought on the 27th and 28th July 1809, when the combined forces under Wellesley completely defeated the French army commanded by Joseph Bonaparte, ex-King of Naples, now King of Spain.

It was for this great victory that Sir Arthur was created a peer under the title of Lord Wellington, and it is well worthy of being recorded that the Gordons had a distinct share in the honours of the day. Nicol's description of the battle is full of interest. He tells us that the army crossed the Guadiana and entered Spain with light hearts. He begins by giving a detailed statement of the officers commanding the various divisions and brigades, and supplies particulars of all the regiments in the army, which had an effective strength of twenty thousand men.

The approach of the Spanish army is well described by Nicol, who says : 'We got into a fine cultivated plain, when the French began to make their appearance in our front.   Sir Arthur with his staff passed us, and we halted an hour at a village, where our cavalry dismounted and cut down some fields of ripe corn for forage.   At this time we began to see great clouds of dust on the right of the plain.   This was the Spanish army advancing.   They had crossed the Tagus by the bridge at Almarez, and were now marching on the high-road to Madrid, driving the French outposts before them. Big words were now spoken by the boasters of taking Madrid, beating the French, and driving them out of Spain—great things that were not accomplished till years after.

'We halted on the 21st, and were ordered to appear as clean as possible, to be reviewed by the Spanish General Cuesta, commanding the army with which we were to act. Our army was drawn up in line.   Sir Arthur and Cuesta, arrived on the ground, escorted by a troop of British and one of Spanish cavalry ; they rode along the line, we paying them all military honours.   Cuesta was a fine stout, rough looking old man.   He said he was happy to see us look so well after so long a march.   We got one day's biscuit served out here ; this was the last regular rations served out to our brigade.

'On the 22nd we marched past the Spanish Grand army, as the French were in front, we were going to set them an example by commencing an attack on the enemy, for we thought that General Victor would give battle in front of Talavera.   The Spaniards amounting it was said, to fifty thousand men, were drawn up on both sides of the road as we passed ; they had some very heavy cannon—too unwieldly for the field—and many waggons, baggage-mules, asses, etc. This day was very warm, with much dust, and little or no water to be got.   On the right side of the road was a stagnant pool ; the cavalry rode through it, and some of our men went up to the knees amongst it drinking, though it was as thick as water-gruel.

CHAPTER III

THE GREAT FIGHT AT TALAVERA

'THE French were drawn up in line about a league from Talavera. The attack was begun about eleven o'clock by the British artillery and our cavalry under General Anson, who turned the right of the French army, while the Spaniards under Duke Albuquerque, one of the best of the Spanish Generals, drove them back and through the town. Some houses and a field of wheat took fire, and the French retreated through the smoke to a position on the other side of the river Alberche, and broke down the bridge. The combined armies bivouacked in the vineyards and olive-grounds; the Spaniards in the town and by the side of the river Tagus, over which was a wooden bridge that kept communication with the country on the right bank of the river. Sir Arthur had a narrow escape this day. While reconnoitring, a cannon-shot was fired at him which carried away a branch of the tree under which he stood, within a few inches of his head—a lucky escape for him. He was fully determined to bring General Victor to action on the morning of the 23rd, and we were in readiness to march off the ground at five o'clock, when we were countermanded—to our disappointment. The Spanish General Cuesta, it is reported, would not fight on a Sunday. Well, he might be a very good Christian General, but he was no match for the French unless he could take, at any time, any advantage that might occur. This was an opportunity lost, for during the night the French retreated to St Olala, falling back upon their own strength.

'On the 24th, Monday, the Spanish General was surprised to find that the French had left their position. He now marched to pursue them and drive them out of Madrid, and fight them wherever he could find them. Sir Arthur explained that the British had no provisions, and that we could not

THE LION AT HOME

Facing page 9

move until these were supplied. But the Spaniard was obstinate, and crossed the river after the French; he was to do great things with the Spanish army since he got the French on the retreat. This day we waited patiently for a supply of biscuit, but none came. In the evening two pounds of beef each man were served out; this kept us cooking most of the night.

'On the 25th—We advanced to the Alberche and moved a division of cavalry and foot, under command of General Sherbrooke, across the river, to keep communication with the Spaniards and Sir Robert Wilson's division of Portuguese, who were far advanced on the road to Madrid, to our left. This division occupied the position the French had retreated from at Casalegas. We then returned to our old ground, and sent out parties in search of bread or wine, others being sent to gather wheat and peas in the fields. Very hard times these. In the evening our foragers returned, and brought a mule with two skins of good wine and some bread. This was distributed among the company.

'News reached us that General Cuesta and his Spaniards were in full pursuit of the enemy as far as Torrejos, and that Marshal Victor had gone on the Toledo road, where he was joined by General Sebastiani and his army. At this place the French, hearing that the British army was still at Talavera, faced about on the poor Spaniards. On the 26th news arrived almost every hour from the Spanish army that they had been attacked and beaten with great loss, and were retreating in confusion. I saw one of our officers who had been as far as St Olala; he stated that the streets of that town were entirely blocked up with the Spanish artillery, bread-wagons, baggage, etc., and that whole regiments were running like a rabble or a mob. We began to hear a cannonading at a distance, rolling nearer to us.

'On the 27th the Spaniards began to arrive; they took up the ground on our right, in two lines, and entrenched themselves and made batteries on the high-road leading from the town to the bridge over the Alberche, and planted their heavy cannon in front of a chapel at our right. We expected a general attack, and our line was drawn between the river and the hill, a distance of about two or three miles. General Sherbrooke was called in from Casalegas, and General MacKenzie was stationed with a strong advanced-post at some houses in a wood. I was sent with a working-party to

G

raise a battery on some rising ground among the olive-trees.
About two o'clock the French arrived at the side of the
Alberche, and opened fire on our advance-guard, fording the
river at the same moment. We kept them in check ; but
from where I was I could see that our people were suffering
much, and retiring to take up their position in the line. The
working-parties were ordered to stand to their arms, as the shot
from the French was coming thick among us. We were then
ordered to join our regiments as quickly as possible, and we
joined our battalion on the side of the hill to the left of the
line.

'A dreadful cannonade commenced on the British right, and
the enemy attacked the Spaniards with their cavalry, thinking
to break their lines and get into the town ; but the Dons
repulsed them manfully. The firing ceased on the right after
dark, when the French had made a charge of infantry without
success. From the place where we stood we could see every
movement on the plain.

'At this time our brigade got a biscuit each man served
out, when a cry was heard, "The hill ! the hill !" General
Stewart called out for the detachments to make for the top of
the hill, for he was certain that no regiment could be there
so soon as we. Off we ran in the dark, and very dark it was ;
but the French got on the top of the hill before us, and some
of them ran through the battalion, calling out, "Españioles,
Españioles," and others calling "Allemands."

'Our officers cried out "Don't fire on the Spaniards." I
and many others jumped to the side to let them pass down
the hill, where they were either killed or taken prisoners in
our rear. I saw those on the top of the hill by the flashes
of their pieces ; then we knew who they were ; but I and
many more of our company were actually in rear of the
French for a few moments, and did not know it until they
seized some of our men by the collar and were dragging them
away prisoners. This opened our eyes, and bayonets and the
butts of our firelocks were used with great dexterity—a dreadful mêlée. The 29th Regiment came to our assistance,
charged, and kept possession of the top of the hill. This
regiment lost a number of men on the highest point of the
hill, where the French had a momentary possession, and
affairs hung in the balance ere it was decided who should have
this key of the position. The enemy tried it a second time,
coming round the side of the hill ; but as we now knew who

they were, to our cost, a well-directed running fire, with a charge, sent them into the valley below, their drums beating a retreat.

'General Hill's division arrived, with two guns, after the affair was over, and, I was told, got credit for this hard contest, though really they were dragging their guns about the foot of the hill and did not fire a shot here until next morning. The firing ceased on this point before eleven o'clock ; all was silent on the plain long before. Our brigade got into formation as well as it could, with our left to the top joining General Hill ; a deep ravine or hollow was to our front. Some other regiments came on the side of the hill and formed a second line, and some guns were posted to the right of our brigade. I believe it was only after nightfall that our Generals found the importance of this post. We got ammunition served out, and had time to count our loss, which was very great. Vedettes were placed a few yards in front, and we sat down in the ranks and watched every movement of the enemy. About one in the morning we could hear and see the French moving their artillery on the other side of the hollow about two hundred yards from us. Some firing commenced ; it ran from the left to the right for we could see every flash in the plain below us.

'Order was restored, and a deathlike silence reigned among us. The French kindled great fires in rear of their lines. I had a sound sleep for a short time, being one of those who could sleep half an hour or twenty minutes at any time or place and feel myself much refreshed.

'When daylight appeared each army gazed on the other and viewed the operations of last night. Round the top of the hill many a red coat lay dead ; about thirty yards on the other side the red and blue lay mixed, and a few yards farther, and down to the valley below, they were all blue. The French fired one gun from the centre as a signal for all their line to commence action. Their guns began to pour grape-shot and shell into our lines, and three columns came bearing for the hill.

'We were ordered to lie close to the ground, but when the enemy was about fifty yards from us we started to our feet and poured in a volley, then charged with the bayonet, and ran them down into the valley, cheering and firing upon them, for they proved better runners than we. They retreated across the valley to our left, leaving many killed and wounded behind them, we took some ammunition-waggons, from one of which I took two three-pound loaves of bread. This was a noble prize where there were so many hungry men.

'We were ordered to pursue no further than the rising ground at the foot of the left side of the hill. They crossed the valley and formed on some rocks on the other side, and threatened to turn our left. Two Spanish battalions were sent over to them, which kept them in check, and they kept up a popping fire at each other most of the day. Our guns on the top and side of the hill kept blazing away upon the French guns and columns within reach.

'After the march was over here, we heard some heavy firing down on the plain among the olive-grounds, but from where we now were we could not see what was going on; the 48th Regiment and some others were withdrawn from the hill to the plain. About eleven o'clock the enemy, being baffled in all his attacks upon our lines, withdrew his troops a little. As we did not move to follow them they deliberately piled arms and set about kindling fires and cooking their victuals. A brook ran through the plain; to it both armies went for water as if truce was between us, looking at each other, drinking, and wiping the sweat from their brows, laughing and nodding heads to each other; all thoughts of fighting for the time being forgotten. Water was in great demand by our brigade, and parties were sent off for it; others were sent to bury the dead that lay thick about us, and to assist the wounded to the rear.

'Our brigade took up the ground it had quitted in the morning and the 48th and 66th Regiments took up our ground, for we expected the enemy to make another rush for the top of the hill, and in this we were not deceived. About one o'clock the French army was in motion again, and three divisions were on their way to the hill, one on each side, the other to the front. Our guns on the hill opened upon them, but did little execution to what we expected; it was said, "They are the German Legion artillery." The enemy's right division got under shelter of a large house in the valley, where they stood in close column and sent forward their sharpshooters to within a few yards of us.

'At this time the British cavalry entered the valley to check the French right. The 23rd and German hussars formed across the valley, and, supported by the heavy dragoons, charged the right division of the enemy. This charge, though nobly executed, had not the effect intended, for the French opened a steady fire upon them, killed and wounded and took many of the 23rd Light Dragoons prisoners, and forced the remainder back on General Anson's heavy brigade, which kept this division of the enemy from advancing any farther.

'We stood looking at the affray for a few moments, until General Stewart's brigade was ordered to advance to the top of the hollow, when all the others were ordered to lie close to the ground, as the French had taken up a position with their heads above the rise, and were doing much mischief. We sustained a heavy fire from the enemy's guns on the other side of the hollow; they were making lanes through us, and their musketry attacked us on our flanks. We cleared the enemy from our front and right, but they maintained the heights on the other side; and, as we were lower than they, they punished us severely. All the other troops were brought into action, and the battle raged along the lines from right to left, and nothing could be heard but the long roll of musketry and the thunder of the artillery intermixed. Captain MacPherson of the 35th Regiment, who commanded our company this day, was down, and my right file was taken off by a cannon-shot. William Bowie and John Shewan were killed on my left, and Adam Much lay in the rear, wounded.

'About four o'clock I was struck by a musketball, which grazed my left knee and passed through my right leg about two inches below the cap of the knee. I finished my loading and fired my last shot at the man who wounded me, for I could plainly see him on a height a few yards to my front; I think I should have known him if he had come in my way afterwards. I called out to Sergeant John Gordon that I was wounded; he was the only non-commissioned officer belonging to the regiment I saw at his post. I made along the side of the hill as well as I could, using my firelock as a crutch.

'I now looked back at the brigade, and saw it was much cut up. I passed Colonel Alexander Gordon, formerly captain in our regiment, killed; and Brigade-Major Gardener, who had been an active officer in our brigade all morning— he and his horse lay dead together; Major Ross, 38th, and Captain Bradley, 28th Light company, (I knew him in the light battalion in Dublin), badly wounded. I stepped over many men lying on the ground here to rise again no more. The shot was tearing up the ground on my left and right, as the French cannon were doing great execution at this time, and their shells had set the cornfields on fire in the plain, and brushwood and long grass were blazing on the sides of the hill ; and many wounded men, unable to get away, were burned to death. If I had sat down no doubt the same lot would have been mine, so I kept hopping along until I came to a large white house where many wounded men were waiting to be dressed. Here I found the surgeon of the Gordons, Dr Beattie, who came at once to me and dressed my leg and put a bandage on it. He then gave me a drink of water, and told me I had got it at last. I, smiling, replied, 'Long run the fox, but he is sure to be caught at last.' This made many smile whose bones were sore enough.

'I had now time to look about me, and I saw that we were going on in the plain little to our advantage. Some of our guns were drawn to the rear to take up a fresh alignment. Feeling very weak, I took a mouthful of water and a slice of the loaf that I got in the morning, when I found a musket-ball in it, which had pierced my haversack and lodged in the loaf. I sincerely returned thanks to God for preserving me in the dangers to which I had been exposed, and gave myself great credit for all I had done. Thus pleased with myself, I got up and hopped along for the town of Talavera.

'I trudged along in the rear of the line towards the town with some more men in the same condition, although about this time it seemed rather doubtful whether the French would be there before us. I felt myself getting very weak through loss of blood, and had to make many halts among the olive-trees ; and I was vexed to see so many men of different regiments, especially of the King's German Legion, skulking in the rear when they should have been doing their duty in front with their comrades—going prowling about with bad intentions I knew by their looks. And as for the Spaniards, some battalions of them had left the field in mobs during the action ; not those actually engaged, but those in the second and third lines. This was disgraceful conduct.

'I reached the town and sat down on the steps of a door, when a young woman brought me a pitcher of water and vinegar, and many a pull I took of it before I let it out of my hands. I then went to the general hospital, a large convent, where hundreds of men were lying in the courts and passages, and on the stairs. I lay down and put my head on the dead body of a man of the 61st Regiment, and slept amid all the uproar and bustle. I awakened about dark, and got into one of the large rooms. I saw no one I knew but Adam Much of our regiment, who was wounded about the same place as myself. I lay down beside him. We slept soundly until morning, when I was wakened by the surgeons performing their operations, cutting off legs and arms. I found myself stiff and sore. Dr Beattie came and dressed our wounds On the afternoon of the 29th Adam Much's wife found him ; this was a joyful meeting, as he was supposed to be killed. I got about two glasses of wine from her, which greatly revived me ; this was a glass in need, not to be forgotten.

'On the 30th we were carried to the battalion hospital, situated in a church. I got plenty of clean straw, and had one of the steps of the high altar for a pillow, and had some good soup, of which I had much need. Here I learnt the particulars of both armies. The firing was kept up until evening, and we kept our ground and no more on the 28th. Early on the morning of the 29th, when a fresh attack was expected, the French crossed the Alberche and retreated in good order to their old positions.

'Thus, although commanded by King Joseph in person, and Marshals Victor and Jourdan, and General Sebastiani, with about forty-eight thousand men, they could make no impression on the British lines, and we were the mainstay of the Spaniards. In this action our loss was very great. Generals MacKenzie and Langworth were killed in the field. According to a statement which I saw, the number of killed and wounded was : officers, three hundred and thirty-seven ; sergeants, two hundred and eight ; drummers, twenty-nine ; rank and file, four thousand eight hundred and ninety-two— a total of five thousand four hundred and sixty-six. Of the first battalion of detachments there were above three hundred men killed and wounded. Our company had forty-eight men in the field, of whom six were killed and twenty-four wounded.' *

* Oman, in his *History of the Peninsular War*, gives the total British casualities as five thousand three hundred and sixty-three ; killed, thirty-four officers, seven hundred and sixty-seven men ; wounded, one hundred and ninety-six officers, three thousand seven hundred and nineteen men ; missing, eight officers, six hundred and thirty-nine men. The French casualities were seven thousand two hundred and sixty-eight.

CHAPTER IV

THE FRUITS OF VICTORY

'The French army must have suffered much more than we did ; we may safely add one-half more. Some cannon fell into our hands, with a very few prisoners. The Spanish loss was about one thousand two hundred killed and wounded ; what they had missing no one could tell, as they went off to the rear in droves. Thus we may say a great battle was fought or trial of strength made for no important end whatever. The day after all this was over, a light brigade, three thousand strong, and a troop of horse artillery arrived from Lisbon under Brigadier-General Crawford. I suppose the French had got intelligence of this, which made them draw off and put the river Alberche betwixt us, and some despatches from General Jourdan fell into our hands, telling Marshal Soult to march from Salamanca speedily by the Puerta del Banos and Placencia, there to be joined by the divisions under Ney and Mortier, and then fall on the rear of the British army. This opened our eyes. There was only one way of avoiding this snare, and that was to retreat immediately across the Tagus by the bridge of Arzobispo, and take up a defensive position where provisions could be got for the army. I never received any correct intelligence of our army after the retreat, not so much even as a flying report.

'On the 31st July, Colonel Bunbury, commanding our battalion, got bread and aguardiente, which he divided himself among the wounded men in hospital. He expressed his satisfaction with our behaviour in the different actions in which he had had the honour to command us ; and Sir Arthur, he said, had expressed his thanks to the first battalion of detachments for their bravery and good conduct in the night attack upon the hill and during the whole of the 28th, and he would not fail to represent it to His Majesty. Next day he sent a doubloon's worth of bread and two skins of wine for the use of the wounded. This was of more benefit to us than the fine speech he made yesterday, and was a great relief to every man in the hospital. He ordered all the battalion to be paid to 24th July—the last money I received for many a day; and he waited in the hospital until he saw the wounded men get their money, and was exceedingly attentive to us as far as lay in his power. Large parties of Spaniards were sent to gather the dead men and horses into heaps and burn them, for fear of causing a plague about the town.

'On the 2nd of August all the British troops marched off by daybreak—we thought to attack the enemy; but, to our horror, we found they had retreated, leaving us wounded men in a dreadful condition, without provisions, only a few surgeons, little medicine, and no attendants. About twelve o'clock Dr Beattie came in and desired every man that was able to make the best of his way after the army, for he expected the French in the town in a few hours. This caused a great consternation among us. I had been very cheery in the morning, but this made me change my tune. Spanish officers came through the church among us, bringing in mules and asses for those that were able to ride. Many tried to leave the place, but had to return before night; and many were obliged to lie down in the fields who never rose again. Sergeant MacBean got a mule for himself and me, but by this time I could neither sit nor stand, my wound was so bad and my leg swollen. He got on and pranced down the centre of the church like a mounted hussar. I bade him God speed and asked him to tell my comrades—if ever he reached the regiment—where he had left me. When it was growing dark, who should come into the church, crawling on all-fours, but Sergeant MacBean! He crept in among the straw beside me, and we kept together until our wounds were healed over. So we were obliged to content ourselves and remain at the mercy of the French.

'There were about thirty French wounded men in the church, and well they could observe what was going on. They were in great terror for the Spaniards. Some of them got red coats, caps, Highland bonnets, etc., that they might pass for British. One tall, fine looking man got on a kilt, hose, and big coat. He was wounded in the shoulder, but could make good use of his legs, and was water-carrier for all about our corner, and was ready to help every one ; he would answer to no name but Grenadier " Sansculotte."

'On the 4th the Spanish troops left the town, and took their own wounded with them, but none of the British, who were left in a very helpless condition, more especially those belonging to our battalion, as we had nobody to take charge or yet attend us. I certainly blame Dr Beattie for this, as other corps left their assistant-surgeon, orderlies, hospital sergeant etc., while we were destitute of any assistance. On the 5th John Murray, who had been in the general hospital with the fever, came and found us in this helpless condition ; and, poor fellow, although weak himself, yet having the use of his limbs, he did all he could to make us comfortable. He got us removed to the general hospital, a large convent in a fine airy situation. We stationed ourselves in one of the passages on the second floor, and here we were for many a day beside some men of the 2nd battalion 24th Regiment. There were only four of our regiment left here that we knew of—namely, Sergeant Alexander MacBean, Donald Johnston, John Murray and myself. Murray recovered strength rapidly, and was made cook in the hospital ; yet whenever his time permitted he gave us all the attention in his power. We were visited frequently by the general doctor, Higgins, who ordered us to dress each other's wounds morning and evening.

'On the 6th the French entered the town and carried on a regular system of plunder, breaking open every shut door they found, and every article that was of value to them was carried off. A great quantity of provisions found hidden in the houses of the town from our armies was now distributed with a liberal hand by the French soldiers who did not forget their English enemies. I got a mattress and a set of red window curtains, which served me as blankets until I entered France. The indefatigable John Murray let us want for nothing he could get ; he brought us soap, linen to dress our wounds, etc. The French mounted a guard over this large convent, as much as to say, "You are prisoners of war." All who were able had liberty to go out and in through the day, and Marshal Victor gave strict orders to use us civilly, and not to take any article from us, but to purchase anything we had to dispose of. For a few days our hospital was crowded from morning to night with French soldiers come to get a sight of the English wounded, and some to purchase shoes, which were in great demand. I sold a new pair for a dollar, not to be troubled any more, for I saw some taking them by force, and I remembered the order given to some of the British at Braga, to strip every French prisoner they saw with a good pair of shoes. On 7th August we got rations from the French, three pounds of coarse bread for every eight men, and a very small quantity of beef to make soup (boullion, as they called it), without salt or vegetables. The French got a regular market established in the town, which was more than the British or Spaniards could do while they had command of it ; and it surprised us much that the people of the country would hide stores of provisions from their own army and ours, who were willing to pay ready-money for them. However, the French are good foragers, and I have seen at times much good come out of intended evil. Plenty of white bread, fruit, wines, etc., were brought into the market and sold for ready money.

'On 15th August we were alarmed by the French artillery firing—thought it to be some attack ; but it turned out to be the birthday of the French Emperor. They fired at day-break, mid-day, and sunset. On the 27th fever got in amongst us and swept away great numbers, especially men who had limbs amputated or were wounded, so as to be unable to attend to themselves ; for men get selfish in the midst of misery, and if a man could not help himself, alas for him ! About this time a waggon attended every morning to take away the dead. The driver of this waggon I shall never forget. He was a very tall man in the dress of a French prisoner, with long black beard and moustaches—an ugly man. He stood in the middle of the passages and bawled out, making the place ring again, ' *Combien de mort Anglais le jour ?* ' which is nearly, 'How many dead Englishmen to-day ? ' If there were none he would shrug his shoulders and mutter a curse ; if one or more he seemed happy, saying ' *Bon !* ' (Good). Then the wretch would seize the dead by the ankles and drag him off to his waggon. I heard he got a franc for every corpse he took out of the convent.

'According to report, there were two thousand six hundred British left here ; but we were getting thinned rapidly by death and desertions. The French caused a general muster to be made, as some of our people had been caught and brought back while trying to make their escape. All who could walk were mustered and forty cartloads of wounded were sent off

to Madrid ; this gave us more room, but we were more strictly
looked after by the French.   My leg and thigh swelled to an
alarming extent.   The general doctor and Dr Taylor of the
Sixty-sixth Regiment were for cutting it off ; but to this I
objected, and told them I might as well go to the grave with
two legs as one.   I continued poulticing the wound with the
bread that should have gone into my belly, and I suffered
great pain.   But I was relieved in an extraordinary manner.
One night after it was dark a French drummer was pursuing
a woman belonging to the Twenty-fourth Regiment in full
flight along the passage, when she fell right on my wounded
leg.   I roared out, the woman shrieked, and the drummer,
thinking he was to be attacked, drew his sword and went off
cursing.   I was in great distress and in a high fever all night ;
but next morning, on dressing my wound, seven small pieces
of bone came out of it, some of them about the size of the
teeth of a dressing-comb, and a piece of my trousers that had
been driven in by the ball.   From this time I mended every
day.   I was well attended by Sergeant MacBean, who was
wounded in the hip which had now healed, and he could
limp about on a stick, bring water, wash our linen, etc. ; but
one day he fell in the cook-house, and had to take to his bed,
to my great loss and his own.   However, this accident was
fortunate for him, for his wound broke out afresh, and two
pieces of his trousers were discharged.   In a few days he was
on his feet again, and he cut me some young olive-trees to
make me a pair of crutches, and did everything in his power
to get me mounted on these.   My wound was skinned over
on the 2nd of October, two months after I received it, and I
began to look forward a little, for some weeks I had not
expected to leave the convent but by the help of *Combien de
mort*, the French waggoner.   My first start out of doors was
to the river Tagus, which ran past the foot of the garden, to
wash my shirts.   I sat in the sun till I got sick, and had to
keep my bed with a kind of fever and ague, which went
through amongst us.

   'On the 5th November, Sunday, the hospital was visited
by Marshal Mortier and his staff.   He was a tall, stout man,
with a star on his breast.   He told us he was sorry it was not
in his power to supply us with many things we stood in need
of, but while bread was to be got for his own troops we
should be first served.   He said the French had used us
better than our own army had done, in leaving us in the state

they found us ; for the Spaniards, being our friends, could
have provided the means of transporting the wounded if our
commanders chose; but instead of this we had been left a
burden to the French army. He also told us that many
British had made their escape ; but some had been shot, and
if any of us were caught in future a mile from the town we
might expect to be served in the same manner. All this he
said in English, and left, it is said, one hundred and sixty
doubloons to purchase wine, rice, etc., for the use of the
hospital. I believe it was entrusted to bad hands, and not
half of it was expended in the use it was intended for.

'On the 7th November the French seemed in a bustle :
drums beating, cannons driven to and fro, and planted in
position on the roads leading from the town and by the riverside. A battery had been built at the end of the bridge across
the Tagus, which had been repaired ; but now the planks of
the centre arch were removed and the French stores packed
up. On our going for rations the commissary told us to
reste tranquille, and the Spaniards would serve us out to-
morrow. The Spanish troops remained in sight all day, and
we thought they meant to attack the town and set us at
liberty ; but no such thing. The French marched out at
night ; we could see the fires of both armies, and supposed
the French meant to begin the attack in the morning. But
the Spaniards moved off; the French repaired the bridge in
quick time, and sent troops after them, and more arrived from
Madrid. Sergeant MacBean and many others resolved to
make their escape ; as the Spaniards were in the neighbourhood, they thought they might fall in with them before long.
On the evening of the 9th MacBean took leave of me for the
second time. I gave him a loaf of bread, a small map of the
country, and a letter to my mother. I never was more vexed
in parting from any man, yet I advised him to start, he being
married and a persevering man, and likely to succeed in anything he took in hand. Next day I got out to market and
bought some bread and grapes, etc., and found my money
getting very small ; yet I never spent money to such good
purpose as at Talavera. There seemed to be a blessing in it,
and I often had something extra when feeling badly.

'The French General discovered that many of our men
had escaped since the Spanish troops came near. Early on
the morning of the 12th, without previous notice, all the
British officers, doctors, and every man that was expected to

live were turned out to the square, and were put on bullock-
carts, and driven out of the town on the road to Madrid. We
crossed the well-contested plain and the river Alberche, and
saw many dead men's bones picked bare on both sides of the
bridge, which was now repaired. Reached St Olala after it
was dark ; this town was nearly deserted by its inhabitants.
The French guard were very kind to our wounded men,
carrying those unable to walk from the carts into some stables,
with their baggage, etc. Those troops that had fought in the
field with us were always the kindest and readiest to assist
us ; when we had a guard of young conscripts they were very
troublesome to every one.

'13th.—To Ventas. It was dark before we reached it,
although the French soldiers pricked the bullocks with their
bayonets to get the carts on. This is a very slow method of
travelling, and we all were very tired sitting huddled on the
carts. Two of our people died on this day's march through
fatigue and want of sustenance. We passed through a dreary,
uncultivated country, with no houses between the stages, and
no food could be got. In the afternoon we saw from a height
the spires and part of the ancient city of Toledo, across an
uncultivated plain to our right.

'14th.—To Pitho, a village within three leagues of the
capital. The country begins to be better cultivated and more
sheltered with trees, etc. ; we had passed over but a barren
waste since we crossed the Alberche.

'15th.—Started before daylight to get early into the city.
The French soldiers seemed very happy to get there, and so
were we poor wounded prisoners ; although we knew not what
our condition was to be, we knew it could not be worse than
it had been. We viewed the majestic appearance of the city,
with its fine spires, domes, and churches, with the sun shining
brilliantly upon them, as we approached it from the west, there
being no hill to hide it from our view. The French cavalry
was quartered in all the villages along the road, and sentries
were placed on the tops of some of the churches and high
houses to observe the plain country, for fear of being surprised
by the Spaniards.

'We crossed a shallow river by a stone bridge on the west
side of the city. There we saw hundreds of women washing
on both sides of the river as far as we could see ; each dame
on her knees with a board in front of her, rubbing and
washing, and singing cheerily. A hardy race of ladies, I could

see from their countenances ; they sympathised much with us in our distress.   We passed some avenues of trees up to the city, which is surrounded by an earthen wall, with gates and a strong guard of French at each entrance.   We halted. Notice of our arrival was sent to the commandant, who ordered us round to the Puerta del Sol, a spacious square with many streets leading from it.   Crowds of people came round, asking when and where we were taken, and giving us bits of bread, money, etc., until the French soldiers drove them off with the butts of their firelocks.   We were lodged for the night in the great military hospital.   Each man received a small measure of wine and a piece of bread, of which we had much need.   We thought the first stage of our misery was over.'

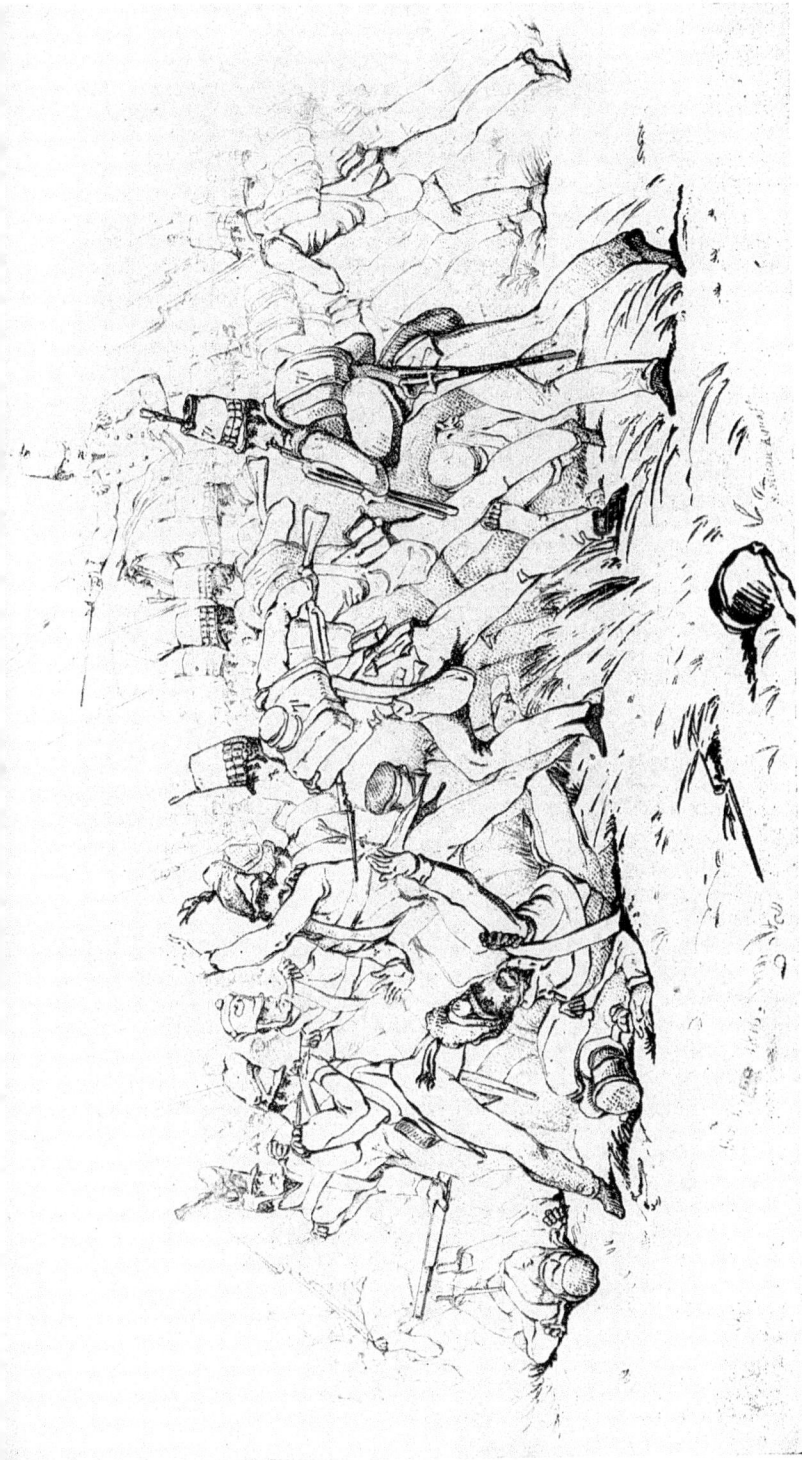

71ST HIGHLANDERS AT QUATRE BRAS

Facing page 112

IV

HOW THE BRITISH STROMED ARAY DEL MOLINOS

FROM THE JOURNAL OF SERGEANT D. ROBERTSON

HOW THE BRITISH STORMED ARAY DEL MOLINOS

WE remained, says Sergeant Robertson, writing of the year 1811, in winter quarters till the 4th of March, when the French broke up from Santarem, and went into the north of Portugal. On their march they committed the most wanton outrages and cruelty, destroying everything that came in their way. At Bombal they ham-stringed every beast of burden in the place, so that the poor creatures were rendered quite useless.

As our advanced guard and the rear guard of the French army were in contact every day, frequent skirmishes occurred, in which there were some lives lost. The Portuguese peasantry stripped the dead and wounded naked, after which they collected the bodies of men and horses into heaps and burned them to ashes without distinction. We again began to feel the effects of a forced march. Our Commissary was not provided with the means of transport to keep us in provisions, and we had nothing to live upon but cattle, which were killed as they were needed. For fourteen days we did not taste a bit of bread—nothing but beef without salt. One day, as an especial favour we got two ounce of rice per man. Indeed so hard pressed were we at this time, that the women were known to pick up the unbroken corn that fell from the horses and eat it. While we were enduring all these privations, Lord Wellington gave the Commissary-General his thanks in general orders for his attention in getting forward supplies !

After arriving on the frontiers of Spain, we went into cantonments. A few days afterwards the bread that we should have received on our march at length reached us ; but being newly baked when it was packed up, it was quite unfit for use. However we did not need it now for there was a market in the place and every thing that we wanted could be got in abundance. We remained here till the 1st of May 1811, when the French showed a disposition to relieve Almeida and passed the Aguada for that purpose. We turned out and lay under arms till the evening, when we marched to cover the fortress. On the 2nd, we formed line and on the 3rd the light companies and the French riflemen exchanged some shots, by which we had two killed and five wounded. The 4th was spent in the marching and the countermarching of the different columns to their positions with occasionally the exchange of a few shots, without much injury being done on either side. On the morning of the 5th we were again badly off for provisions and had to be supplied from the haversacks of the Scots Guards with what they could spare out of their own allowance. About eight o'clock the French began to push forward their left in strong columns on perceiving which we wheeled into line to receive them. The place which we occupied was the boundary line between Spain and Portugal on a road that connects the two countries. The 50th and 71st were taken to the left, while our picquet, the light company, and what remained were left to cover and protect the artillery which were stationed in a temporary battery near the right, on a piece of rising ground. When the firing commenced that part of the 92nd posted here was formed into a line by itself a little in advance, and on the extreme right, to cover the artillery in position. We were ordered to lie down to be out of danger from the enemy's shot as much as possible. A body of French cavalry made an attempt to charge and take the guns from the artillery, when we started up and gave them a few rounds which made them wheel to the right about. They repeated this several times but with as little success as at first. The French did us considerable damage with their shells which were now beginning to fall thick and fast about us. One of them burst among the company to which I belonged when we were in the act of lying down and killed and wounded four of our men, while another fell among a different company and killed an officer and eleven men. While this was going on another attempt was made by the enemy to carry off our guns, but all their efforts were unavailing ; for so firmly did we maintain our ground, and so well directed was our fire, that they were compelled to retire with considerable loss. We still retained our position and took every precaution lest they should renew

DEATH OF COLONEL MACARA OF THE 42ND HIGHLANDERS AT QUATRE BRAS

the attack in the morning. Our precautions however, proved useless, for the next morning not a French soldier was to be seen. We had lost thirty killed on the spot, besides a great number who died of their wounds on the following two days.

We then broke up and went into cantonments, where we remained until the 26th, when we were ordered to march and pass the Tagus, from which we were distant about five days' journey. As it was intended that the whole army should cross to assist General Beresford, we started off at five o'clock in the evening and marched two days and nights before we halted. A great many of the men were quite done up and unable to come forward ; and as Soult had withdrawn from Badajoz, we were allowed to rest for a day. All the army of the north was ordered back to its old cantonments, with the exception of our brigade, which was ordered to join the second division of the army under the command of General Hill, on the south side of the Tagus.

We marched by easy stages till we reached Albuera, where we made an attempt to relieve Badajoz. When we came to this place the Spaniards had set the fields on fire by which the wounded were severely burned before we could get them conveyed away. It being in the month of June, every thing was scorched with the drought, and the flames spread rapidly in all directions.

We remained only a week here, when we had to raise the siege of Badajoz and retire into Portugal, where we took up our ground in rear of the fortifications of Elvas and at Torea de Morea. The French made different sallies at Badajoz on purpose to keep us in alarm, but did not effect anything of consequence, except taking a picquet of the 11th dragoons. In this camp we remained till the 21st of July, when we went into quarters in a village in the rear of our position. Our brigade and a Portuguese one occupied Barbeo, a neat little place, in which a market was held every day we were there.

On the 1st September we marched to Portalegra, in which city the whole division was quartered. We moved from Portalegra on the 22nd October, leaving the women, sick, and baggage behind, and took the road to Albuquerque, in Spain, and thence to Aray del Malina, where a considerable body of the French was assembled, under the command of Generals Gerard and Le Brune, and the Duke de Amburgo. On our march we were joined by a number of Spanish troops of a very unsoldierlike appearance, being habited in the old Spanish costume fashionable in the days of Pizzaro and Don Quixote. They were called the Estramadura Legion and were under the command of General Downie.

On the evening of the 27th, we had approached so near the French that we durst not kindle fires ; and as it rained exceedingly heavy, we were drenched to the skin. By the neglect of the Commissary, we were again without supplies of bread for three days. Under a torrent of rain we started off before daylight, and marched on till we came to a hill a little way from the town, where the divisions were told off to their respective posts. The storming of the town was assigned to our brigade, while the cavalry and the other brigades were to occupy a wood which lay on the right of the town between the French and the main road, and to intercept the enemy in case they should attempt to move off in that direction. When all the dispositions for the attack were made, we received the signal to advance, which was done in profound silence. As the 92nd was the junior regiment it was placed in the centre, having to keep the highway with orders to proceed to the market square and if not interrupted, to go on to the other side of the town. The 50th was to take the right of the town, go round by the suburbs and meet us ; while the 71st was to take the left and go on to an olive grove, and be ready to act as circumstances might require. The rain was falling on us in abundance when we advanced to the town. When the 71st reached the olive grove, they found a body of French cavalry in it. The dragoons were engaged at the time feeding their horses, and before they were aware of what was going on, the 71st had got hold of the bridles and secured them. By this time we had entered one of the streets and were proceeding along, when the French taken by surprise, came out to see what was the matter. The 92nd kept moving on, the pipers playing ' Hey Johnnie Cope are ye waukin' yet,' till we came to a court were there were two horses standing at a door with a groom beside them. Aroused by the sound of the bagpipes, the Duke de Armburgo came out in a half-naked state, when a sergeant of the 92nd seized him by the arms and made him prisoner. The Duke made some resistance, but the sergeant applying the point of his sword, compelled him to move forward.

By this time a number of the French assembled and threw themselves across the head of the street along which we were marching and commenced firing upon us. Owing to the narrowness of the street, and the compact way in which we were at the time, their shot told with deadly effect. Our front section dashed forward at a rapid pace and quickly dislodged them. The greatest uproar and confusion now prevailed in the town, and the work of death was going on at a fearful rate. The 71st moved down to our assistance while the 50th secured all the passages to the town and captured the French artillery. Our artillery could not be brought into play although we stood much in need of its aid. We now pushed our way through the suburbs and cleared the town of the enemy. They afterwards formed in a field and fired down a lane upon us, by which twenty-three of our men were killed and a great number of officers and men were wounded, among whom were Colonel Cameron, Major Dunbar, and also Captains MacDonald and MacPherson. The French were formed in two columns when we surrounded them and made them prisoners,—a number of stragglers escaping, among whom was General Gerard. The capture included two entire regiments (the 34th and 40th) with banners, etc., but one of the eagles was got off by some means or other. After placing a guard over the two regiments we gave chase to the fugitives and our guns being now brought up we made great havoc among them. We pursued them up a hill, where a great many of them, overcome by fatigue, were not able to get out of the way ; all of these we took prisoners. There were taken General Le Brune, a Commissary-General, a Major-General and a great many subordinate officers. Along with the artillery, we also captured the military chest, which contained a large sum of money, and a chest belonging to a mason lodge with all the jewels and paraphernalia belonging to the order of masonry. There were also a great many horses and mules which were sold, and the proceeds divided amongst the captors. In fact everything fell into our hands. We halted all night in a wood about two leagues from the town, on the road to Morida, where double allowance of soft bread and spirits was served out to us.

V

WATERLOO PAPERS

BY THE LATE E. BRUCE LOW

THE GUARDS AT WATERLOO

HOUGOUMONT

'The success of the battle of Waterloo turned upon the closing of the gates of Hougoumont.'—WELLINGTON

A DISTINGUISHED novelist, Sir A. Conan Doyle, has told, and Sir Henry Irving has realised for us in life-tints on the stage, the story of Corporal Gregory Brewster's daring deed at the great North Gate of Hougoumont, in dashing through the flames with a waggon-load of ammunition for the defenders ; but another heroic incident took place at the same spot, which was of even greater interest, and certainly produced results of much greater importance.

All British and French writers agree that the château and farmhouse of Hougoumont formed the key to Wellington's position at Waterloo. When Lord Uxbridge asked the Duke which was the material point of his operations in case any accident should overtake him, the reply was, 'Keep Hougoumont.' Victor Hugo, describing the battlefield, writes : 'Hougoumont : this was the beginning of the obstacle, the first resistance which that great wood-cutter of Europe called Napoleon encountered at Waterloo—the first knot under the blows of his axe. Behold the court, the conquest of which was one of Napoleon's dreams. This corner of earth, could he but have seized it, would perhaps have given him the world likewise.'

To hold this vital point in his line of battle, Wellington chose the Coldstream Guards, under Lieutenant-Colonel Sir James Macdonell, a gigantic, broad-shouldered Highlander from Invergarry ; and to these same broad shoulders and the *perfervidum ingenium Scotorum*, which at the supreme moment and crisis of the assault refused to yield, Wellington after the battle accorded the laurels of victory. [Macdonell had obtained a gold medal for distinguished service at the battle of Maida, Sicily, 1806.] When appealed to, in awarding the prize of five hundred pounds bequeathed to 'the bravest soldier in the British army at Waterloo,' Wellington wrote : 'The success of the battle of Waterloo turned upon the closing of the gates of Hougoumont. These gates were closed in the most courageous manner at the nick of time by Sir James Macdonell. I cannot help thinking, therefore, that Sir James is the man to whom you should give the five hundred pounds.' Like a true Highland gentleman, Macdonell handed over the money to the stalwart sergeant who, shoulder to shoulder with this colonel of the Guards, had-forced back the door on its hinges in face of overwhelming numbers of the enemy.

The following details of this soul-stirring incident are gathered from the most reliable French and British sources :

The Coldstream Guards, who, with the 3rd or Scots Guards, formed the 2nd Brigade of General Cook's Division of Guards, arrived on the field of battle at five o'clock on the evening of the 17th June, wearied with the long march from Quatre Bras, where they had helped the Highland Brigade to win a costly victory. It was then a fine evening ; but at seven o'clock, when Macdonell's men advanced to take possession of the château and grounds, a tremendous storm of rain, wind, lightning, and loud thunder broke over the country. Nor were they a moment too soon ; for hardly had they closed the gates before a party of French cavalry approached at full speed and sought to seize the orchard. A short and sharp encounter satisfied the enemy that the attempt with their numbers was fruitless.

All that night the small garrison were kept at work by Macdonell in strengthening the buildings for defence ; and in the morning they started to pierce the brick walls of the orchard and garden for loopholes, and to erect low platforms for the second firing-line which should shoot over the walls. All the gates giving access to the château or the farm were barricaded with flagstones, beams, broken waggons, and the like ; but the great North Gate leading to the British ridge was left open to allow of free ingress for ammunition and reinforcements if necessary. This open gateway constituted a source of much danger, as by a rush the enemy might at

SIR THOMAS PICTON ORDERING SIR JAMES KEMPT'S BRIGADE TO CHARGE AT QUATRE BRAS

Facing page 124

any moment force an entrance before a sufficient number of the defenders could rally to the spot.

Early in the morning of the 18th, Wellington and his staff rode down to the spot. Müffling, the Prussian officer, and other foreigners were with them. Taking a survey of the defences, the Duke expressed himself well satisfied. 'Now Bonaparte will see how a general of Sepoys can defend a position,' he said ; and was about to remount, when Müffling expressed some doubt as to the possibility of the post being held against assault. Wellington merely pointed to Macdonell, to whom he had been giving some final instructions, and remarked, 'Ah! you do not know Macdonell.' After the battle—after Napoleon had sent his brother Jerome against Hougoumont ; after the divisions of Foy, Guilleminot, and Bachelu had hurled themselves against it ; after nearly the entire army corps of Reille had been employed against it, and had miscarried ; and Kellerman's iron hail had exhausted itself on this heroic section of wall—Wellington again met Müffling near the château, and shouted exultingly to him, 'Well, you see, Macdonell held Hougoumont after all.'

The first French gun was fired at half-past eleven, and was the signal for a general advance of their 6th Division, under Jerome Bonaparte, which attacked the wood on the south side of the position with great impetuosity, in the face of a heavy artillery fire from Major Bull's howitzer horse battery—to whom the Duke gave orders in person—with the effect that the French columns were twice checked ere they entered the wood and drove off the Hanoverians and Nassauers posted there. Time after time the attack was renewed, the defenders contesting every inch of ground and making a rapid advance at the first indication of hesitancy in the attack.

Slowly and surely the French infantry pressed back the skirmishers of the Guards through the beechwood into the alley of holly and yew trees running round the north and west sides of the position. Under the belief that this hedge formed the only obstacle to a rush into the garden and orchard, the Frenchmen, mistaking the red colour of the brick wall for the British uniform, sprang rapidly forward only to find themselves the target for a deadly fire, which burst upon them from loopholes and platforms along the garden wall. Though staggered for a time, the assailants, rendered frantic by the unexpected obstacle, and constantly reinforced from the main body, rallied, and obtaining a vast preponderance of force, swept round the flanks of the farmhouse, and, like the onward sweep of a tidal wave, carried all opposition before them. The French had ascertained that the defenders received their supplies of ammunition and were being reinforced from time to time by way of the great North Gate. It was therefore determined to make a fierce onslaught on this portion of the line of defence. To this point, accordingly, General Bauduin, the Commander of the first Brigade of Jerome's Division, directed the advance of the 1st Regiment of Léger Infantry. Later, seeing Bauduin fall mortally wounded just before the gateway was reached, the colonel, Cubières, assumed the direct command, and with loud shouts rode forward towards the one vulnerable spot in the armour of the defence. In order to beat down all opposition he ordered forward a party of Sapeurs, at whose head he placed a brave young officer, the Sous-Lieutenant Legros, but better known among the soldiers as 'L'enfonceur,' otherwise 'the smasher,' who, though at the time an officer of Light Infantry, had served for a period with the Engineers, and was recognised by all as a brave and capable leader for the task in hand.

Seizing a hatchet, and waving his comrades to follow, Legros rushed past the blazing haystack, the dense black smoke from which filled the lane and hid from the defenders the terrible danger which now threatened their position. At this critical moment the group of Guardsmen who had been holding tenaciously to the lane leading to the gateway were compelled by the overwhelming smoke and heat produced by the burning hay, and now by the rapidly increasing pressure of their enemies, to relinquish their post. Seeing themselves about to be outflanked and their retreat cut off by a force now entering the 'friendly hollow way' from the other or east end, the Guards withdrew into the great courtyard of the farm, and hastened to close the great North Gate.

THE FORGOTTEN RANK AND FILE

This handful of Guardsmen, upon whose courage and devotion to duty must now depend the fate of Hougoumont, and, in Wellington's own words, 'the success of the battle of Waterloo': who were they? From contemporary newspapers, from short obituary notices, and from the lists of Yeomen of the Guard, Bedesmen of Westminster Abbey, Tower, and Chelsea Pensioners, and the like, it has been possible to trace a few of these brave men. How difficult the task has become is shown by the fact that Mr Dalton's *Roll-call*, published in 1890, contains the names of but a few out of the many who fought in the rank and file of the regiments of Foot Guards. Thousands are as forgotten as 'autumnal leaves that strew the brooks in Vallombrosa'.

The party now retiring slowly into the courtyard consisted of men from the light companies of the Coldstreams and of the 3rd or Scots Guards. Among them were two brothers, Graham by name, natives of the County Monaghan, also two sergeants of the Scots Guards—Bryce M'Gregor, a native of Argyleshire, who enlisted at Glasgow in 1799, and remained in the service till 1822; and Sergeant-Major Ralph Fraser, a veteran who had served with distinction in Egypt in 1801, in Hanover, at Copenhagen, and in the Peninsula, where he was twice badly wounded. Upon these men then fell the brunt of the determined attack of Cubières' regiment, headed by Legros and his Sapeurs.

A fierce hand-to-hand fight now ensued. Step by step the gallant defenders were forced to give ground. Then, in order to create a diversion, Sergeant Fraser, while his comrades made for the gate, rushed forward into the thickest throng of the enemy, alone and at great personal risk, and attacked the mounted officer whom he saw urging his charger forward with the obvious intention of preventing the heavy gates from being closed. With a powerful thrust of his sergeant's halberd he pulled the officer, who was no other than Cubières himself, from the saddle; and then, with a swiftness which utterly disconcerted the Frenchmen around him, he 'rode into the courtyard on the Frenchman's horse' before the surprised assailants had realised his daring design. Fraser was, however, closely followed by Legros and about a hundred of the enemy, who, parrying the vigorous bayonet-thrusts of the defenders, threw their combined strength upon the partially closed gate; and, mid the crash of falling timbers and the rattle of crumbling masonry, the great North Gate of Hougoumont was captured.

Only for a moment did victory rest with the Frenchmen. Attracted by the loud shouts of 'Vive l'Empereur!' and the counter-cries for help from the hard-pressed defenders

of the gate, Macdonell, calling the three officers near him
to follow, made for the courtyard. The sight which met
his gaze was sufficient to stagger even the bravest heart.
Already a hundred Frenchmen had entered the gateway,
and some had penetrated as far as the wicket-gate of the
inner yard by which he and his party must pass from the
garden to reach the North Gate. Here a dozen Frenchmen
of the 1st Léger Regiment had been surrounded by a number
of Hanoverian infantrymen, who had been driven into the
garden from the orchard by the overwhelming numbers of
the enemy. In a few moments the fight here was over, and
the intruders hunted down; but not before the Frenchmen
had the satisfaction of seeing a young Hanoverian lieutenant,
Wilder by name, pursued by another party of Frenchmen
towards the farmhouse, and, at the moment when he grasped
the handle of the door, cut down by a ferocious Sapeur, who
hewed off his hand with an axe.

On entering the courtyard, Macdonell saw that the
Guardsmen there were defending themselves at the entrance
to the cowhouse and stables which ran eastwards from the
gate, and that several of their number were lying wounded
at the doorway. Among these latter was one of the brothers
Graham of the Coldstreams. From the windows of the
parlour, 'from behind the walls, from the summits of the
garrets, from the depths of the cellars, through all the air-
holes, through every crack in the stones, the Guards, now
in ambush, were firing upon the French in the yard. At the
château, the defenders, besieged on the staircase and massed
on the upper steps, had cut off the lower steps.' To-day,
the ends of these broken stones resemble broken teeth of
some monster as they project from the ruined wall, and
among the nettles around still lie the blue slabs which formed
the steps; above, but inaccessible, are the stairs where the
Guards held their ground. Well may Victor Hugo declare:
'This corner of the earth, could Napoleon have held it,
would have given him the Sovereignty of the world.'

However, it was not to be. Macdonell, as we have
said, was a man of giant stature and breadth of frame;
and when he rushed like an infuriated lion upon the Frenchmen around the gate they scattered before him. With him
were the handful of young officers, whose names have
been honourably preserved to us by Siborne, the Kinglake
of the Waterloo campaign. They were, like Colonel

GALLANT STAND OF THE 28TH AT QUATRE BRAS

Facing page 129

Macdonell, all officers of the Second Battalion of the Coldstreams. Captain Harry Wyndham (afterwards General Sir H.
Wyndham, K.C.B., M.P.) was a son of the third Earl of
Egremont, and had already seen eight general engagements
in the Peninsular war, although on the day of the battle of
Waterloo he was not yet twenty-five years old. Besides
earning immortal fame by the heroic deed which we are now
about to relate, Wyndham is remembered by an incident
which occurred immediately after the battle as darkness was
falling upon the field. Pressing on in the general pursuit
of the French, he saw one of the Imperial carriages attempting to escape, and soon ascertained that the occupant was
none other than Napoleon's brother Jerome against whose
columns he had been fighting all day. Quick as thought he
opened the carriage-door, only to catch a glimpse of Jerome
as he leapt out by the other door and disappeared in the
darkness.

SERGEANT JOHN GRAHAM

Following Wyndham into the courtyard came Ensigns
Gooch (afterwards Colonel) and Hervey; and as they
approached the small tower and well in the centre of the
farmyard they were joined by Sergeant John Graham of
the light company of their regiment, who, as already described,
had, with his now wounded brother and Sergeants Fraser
and MacGregor, been holding the enemy in check and preventing them from setting the stables and barn near the
great North Gate on fire. As this small party approached
the gate there appeared before them, at the further end of
the narrow way, a strong reinforcement of French infantry
pouring in from both flanks. The British officers became
at once roused to frenzy by the thought of the dire calamity
which must befall the whole army if they should fail. With
Hougoumont taken, Napoleon would entrench himself in the
key to the British position, enfilading the right wing and
opening the highway by the Nivelles road direct to Brussels.

The little party of officers no sooner burst in fury upon
the Frenchmen near the gate than they turned tail and broke
up into several parties, some taking refuge in the open cart-
shed adjoining the gate, and others making for the barn,
where many of the British wounded were lying, and through
which there was a direct road to the south or French side of

I

the position. The remainder stood their ground, awaiting the arrival of the reinforcements now in sight. In less time than it takes to relate, Macdonell and Sergeant Graham placed their broad shoulders against the open gates ; and, while their comrades engaged and overcame the daring spirits among the enemy who struggled to resist, the heavy doors were swung together, and—Hougoumont was saved ! Immediately stone slabs, broken beams, and the remains or wagons and farm implements were heaped against the gate, and then the storm of baffled and impotent rage burst against the outside. In another instant the heavy cross-bar which held the doors together was fixed by Graham, and the blows of hatchet and bayonet beat unavailingly on the solid planks of which the gate was composed. Long afterwards the imprint of bloody hands upon the gate-post and timbers told the tale of the frantic disappointment and passion of the assailants, which became fiercer as the cries of the hunted Frenchmen still within the yard became gradually silenced in death. As at Quatre Bras the 42nd Highlanders (the Black Watch) received the French cavalry into the still unformed square, then closing its ranks, turned upon the intruders and exterminated them, so now the Guards at Hougoumont proceeded to dispose of Cubières' Light Infantry one by one.

So fierce now became the pent-up wrath of the baffled enemy that an effort was next made to scale the high brick archway above the gate, and for this purpose a tall French Grenadier, amid the shouts of his comrades, mounted on their shoulders, and leaning over the top, took deliberate aim at Captain Wyndham, who at the moment was holding a musket in one hand while directing Sergeant Graham where to rest a massive beam of wood which Graham had brought to strengthen the gate. Noticing the Frenchman's movement and intention, Wyndham calmly handed the musket to Graham, who was a marksman of note, and with a significant gesture indicated the sharpshooter, whose musket was levelled, and who had merely to draw the trigger. Instantly grasping the situation, Graham took aim and fired. Two shots rang out, but the Frenchman's weapon discharged itself harmlessly in mid-air, and he fell backwards on the heads of his companions, pierced through the brain. At the same moment the assailants were taken in rear by a force of four companies of the Coldstream Guards under Colonel Alexander Woodford, a Peninsular veteran, who afterwards rose to the rank of

Field-Marshal and survived till August 1870. Woodford's men fixed bayonets and charged. The enemy immediately gave way and 'withdrew from the contest, which enabled Woodford to enter the farm by a side-door in the lane. Woodford had come at the personal request of Wellington himself to assist Macdonell; but although senior in rank to that gallant officer, he refused to supersede him.

The French continued during the whole of the day to renew their attack, but at no time were they able to enter the farm. As already stated, the attack had begun at half-past eleven; the assault on the great North Gate took place at one o'clock and was succeeded by a series of determined attacks by the whole of Bachelu's Division till three o'clock, when it became apparent to Napoleon that these troops were being thrown away without result, and that now a different line of action must be adopted. He resolved to make the position untenable by setting the whole of the buildings on fire.

Among the two hundred and fifty pieces of artillery which Bonaparte had brought into the field of battle were a number of howitzers, which he directed to be formed into a powerful battery in order that their fire might be concentrated upon the château and farm. It was not long ere the projectiles thrown among the inflammable materials accumulated in the farm caused them to burst into flame. The great barn, filled, as we have seen, with wounded Guardsmen, was the first to catch fire; then followed the outhouses on the north side of the château and the farmer's house; and, finally, the château itself burned furiously. Amid dense volumes of black smoke, which attracted the attention of the combatants far and near— producing a temporary lull in the general engagement—the roofs of these buildings were seen to fall in, in quick succession, sending vast sheets of flame upwards, with brilliant effect. It speaks well of the discipline of the defenders that, although many of the Guardsmen had brothers and kinsmen lying wounded within the burning buildings, it was recognised by all that the defence of their various posts was the first duty of each man, and not one left his rank, terrible as was the anxiety to save the wounded, until the permission of the officer in command had first been obtained.

It was at this moment that Sergeant Graham, whose post was now at the hastily improvised banquette composed of benches, tables, chairs, and other like materials, appealed to Colonel Macdonell to allow him to withdraw from the fighting-line. Macdonell consented ; but he asked Graham, whose bravery was well known to him, why he should retire when matters were at such a critical point. 'I would not,' said Graham, 'only my brother lies wounded in that building which has just caught fire.'

Leave was cheerfully granted ; and Graham, laying down his musket, ran into the blazing building, lifted his brother to a place of safety in a ditch close by, and was back at his post almost instantly. Graham's wounded brother survived to thank his commanding officer, who in his turn repeatedly expressed his admiration for the high sense of duty and the brotherly affection shown by these lads from County Monaghan.

Nor did Macdonell forget the sergeant's gallant behaviour ; for not only did he keep him in mind in various ways till Graham died at Kilmainham on 23rd April 1843, but when the Duke of Wellington awarded the Norcross bequest of five hundred pounds to Colonel Macdonell as 'the bravest soldier at Waterloo,' it was to Graham that he passed on the gift, with the remark, 'I cannot claim all the merit due to the closing of the gates of Hougoumont ; for Sergeant John Graham, who saw with me the importance of the step, rushed forward, and *together* we shut the gates.' The other brave fellows who had held the post at the lane and gate till succour arrived were not altogether forgotten ; for it appears that Sergeant-Major MacGregor retired after twenty-two years' service with a considerable pension, and was selected as one of the Yeomen of the Guard, and was thus well provided for till his death on 27th November 1846. Sergeant-Major Ralph Fraser was, after his discharge in 1818, appointed a Bedesman in Westminster Abbey, where he continued till he was over eighty years of age.

Besides receiving from Wellington the high honour of being credited with the 'success won at Waterloo' through his stout defence, Macdonell was recognised by the Prince Regent and by the Emperor of Austria, who made him a Knight of the Order of Maria Theresa. He afterwards became General Sir James Macdonell, G.C.B., Colonel-in-chief of the Highland Light Infantry. Of this officer, it is interesting to note that his family, the Macdonells of Glengarry, Inverness-shire, were of very ancient descent from the Lords of the Isles, and that Colonel Alexander, the eldest brother of Sir James, was the Fergus MacIvor of Sir Walter Scott's *Waverley*. The family were much reduced and the estates heavily mortgaged in consequence of the prominent part taken by them in the Jacobite risings of 1715 and 1745, when, as official documents show, they brought five hundred clansmen into the field. The result was that at the death of Colonel Alexander Macdonell, in 1828, the whole of the estates were sold, and the chieftain's son and immediate followers emigrated to Australia. The hero of Hougoumont survived till 15th May 1857, and with him ended the direct male line.

On the French side, General Baron Bauduin died of the wounds received in the attack, aged forty-seven ; and at the door of the little chapel of the château, to which, when the gate was closed, he had fled for safety, was found the corpse of Sous-Lieutenant Legros of the 1st Léger Regiment, still holding the axe in his hand with which he had beaten in a panel of the massive gate.

A FINE INCIDENT

Legros' colonel, Baron de Cubières, afterwards made General and Governor of Ancona in 1832, was loud in his praise of the British soldiers, who, when he was unhorsed by Sergeant Fraser and fell severely injured, 'forbore to fire upon him, and to this he declared he owed many good years since the battle,' as Sir Alexander Woodford tells us.

To-day the great North gateway still stands much as it stood on the day of the battle, though the brick arch and massive beam on which it rested have long since disappeared. A bit of the north door, broken by the French, hangs suspended to the wall of the farmhouse. This consisted, till recently, of four planks nailed to two cross-beams, 'on which the scars of the attack are visible,' says Victor Hugo. He adds : 'Bauduin slain, Foy wounded ; conflagration, massacre, carnage ; a rivulet formed of English blood, French blood, German blood, mingled in fury ; a well crammed with corpses ; the regiment of Nassau and the regiment of Brunswick destroyed ; Duplat killed, Blackman killed, the British Guards mutilated, twenty French battalions, besides the forty from Reille's Corps, decimated ; three thousand men in that hovel of Hougoumont alone cut down, slashed to pieces, shot, burned—and all this so that a peasant can say to-day to the traveller, "Monsieur, give me three francs, and if you like I will explain to you the affair of Waterloo." '

VI

THE GREYS AT WATERLOO

REMINISCENCES OF THE LAST SUR-
VIVOR OF THE FAMOUS CHARGE
BY THE LATE E. BRUCE LOW

THE GREYS AT WATERLOO

REMINISCENCES OF THE LAST SURVIVOR OF THE FAMOUS CHARGE

The Greys at the glorious Waterloo fight
Put ten thousand men of Count D'Erlon to flight,
Then eagle and banner by Ewart were won,
And the deils o' Dundee proved they're 'Second to None.'

SERGEANT-MAJOR DICKSON of the Scots Greys from whose lips many of the details of the battle of Waterloo here given were obtained by members of his family, was the last who survived of those who fought in the regiment at Waterloo. He was a native of Paisley, born in the Revolution year of 1789. He enlisted at Glasgow in 1807 when barely eighteen, and remained in the service till 1834. At Waterloo he was corporal in Captain Vernon's troop, and his sabre and other regimentals bear evidence that his number was 57 of F troop. He was promoted sergeant after Waterloo for his services, and took the place of Sergeant Charles Ewart, who received a commission in the Fifth Veteran Regiment for the brave deed narrated here.

On retiring from the Greys Sergeant Dickson joined the Fife Light Horse, and his long residence in Crail is fresh in the memory of many of the inhabitants. He died at the age of ninety on 16th July 1880, survived by three children and several grandchildren. His army papers bear witness that during his service of twenty-seven years in the Greys his character was 'excellent,' and he was awarded a medal for long service and good conduct in addition to his Waterloo medal. He was a typical yeoman—tall, of ruddy complexion, brown hair, and hazel eyes, as the army record tells us—and his descendants still farm the acres in East Lothian which their ancestors have held from Lord Wemyss for generations.

Seated within the coffee-room of the little Fifeshire inn, a merry party of villagers and visitors met in the summer evening to do honour to their veteran host John Dickson, on the anniversary of Waterloo, in the year 1855. The news from the Crimea portended another attack upon Sebastopol, which in truth was taking place at that very moment ; and as the thoughts of the people were with their kinsmen in the trenches, the genial host was induced to relate his experiences of forty years ago.

Taking his 'yard of clay' pipe in hand, he seated himself at the table, at the head of which sat the village banker ; for, be it known, 'Waterloo Day' was a high day in the village, kept in ripe memory by the flags flying and the procession of school children, decked in summer attire and gay with flowers, to do honour to 'mine host,' whose deeds of valour were on every tongue. When the toddy-glasses had been filled it only required the key-note to be sounded by the inquiry of the president, 'By-the-bye, sergeant, what might you be doing just at this time forty years ago ?' to draw forth the great story of the charge of the Union Brigade. The sergeant smoked for a time in silence ; then, with a far-away look in his eyes, he began :

'Well, you all know that when I was a lad of eighteen, being a good Scotsman, I joined the Greys, the oldest regiment of dragoons in the British army, and our only Scottish cavalry corps.

'When news came that Napoleon Bonaparte had landed in France, we were sent across to Belgium post-haste, and there had a long rest, waiting for his next move. I remember how the trumpets roused us at four o'clock on the morning of Friday the 16th June 1815, and how quickly we assembled and fell in !

'Three days' biscuits were served out to us ; and after long marches—for we did fifty miles that one day before we reached Quatre Bras—we joined the rest of our brigade under Sir William Ponsonby.

'Besides our regiment there were the 1st Royals and the Enniskillens, and we were known as the Union Brigade because, you see, it was made up of one English, one Irish and one Scots regiment.

'On the day before the great fight—that was Saturday, for you know the battle was fought on the Sunday morning, the 18th June—we were marched from Quatre Bras along the road towards Brussels. We thought our Iron Duke was taking us there ; but no. In a drenching rain we were told to halt and lie down away in a hollow to the right of the main road, among some green barley. Yes, how we trampled down the corn ! The wet barley soon soaked us, so we set about making fires beside a cross-road that ran along the hollow in which we were posted. No rations were served that night. As we sat round our fire we heard a loud, rumbling noise about a mile away, and this we knew must be the French artillery and waggons coming up. It went rolling on incessantly all night, rising and falling like that sound just now of the wind in the chimney.

'One thing I must tell you : though there were more than seventy thousand Frenchmen over there, we never once saw a camp-fire burning all the night and until six o'clock next morning. Why they weren't allowed to warm themselves, poor fellows ! I don't know. Well, about eleven o'clock that night a fearful storm burst over us. The thunder was terrible to hear. It was a battle-royal of the elements, as if the whole clouds were going to fall on us. We said it was a warning to Bonaparte that all nature was angry at him.

'Around the fires we soon fell asleep, for we were all worn out with our long march in the sultry heat of the day before.

'I was wakened about five o'clock by my comrade MacGee, who sprang up and cried, " D—— your eyes, boys, there's the bugle ! " " Tuts, Jock ! " I replied, " it's the horses' chains clanking." " Clankin' ? " said he. " What's that, then ? " as a clear blast fell on our ears.

'After I had eaten my ration of " stirabout "—oatmeal and water—I was sent forward on picket to the road two hundred yards in front, to watch the enemy. It was daylight, and the sun was every now and again sending bright flashes of light through the broken clouds. As I stood behind the straggling hedge and low beech-trees that skirted the high banks of the sunken road on both sides, I could see the French army drawn up in heavy masses opposite me. They were only a mile from where I stood ; but the distance seemed greater, for between us the mist still filled the hollows. There were great columns of infantry, and squadron after squadron of Cuirassiers, red Dragoons, brown Hussars, and green Lancers with little swallow-tail flags at the end of their lances. The grandest sight was a regiment of Cuirassiers dashing at full gallop over the brow of the hill opposite me, with the sun shining on their steel breastplates. It was a splendid show. Every now and then the sun lit up the whole country. No one who saw it could ever forget it.

'Between eight and nine there was a sudden roll of drums along the whole of the enemy's line, and a burst of music from the bands of a hundred battalions came to me on the wind. I seemed to recognise the "Marseillaise," but the sounds got mixed and lost in a sudden uproar that arose. Then every regiment began to move. They were taking up position for the battle. On our side perfect silence reigned ; but I saw that with us too preparations were being made. Down below me a regiment of Germans was marching through the growing corn to the support of others who were in possession of a farmhouse that lay between the two armies. This was the farm of La Haye Sainte, and it was near there that the battle raged fiercest. These brave Germans ! they died to a man before the French stormed it, at the point of the bayonet, in the afternoon. A battery of artillery now came dashing along the road in fine style and passed in front of me. I think they were Hanoverians ; they were not British troops, but I don't remember whether they were Dutch or German. They drew up close by, about a hundred yards in front of the road. There were four guns. Then a strong brigade of Dutch and Belgians marched up with swinging, quick step, and turned off at a cross-road between high banks on to the plateau on the most exposed slope of our position. They numbered at least three thousand men, and looked well in their blue coats with orange-and-red facings. After this I rode up to a party of Highlanders under the command of Captain Ferrier, from Belsyde, Linlithgow, whom I knew to belong to the Ninety-second or "Gay Gordons," as we called them. All were intently watching the movements going on about them. They, with the Seventy-ninth Cameron Highlanders, the Forty-second (Black Watch), and First Royal Scots formed part of Picton's, "Fighting Division." They began to tell me about the battle at Quatre Bras two days before, when every regiment in brave old Picton's division had lost more than one-third of its men. The Gordons, they said, had lost half their number and twenty-five out of thirty-six officers. Little did we think that before the sun set that night not thirty men of our own regiment would answer the roll-call.

'I seem to remember everything as if it happened yester-

day.   After the village clocks had struck eleven the guns on
the French centre thundered out, and then musketry firing
commenced away to the far right.   The French were seen to
be attacking a farmhouse there in force.   It was called
Hougoumont.   I noticed, just in front of me, great columns
of infantry beginning to advance over the brow of the hill
on their side of the valley, marching straight for us.   Then
began a tremendous cannonade from two hundred and fifty
French guns all along the lines.   The noise was fearful ; but
just then a loud report rent the air, followed by a rolling
cheer on our side, and our artillery got into action.   We had
one hundred and fifty guns in all ; but half of these belonged
to the Dutch, Germans, or Belgians, who were hired to fight
on our side.   The French had about ten thousand men more
than we had all that day, till, late in the afternoon, the
Prussians arrived with forty thousand men to help us.   I
was now drawn back and joined our regiment, which was
being moved forward to the left under better cover near
a wood, as the shot and shell were flying about us and
ploughing up the earth around.   We had hardly reached our
position when a great fusillade commenced just in front of
us, and we saw the Highlanders moving up towards the road
to the right.   Then, suddenly, a great noise of firing and
hisses and shouting commenced, and the whole Belgian
brigade, of those whom I had seen in the morning, came
rushing along and across the road in full flight.   Our men
began to shout and groan at them too.   They had bolted
almost without firing a shot, and left the brigade of Highlanders to meet the whole French attack on the British left
centre.   It was thought that the Belgians were inclined
towards Napoleon's cause, and this must account for their
action, as they have shown high courage at other times.

'Immediately after this, the General of the Union Brigade,
Sir William Ponsonby, came riding up to us on a small bay-
hack.   I remember that his groom with his chestnut charger
could not be found.   Beside him was his aide-de-camp, De
Lacy Evans.   He ordered us forward to within fifty yards
of the beech-hedge by the roadside.   I can see him now in
his long cloak and great cocked hat as he rode up to watch
the fighting below.   From our new position we could descry
the three regiments of Highlanders, only a thousand in all,
bravely firing down on the advancing masses of Frenchmen.
These numbered thousands, and those on our side of the

Brussels road were divided into three solid columns. I have read since that there were fifteen thousand of them under Count D'Erlon spread over the clover, barley, and rye fields in front of our centre, and making straight for us. Then I saw the Brigadier, Sir Denis Pack, turn to the Gordons and shout out with great energy, "Ninety-second, you must advance! All in front of you have given way." The Highlanders, who had begun the day by solemnly chanting "Scots wha hae" as they prepared their morning meal, instantly, with fixed bayonets, began to press forward through the beech and holly hedge to a line of bushes that grew along the face of the slope in front. They uttered loud shouts as they ran forward and fired a volley at twenty yards into the French.

'At this moment our General and his aide-de-camp rode off to the right by the side of the hedge; then suddenly I saw De Lacy Evans wave his hat, and immediately our colonel, Inglis Hamilton,* shouted out, "Now then, Scots Greys, charge!" and, waving his sword in the air, he rode straight at the hedges in front, which he took in grand style. At once a great cheer rose from our ranks, and we too waved our swords and followed him. I dug my spur into my brave old Rattler, and we were off like the wind. Just then I saw Major Hankin fall wounded. I felt a strange thrill run through me, and I am sure my noble beast felt the same, for, after rearing for a moment, she sprang forward, uttering loud neighings and snortings, and leapt over the holly-hedge at a terrific speed. It was a grand sight to see the long line of giant grey horses dashing along with flowing manes and heads down, tearing up the turf about them as they went. The men in their red coats and tall bearskins were cheering loudly, and the trumpeters were sounding the "Charge." Beyond the first hedge the road was sunk between high, sloping banks, and it was a very difficult feat to descend without falling; but there were very few accidents, to our surprise.

'All of us were greatly excited, and began crying, "Hurrah, Ninety-Second! Scotland for ever!" as we crossed the road. For we heard the Highland pipers playing among the smoke and firing below, and I plainly saw my old friend Pipe-Major Cameron standing apart on a hillock

* Of Murdestone, Lanarkshire.

coolly playing "Johnny Cope, are ye waukin' yet?" in all the din.

'Our colonel went on before us, past our guns and down the slope, and we followed; we saw the Royals and Enniskillens clearing the road and hedges at full gallop away to the right.

'Before me rode young Armour, our rough-rider from Mauchline (a near relative of Jean Armour, Robbie Burns's wife), and Sergeant Ewart on the right, at the end of the line beside our cornet, Kinchant. I rode in the second rank. As we tightened our grip to descend the hillside among the corn, we could make out the feather bonnets of the Highlanders, and heard the officers crying out to them to wheel back by sections. A moment more and we were among them. Poor fellows! some of them had not time to get clear of us, and were knocked down. I remember one lad crying out, "Eh! but I didna think ye wad ha'e hurt me sae."

'They were all Gordons, and as we passed through them they shouted, "Go at them, the Greys! Scotland for ever!" My blood thrilled at this, and I clutched my sabre tighter. Many of the Highlanders grasped our stirrups, and in the fiercest excitement dashed with us into the fight. The French were uttering loud, discordant yells. Just then I saw the first Frenchman. A young officer of Fusiliers made a slash at me with his sword, but I parried it and broke his arm; the next second we were in the thick of them. We could not see five yards ahead for the smoke. I stuck close by Armour; Ewart was now in front.

'The French were fighting like tigers. Some of the wounded were firing at us as we passed; and poor Kinchant, who had spared one of these rascals, was himself shot by the officer he had spared. As we were sweeping down a steep slope on the top of them, they had to give way. Then those in front began to cry out for "quarter," throwing down their muskets and taking off their belts. The Gordons at this rushed in and drove the French to the rear. I was now in the front rank, for many of ours had fallen. It was here that Lieutenant Trotter, from Morton Hall, was killed by a French officer after the first rush on the French. We now came to an open space covered with bushes, and then I saw Ewart, with five or six infantry men about him, slashing right and left at them. Armour and I dashed up to these half-dozen Frenchmen, who were trying to escape with one of their standards. I cried to Armour to "Come on!" and we rode at them. Ewart had finished two of them, and was in the act of striking a third man who held the Eagle; next moment I saw Ewart cut him down, and he fell dead. I was just in time to thwart a bayonet-thrust that was aimed at the gallant sergeant's neck. Armour finished another of them.'

Our host here pointed out to his little company of intent listeners a print of the well-known picture of the incident which hung on the wall, and of which he was very proud; then he continued:

'Almost single-handed, Ewart had captured the Imperial Eagle of the 45th "Invincibles," which had led them to victory at Austerlitz and Jena. Well did he merit the commission he received at the hands of the Prince Regent shortly afterwards, and the regiment has worn a French Eagle ever since.

'We cried out, "Well done, my boy!" and as others had come up, we spurred on in search of a like success. Here it was that we came upon two batteries of French guns which had been sent forward to support the infantry. They were now deserted by the gunners and had sunk deep in the mud.

'We were saluted with a sharp fire of musketry, and again found ourselves beset by thousands of Frenchmen. We had fallen upon a second column; they were also Fusiliers. Trumpeter Reeves of our troop, who rode by my side, sounded a "Rally," and our men came swarming up from all sides, some Enniskillens and Royals being amongst the number. We at once began a furious onslaught on this obstacle, and soon made an impression; the battalions seemed to open out for us to pass through, and so it happened that in five minutes we had cut our way through as many thousands of Frenchmen.

'We had now reached the bottom of the slope. There the ground was slippery with deep mud. Urging each other on, we dashed towards the batteries on the ridge above, which had worked such havoc on our ranks. The ground was very difficult, and especially where we crossed the edge of a ploughed field, so that our horses sank to the knees as we struggled on. My brave Rattler was becoming quite exhausted, but we dashed ever onwards.

'At this moment Colonel Hamilton rode up to us crying, "Charge! charge the guns!" and went off like the wind up

SHAW THE LIFEGUARDSMAN AT WATERLOO

Facing page 144

the hill towards the terrible battery that had made such deadly work among the Highlanders. It was the last we saw of our colonel, poor fellow! His body was found with both arms cut off. His pockets had been rifled. I once heard Major Clarke tell how he saw him wounded among the guns of the great battery, going at full speed, with the bridle-reins between his teeth, after he had lost his hands.

'Then we got among the guns, and we had our revenge. Such slaughtering! We sabred the gunners, lamed the horses, and cut their traces and harness. I can hear the Frenchmen yet crying "*Diable!*" when I struck at them, and the long-drawn hiss through their teeth as my sword went home. Fifteen of their guns could not be fired again that day. The artillery drivers sat on their horses weeping aloud as we went among them; they were mere boys, we thought.

'Rattler lost her temper and bit and tore at everything that came in her way. She seemed to have got new strength. I had lost the plume of my bearskin just as we went through the second infantry column; a shot had carried it away. The French infantry were rushing past us in disorder on their way to the rear, Armour shouted to me to dismount, for old Rattler was badly wounded. I did so just in time, for she fell heavily the next second. I caught hold of a French officer's horse and sprang on her back and rode on.

'Then we saw a party of horsemen in front of us on the rising ground near a farmhouse. There was "the Little Corporal" himself, as his veterans called Bonaparte. It was not till next night, when our men had captured his guide, the Belgian La Coste, that we learned what the Emperor thought of us. On seeing us clear the second column and commence to attack his eighty guns on the centre, he cried out, "These terrible Greys, how they fight!" for you know that all our horses, dear old Rattler among them, fought that day as angrily as we did. I never saw horses become so ferocious, and woe betide the blue coats that came in their way! But the noble beasts were now exhausted and quite blown, so that I began to think it was time to get clear away to our own lines again.

'But you can imagine my astonishment when down below, on the very ground we had crossed, appeared at full gallop a couple of regiments of Cuirassiers on the right, and away to the left a regiment of Lancers. I shall never forget the sight. The Cuirassiers, in their sparkling steel breastplates and

K

helmets, mounted on strong black horses, with great blue rugs across the croups, were galloping towards me, tearing up the earth as they went, the trumpets blowing wild notes in the midst of the discharges of grape and canister shot from the heights. Around me there was one continuous noise of clashing arms, shouting of men, neighing and moaning of horses. What were we to do ? Behind us we saw masses of French infantry with tall fur hats coming up at the double, and between us and our lines these cavalry. There being no officers about, we saw nothing for it but to go straight at them and trust to Providence to get through. There were half-a-dozen of us Greys and about a dozen of the Royals and Enniskillens on the ridge. We all shouted, " Come on, lads ; that's the road home !" and, dashing our spurs into our horses' sides, set off straight for the Lancers. But we had no chance. I saw the lances rise and fall for a moment, and Sam Tar, the leading man of ours, go down amid the flash of steel. I felt a sudden rage at this, for I knew the poor fellow well ; he was a corporal in our troop. The crash as we met was terrible ; the horses began to rear and bite and neigh loudly, and then some of our men got down among their feet, and I saw them trying to ward off the lances with their hands. Cornet Sturges of the Royals—he joined our regiment as lieutenant a few weeks after the battle—came up and was next me on the left, and Armour on the right. " Stick together, lads ! " we cried, and went at it with a will, slashing about us right and left over our horses' necks. The ground around us was very soft, and our horses could hardly drag their feet out of the clay. Here again I came to the ground, for a Lancer finished my new mount, and I thought I was done for. We were returning past the edge of the ploughed field, and then I saw a spectacle I shall never forget. There lay brave old Ponsonby, the General of our Union Brigade, beside his little bay, both dead. His long, fur-lined coat had blown aside, and at his hand I noticed a minature of a lady and his watch ; beyond him, our Brigade-Major, Reignolds of the Greys. They had both been pierced by the Lancers a few moments before we came up. Near them was lying a lieutenant of ours, Carruthers of Annandale. My heart was filled with sorrow at this, but I dared not remain for a moment. It was just then I caught sight of a squadron of British Dragoons making straight for us. The Frenchmen at that instant seemed to give way, and in a minute more we were safe ! The Dragoons gave us a cheer and rode on after the Lancers. They were the men of our 16th Light Dragoons,* of Vandeleur's Brigade, who not only saved us but threw back the Lancers into the hollow.

'How I reached our lines I can hardly say, for the next thing I remember is that I was lying with the sole remnants of our brigade in a position far away to the right and rear of our first post. I was told that a third horse that I caught was so wounded that she fell dead as I was mounting her.

'Wonderful to relate Rattler had joined the retreating Greys, and was standing in line riderless when I returned. You can imagine my joy at seeing her as she nervously rubbed shoulders with her neighbours. Major Cheney (who had five horses killed under him) was mustering our men, and with him were Lieutenant Wyndham † (afterwards our colonel) and Lieutenant Hamilton,‡ but they were both wounded. There were scarcely half a hundred of the Greys left out of the three hundred who rode off half an hour before.§ How I escaped is a miracle, for I was through the thick of it all, and received only two slight wounds, one from a bayonet and the other from a lance, and the white plume of my bearskin was shot away. I did not think much of the wounds at the time, and did not report myself ; but my poor Rattler had lost much blood from a lance-wound received in her last encounter.

'Every man felt that the honour of our land was at stake, and we remembered that the good name of our great Duke was entrusted to us too ; but our main thought was, "What will they say of us at home?" It was not till afterwards that we soldiers learned what the Union Brigade had done that day, for a man in the fighting-ranks sees little beyond the sweep of his own sword. We had pierced three columns of fifteen thousand men, had captured two Imperial Eagles, and had stormed and rendered useless for a time more than forty of the enemy's cannon. Besides, we had taken nearly three

* Under Colonel James Hay, afterwards Colonel-in-Chief of the 79th Cameron Highlanders.

† Colonel Wyndham was the last survivor among the Greys' officers, and Sergeant-Major Dickson attended his funeral in 1872 in the Tower of London, where he had been the Keeper of the Crown Jewels for twenty years.

‡ Son and heir of General John Hamilton of Dalzell, Lanarkshire, and father of Lord Hamilton.

§ We lost sixteen officers out of twenty-four on the field.

thousand prisoners, and, when utterly exhausted, had fought our way home through several regiments of fresh cavalry. That, my friends, is why, from the Prince Regent to the poorest peasant, from the palace to the lowliest cottage, the name of the Union Brigade was honoured throughout the land.'

When the sergeant had finished his story the toddy had cooled in the tumblers ; but there was time to fill them and drink 'Long life to the Sergeant' and to the Union Brigade of our own time, whose charge on Balaklava Day proved that they were worthy successors of the Heroes of Waterloo.

Facing page 149

CHARGE OF THE UNION BRIGADE AT WATERLOO

VII

WHAT THE GORDONS DID AT WATERLOO

FROM THE JOURNAL OF SERGEANT ROBERTSON

WHAT THE GORDONS DID AT WATERLOO

FROM THE FORGOTTEN DIARY OF SERGEANT D. ROBERTSON

Sergeant Robertson in his Journal says, 'On the 26th of January 1815, we marched to Cork again with the intention of embarking for Scotland but, owing to certain circumstances we were detained until the 1st of May when, instead of embarking for our native country, we were ordered off to Belgium again to take up our quarters in the tented field. We weighed anchor on the 3rd and on the 8th landed at Ostend and disembarked next day. We halted here and got three days' rations served out which we managed to get cooked. In the evening we embarked on board the boats on the canal and proceeded to Ghent, where we arrived on the 11th at daybreak.

It happened to be the weekly market day when we landed, and none of us ever saw such a sight before. The day was beautiful, and the people were coming in boats from all directions to the centre of the city, which caused great stir and bustle ; and to add to the effect of the scene, we were disembarked at the large market-place. If the novelty of what we saw made an impression on our minds, the Belgians were no less surprised at our strange appearance as, I believe, none of them had ever seen any clad in the Highland garb before.

We were all regularly billeted upon the inhabitants without distinction, and were civilly used by them. In a few days we were joined by the Royal Scots, 42nd, and 79th, and were pleased at meeting with so many Scotchmen, more especially those brave fellows with whom we had fought side by side in Egypt and Denmark, at Corunna, Fontes, and Vittoria ; among the Pyrenees, at Bayonne and Toulouse :

'Brothers in arms, but rivals in renown.'

We remained in Ghent till the 28th of the month, without

the occurrence of anything worthy of notice, when we marched
to Brussels, where the Duke of Wellington had his headquarters, and were put in divisions under the command of
Sir Thomas Picton, Sir James Kempt, and Sir Denis Pack.
When we came to Alast, half way between Ghent and
Brussels, we found the Duke de Berri commanding a body
of French troops that adhered to the Bourbon cause. Almost
all the officers had served in the French army in Spain, and
some of them had been in Egypt. The latter upon seeing
the Highland regiments, immediately came running to meet
us, and asked very kindly 'If they had not seen us before ?'
When we answered in the affirmative, they went and told the
Duke, who expressed his happiness to have such supporters
to aid the cause of his house.

On our arrival at Brussels we were billeted throughout
the city. The 28th, 32nd, 34th, 95th, and two battalions of
the Hanoverian militia joined us here, which were paraded
in brigade every second day. While here we had a grand
review, which was attended by all the resident Belgian and
English nobility. Recruiting for the Belgian army was going
on with great activity, and hundreds daily marched to the
different depots. They were mostly all good-looking young
fellows and had a very soldier-like appearance. We were
now served with four days' bread, and supplied with camp
kettles, bill hooks and everything necessary for a campaign,
which according to all accounts was fast approaching. The
inhabitants, like those of Ghent, were very civil and kind to
us, and we in turn were the same to them. We were kept
in a state of alarm for some days from reports that appeared
in the Belgian papers to the effect that the French troops
were moving on to the frontiers.

In order to avoid being taken unawares, the orderly
sergeants were desired to take a list of the men's quarters,
with the names of the streets, and the numbers of the houses.
It was also arranged that every company and regiment should
be billeted in the same or the adjacent streets to prevent
confusion if called out at a moment's warning.

On the evening of the 15th of June, the sergeants on
duty were all in the orderly room till ten o'clock at night ;
and no orders having been issued, we went home to our
quarters. I had newly lain down in bed when the bugle
sounded the alarm, the drums beat to arms, bagpipes played
and all was in commotion, thus stunning the drowsy ear of

night by all kinds of martial music sounding in every street. Upon hearing this, sergeants and corporals ran to the quarters of their respective parties to turn them out. I went to the quarter-master for bread and four days' allowance was given out of the store, which was soon distributed among the men, every one getting his share and speedily falling into rank. So regular and orderly was the affair gone about, that we were ready to march in half an hour after the first sound of the bugle.

Colonel Cameron had that day been invested with the Order of the Bath by the title of Sir John Cameron of Fassifearn and was present at a splendid ball given by the Duchess of Richmond, daughter of the seventh Duke of Gordon who was brother to the Marquis of Huntly. She had invited some sergeants of the 92nd to show the company especially the Belgians, the Highland reel and sword dance, which they did. When the alarm sounded, the Duke of Wellington was quickly at our head and we commenced our march at daybreak, leaving the city by the Lamour gates, followed by the inhabitants to whom we gave three farewell cheers.

When we had got a few miles from Brussels we entered a wood, the trees of which were remarkably tall, and although the road was very wide it was wet and soft, as the sun did not strike upon it to make it dry. During our march we had several times to diverge to the right and left, to avoid the bad parts of the road. When we had got a good way into the wood we met a number of waggons conveying Prussian soldiers who had been wounded the day before, who told us that the French were driving all before them, and that we were greatly needed. As we were too apt to entertain bad opinions, we suspected treachery on the part of the foreigners, and that we should have to retreat ; for we did not credit much what the Prussians told us of the affair.

We continued our route until we came to the skirt of the wood, into which we were marched, and ordered to lie down and rest ourselves for two hours, but not to kindle any fires, and on no account to move out of our places We lay down and slept for some time, when the Duke of Wellington and his staff rode by, which made us move, but we were not called upon to march. While lying here we were joined by a great many Hanoverians and Brunswickers, all of whom were formed up in the wood. When we emerged into open ground, we found ourselves at the village of Waterloo. About eleven o'clock we fell in and marched on.

The day was oppressively warm and the road very dusty. We moved on slowly till we reached the village of Geneppe, where the inhabitants had large tubs filled with water standing at the doors, ready for us, of which we stood in great need. They told us that a French patrole had been there that morning. We had hardly got out of the town when we heard the sound of cannon at no great distance which proceeded from the place where the conflict was going on between the French and the Belgians. The sound had a stimulating effect upon us ; for so eager were we to enter the field of action, that we felt as fresh as if we had newly started. In fact we were all anxious to assist the poor Belgians, who were but young soldiers, and consequently little experienced in military affairs. 'Forward,' was now the word that ran through all the ranks ; but the Colonel had more discretion, and would not allow us to run, lest we should exhaust ourselves before the time. He issued peremptory orders that every man should keep his rank as if on parade, and not march above three miles an hour. The firing seemed to be coming nearer as we approached a farm and public-house, called Quatre Bras.

THE TERRIBLE BATTLE OF QUATRE BRAS

We now went off the road to the left of the house and closed up upon the front division in columns of battalions ready to form line. Before many minutes had elapsed, we received some shots from the French artillery which galled us considerably, as we had none up yet to return the compliment. The French made a movement to their own right ; and the 42nd and 79th were ordered to oppose them, in a field on which was growing a crop of long wheat or rye. As those regiments were moving on to take possession of a wood to the left, a little in front of our position, they were attacked by a strong body of cavalry, which made considerable havoc among them. The 92nd was now brought to the front of the farmhouse and formed on the road, with our backs to the walls of the building and garden, our right resting upon the crossroads, and our left extending down the front. We were ordered to prime and load and sit down with our firelocks in our hands, at the same time keeping in line. The ground we occupied rose with a slight elevation, and was directly in front of the road along which the French were advancing.

Shortly after we had formed here the Duke of Wellington and his staff came and dismounted in rear of the centre of our regiment, and ordered the grenadier company to wheel back on the left and the light company on the right; so that the walls of the house and garden in our rear with the eight companies in front, joined in a square, in case any of the enemy's cavalry should attack us. We had not been long in this way, when a column of Brunswick hussars, with the Duke of Brunswick at their head, made a charge down the road on the right. In this, however, they were unsuccessful, and were driven back with considerable loss, the Duke being among the slain. The column of French cavalry that drove back the Brunswickers retired a little, then re-formed, and prepared to charge our regiment; but we took it more coolly than the Brunswickers did. When the Duke of Wellington saw them approach, he ordered our left wing to fire to the right, and the right wing to fire to the left, by which we crossed the fire; and a man and horse affording such a large object for an aim, very few of them escaped. The horses were brought down and the riders, if not killed, were made prisoners. Some of them had the audacity to draw their swords upon the men when in the act of taking them, but such temerity only served to accelerate their own destruction; for in the infuriated state of mind in which we were at the moment, those guilty of such conduct fared a worse fate than those who submitted without a murmur.

We were informed by the prisoners that Napoleon himself was in the field, so were also our old friends Soult and Ney; and that Ney was directly in our front, and had ordered a charge to be made upon us. We were very happy on hearing this intelligence, as the thought that the two great generals of the time were to meet each other on the field of battle, stimulated us to do our utmost to maintain unsullied the hard-earned reputation which the British army had gained in many a bloody battle field.

As far as I am aware this was the first time that ever the Emperor had been personally engaged with us and we were anxious to know if the same good fortune which attended his former campaigns still awaited him, and whether he would be able to re-enact the splendid achievements of Lodi, Marengo, and Austerlitz, when brought into the arena

against an army for the most part composed of veteran
troops, and commanded by brave and experienced generals.
We wished to show him that we were made of sterner stuff
than those whom he was wont to chase over the length and
breadth of Europe.

Immediately after the enemy's cavalry had been driven
back and partially destroyed, a column of infantry was sent
round to a wood on our right and another to push us in
front.   At this time the 30th, 69th, and 73rd regiments
joined us, upon which we left our ground to charge down the
road, led by General Barnes and Colonel Cameron.   Just as
we had taken our stand, a volley was fired at the Duke of
Wellington from behind a garden hedge.   As I was the first
sergeant he observed on turning round, he ordered me to take
a section and drive them out.   I accordingly got a section and
we went into the garden when, after a short contest, we
succeeded in driving them out, after having killed a good
many of them.   By the time I got out of the garden and came
to the road the regiment was closely engaged with the bayonet.
The lieutenant-colonel at this time was coming up as fast as
he could ride having been shot through the groin.   We
immediately joined the regiment at the foot of the garden
and advanced at full speed, the French having by this time
given way.   In the impetuosity of our charge we had advanced
too near the enemy's guns and were obliged to move off to
the right to the skirts of the wood.   We then advanced
rapidly on the right and turned the left flank of the French.

We now made a determined attack to seize two of the
enemy's guns, which gave us considerable annoyance, but
were foiled in the attempt.   At this time the Guards came up
and the action began to be general.   We, however, still
sustained considerable loss from the enemy's cannon, as we
had none with which to oppose them ; and as so few of our
troops had come up, we could not form a sufficiently strong
column in one place to enable us to take any of their artillery
from them.   Our regiment was now very much cut up both
in officers and men, as we had been first in the action and,
with the other Highland regiments had for a long time to
resist the attack of the whole French army.   We continued
very warmly engaged until about eight o'clock in the evening,
when we rallied, and made another effort to capture the
enemy's guns.   In this attempt I received a wound in the
head, while in the act of cheering the men forward.   I was

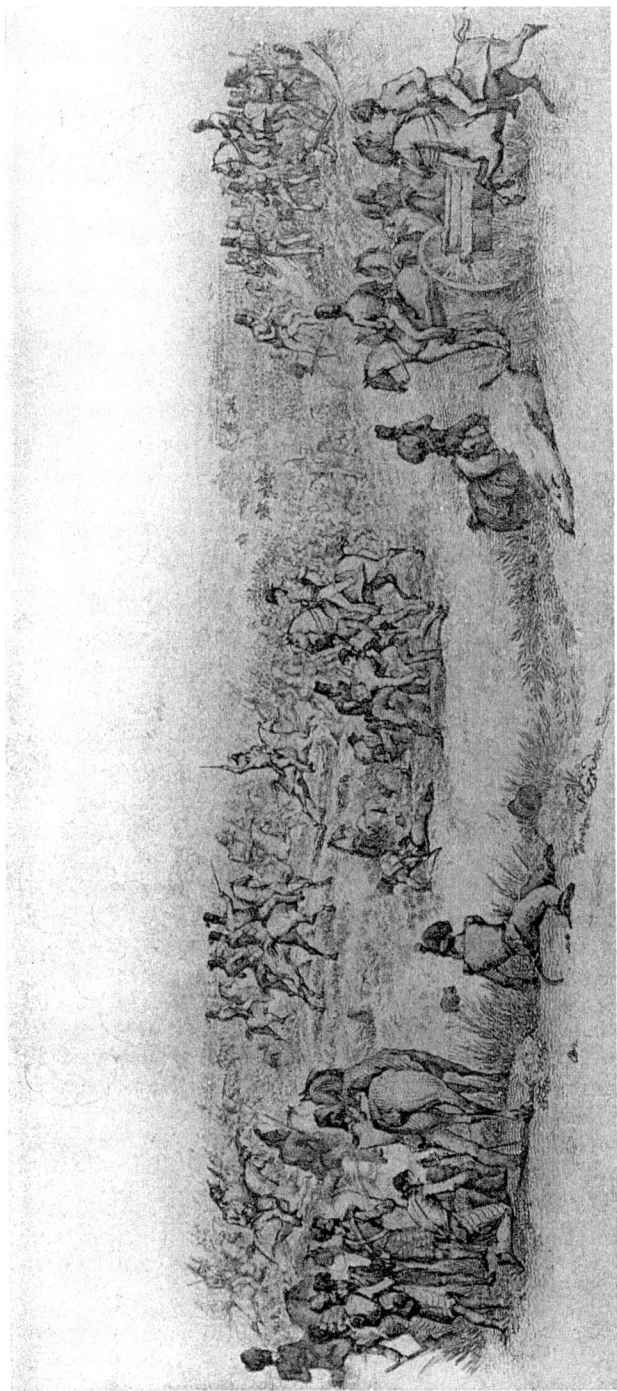

CHARGE OF THE UNION BRIGADE, 2 P.M., WATERLOO

Facing page 156

very sick for a short time, and was sent to the rear under the care of the surgeon, where I got my wound dressed, and remained till morning; when I awoke I found I was able to join the regiment again. On account of this wound I was reported dead and my old companions were rather surprised at my return. On calling over the roll the night previous, it was found that we had lost 1 colonel, 1 major, 4 captains, 12 lieutenants, 4 ensigns, 12 sergeants, and about 250 rank and file.

The regiment was now formed in the rear of the house of Quatre Bras. Before we had time to cook our victuals the Duke of Wellington and his staff came into the midst of us and gave orders for the march of the different divisions. The cavalry by this time were coming up in great strength; and on the arrival of General Hill at their head we all stood up and gave him three hearty cheers, as we had long been under his command in the Peninsula, and loved him dearly on account of his kind and fatherly conduct towards us. When he came among us he spoke in a very kindly manner and inquired concerning our welfare. He also expressed his sorrow that the colonel was wounded; and gave us a high character to the Duke of Wellington who replied that he knew what we could do and that by-and-bye he would give us something to keep our hands in use. We now removed as many of the wounded out of the field as we could and buried all the dead bodies within our reach, especially the officers.

After remaining here till about ten o'clock we fell back to the skirts of a wood near the village of Waterloo, the cavalry forming our rear guard. The French now pushed very hard upon us, but we still managed to keep the road. On coming to the village of Genappe, we found the houses were full of our wounded who had made that length and were not able to go any further. When the French came up they were all taken prisoners. We now heard that Colonel Cameron had died on the road about an hour before we came to Genappe. We still kept moving very slowly, until the French artillery got close to our rear, and were annoying us very much, when the Duke ordered a regiment of Hanoverian infantry to wait and assist our cavalry, who were formed on each side of the road, to protect our flanks which they effectually did.

We arrived at length at the house of Le Hay Saint, a very large building having a great entrance gate on the left hand, where the Brussels road is cut through a small green hill with high banks on each side. On coming to the rear of the house we diverged to the right and left. The right of Sir Thomas Picton's division to which we belonged, rested on the great road; and the left extended on in rear of a double hedge— that is two hedges with a bye-road running between them. It had been raining very hard ever since we commenced our march in the morning and we were drenched to the skin. The ground on which we were formed had been lately ploughed and the corn newly brairded,* so that with the number of men that were treading upon it, the field was reduced to the consistency of mortar. However, we formed line, and the French halted opposite to us much in the same state. The weather soon began to fair up, but still everything round and below was very wet. We now thought of getting our muskets in order for action, for by every appearance we were likely to need them soon. I took the opportunity of going into the hedge to look at the French forming; but such numerous columns I had never looked on before, nor do I believe any man in the British army had ever seen such a host. I must confess that, for my own part, when I saw them taking up their ground in such a regular manner, and everything appearing so correct about all their movements, I could not help wishing that we had had more troops with which to oppose the thousands that were collecting in our front.

Our artillery and a rocket-brigade had now arrived, all the cavalry had come up, and a great number of foreign infantry had already joined us. The evening at length cleared but without any sunshine. We had a fine view of the country round the village of Mount St Jean which stood within half a mile of our rear, and the skirts of the great forest of Soignes lay not much farther off. We could get no fuel here to make fires as everything was soaked with the rain. There was a field of green clover in our rear of which we cut large quantities, and with some branches out of the hedges made a kind of bed on the ground to keep us from the clay. Every regiment sent to its own front a small picquet for the purpose of giving information to the commanding officer in case of alarm. In this condition we stretched ourselves on our uncomfortable lair.

We lay till about twelve o'clock when the alarm was given that the French were coming. We instantly stood to our arms and continued in that posture until the cause of the

* Sprouting above ground.

alarm was found to be groundless ; it arose from a part of the Belgian cavalry going their rounds, having when challenged by our sentries replied in the French language. During all this time it continued to rain very hard. As we had lain down by fours, we had blankets enough to cover us and keep us dry ; but when we got up again we were made as wet as before. The place on which we lay was like a marsh and for the season of the year the rain was very cold. Notwithstanding all these disagreeable circumstances, we lay down again and slept sound, as we were very much fatigued.

THE 'SCOTLAND FOR EVER' CHARGE

We were aroused by daybreak on the morning of the 18th and ordered to stand to our arms, till the line should be reconstructed. During the time I never felt colder in my life ; every one of us was shaking like an aspen leaf. An allowance of gin was then served out to each of us which had the effect of infusing warmth into our almost inanimate frames, as before we got it, we seemed as if under a fit of ague. We remained on the ground till about six o'clock, when we were ordered to clean ourselves, dry our muskets, try to get forward, and commence cooking. We had scarcely got breakfast discussed when a shot from the French killed one of our pioneers who was sleeping. We were now ordered to stand to our arms, prim and load, fix bayonets, wheel into line, and be ready to act in any manner required. By this time the action had begun on the right, and the Duke and his staff had taken up their position on the green height in the rear of Le Hay Saint, where he could see the whole of the line from right to left. Beyond the hedge in our front was a fallow field, having a gentle ascent towards it ; and being placed rather in rear of the slope, the French cannoniers could not hit us with their shot, but they made some shells to bear upon us, which made great havoc in our ranks. As yet we had not fired a shot but what had been discharged by our outposts.

The French were now busy in forming columns to their own right, which was directly in our front, and we were expecting every moment to be attacked, as all on the right of our division were warmly engaged. We were well cautioned to be steady and keep together, as, in all likelihood, we would be first attacked by cavalry, who would try to break our line ; and, above all, to mind what word of command was given—whether to form square or whatever else the order might be. At this time, our men were falling fast from the grape shot and shells that the French were pouring in among us, while as yet we had not discharged a musket. The artillery attached to us had now commenced a brisk fire, which drew a great deal of the French fire upon our ranks, as we were immediately in rear of the artillery. At length a large column of French infantry was seen advancing in our direction. Everyone was now eager to be led on, and as the way they were taking indicated that it was upon that part of the line where the 92nd was stationed that the attack would be made, General Pack ordered us to advance and line the hedge to oppose the advance of the column. But when we got to the side of the hedge we found the French were there as soon as we. We cheered loudly, and called to the Scotch Greys, who were formed up in our rear, 'Scotland for ever!' Upon which, some person in the regiment called out 'charge' when, all at once, the whole regiment broke through the hedge, and rushed headlong on the French column. The onset was so sudden and unexpected, that it threw them into confusion. At this critical moment, the Greys flew like a whirlwind to our assistance, and having got round on the flanks of the column, they placed themselves between the enemy and our own line. While we pushed them hard in front the other cavalry regiments in the brigade, the Royals, Blues, and Enniskillen Dragoons, came at full speed to our aid, when it was fearful to see the carnage that took place. The dragoons were lopping off heads at every stroke, while the French were calling for quarter. We were also among them busy with the bayonet and what the cavalry did not execute we completed ; but, owing to the position taken up by the dragoons, very few of the French escaped. It was here that some of the 92nd and the Greys had a struggle for the eagle which a sergeant of the Greys bore off.

In this charge all the sergeants and one of the officers at the colours were killed. So terrible was the havoc which the Greys had made, and such the fearful impression that they produced on the minds of the French, that nothing was heard from those among them who were literally trodden down but appeals to deliver them from those dragoons. A poor fellow cried out to me to save him, and he would give me his watch and all his money ; but being called to the colours

GREYS AND GORDONS JOIN IN THE 'SCOTLAND FOR EVER' CHARGE AT WATERLOO

I was obliged to leave him. One of our regiment, however, fortunately came to the place where he was, and as he spoke in good English, our fellow thought he was a Briton and conducted him to the rear. We now returned to our old ground as we could not retain possession of what we had acquired.

When we had resumed our old station we found that we had lost a great many in the late affair, and among those that had fallen, was my particular and well-beloved comrade, Sergeant-Major Taylor. As I knew he had a valuable watch upon him, I went out between the fires of the two lines and took it and some other things off him, for the behoof of his widow. We had not time as yet to ascertain the amount of our loss, but I found that our captain had been wounded, and was amissing and that I was left in command of two companies, as we lost all the subaltern officers on the 16th. On the right of our division the French cavalry were making a dreadful push, and we often thought that they would force their way through our lines, but the firm and determined resistance of our troops at last convinced them that their efforts were unavailing.

After the charge already mentioned we were not troubled for a long time nor did we fire any for two hours. During all this time however, we suffered much from the enemy's artillery. We were ordered to sit down and rest ourselves. During this intermission, we had a fine view of what was passing on the right. I could see the French cavalry make those terrible charges which frequently drove ours to the rear, but when our men came to the forest, they faced about and beat them back in turn. And often, when the French cavalry were compelled to pull about, our infantry gave them a dreadful volley on the way when passing. It was, I suppose, at this stage of the action that the French account of the battle stated that they took possession of Mount St Jean ; but, in truth, they did not keep it for one minute, as from where we were seated I had a perfect sight of what was going forward. At this time, the 27th and 40th regiments had arrived from Brussels and were forming column in front of the large farmhouse, on the outside of the village. Although the French cavalry had obtained possession of the village, it would have been impossible for them to have retained it while our cavalry had the support of these regiments.

L

About four o'clock the enemy made another attack on our part of the line, by a large body of lancers, who rode up to our squares with as much coolness as if subjecting us to a regimental inspection. We kept up a smart fire upon them, however, and put them to the right about. But before we had succeeded in turning them they did us considerable damage by throwing their lances into our columns, which, being much longer than the firelock and bayonet, gave them a great advantage over us.

At this time we could distinctly see large columns of infantry forming in our front, with numerous bodies of artillery, and we expected we were to be called upon to sustain a charge from all kinds of arms. We were again ordered to line our old hedge to be in readiness to receive them. When we saw the dense masses collecting in our front ready to rush upon us we looked for nothing but that our line would be broken, and utter discomfiture would be the consequence. The bodies of our artillerymen lay beside the guns which they had so bravely managed and many a cannon had not a gunner left to discharge it. At this time there was scarcely an officer left in our regiment, in consequence of which the command of the company devolved upon me. I now began to reflect on what should be done in case of a retreat becoming inevitable, over a long plain, in front of cavalry. I was aware it would be difficult for me to keep the men together, as they had never retreated before under similar circumstances. In fact, any word of command misunderstood in the smallest degree would be sure to produce disorder. And in the face of peril so imminent, there must always be some persons more afraid than others, whose timidity might infect the rest ; whereas, when advancing to meet the enemy every one becomes emboldened and confusion is not so likely to occur.

While we were in this state, with life and death in the balance, the French column began to move forward. An awful pause ensued. Every man, however, was steady. At length they came within pistol-shot of our lines, when a volley of rockets was let off by the brigade that had been formed in the hedge, which threw them into entire confusion. To complete their disorder we, at the same instant, gave a loud huzza and poured a well-directed volley upon them. This unexpected and rather rough reception made them turn round and run, leaving behind them a number of killed and wounded.

When this brush was over, we sent out a few skirmishers in our front along the hedge, merely to keep up the fire, and give information of what was passing among the French, who were still keeping up a distant cannonade. We now opened our files along the hedge, as the wider they were kept, there was less danger to be apprehended from the round shot, and in this way we remained for a long time. Notwithstanding this precaution they were occasionally taking off some of us.

It was now seven o'clock and by this time there was no officer in the regiment but the commanding officer (whose horse had been shot), the adjutant, and very few sergeants. I had charge of two companies, and was ordered to pay particular attention to any signal or movement I might see in front, for which purpose I was furnished with a spy-glass. In a short time one of our skirmishers came running in, and called to me to look at the French lines, as something extraordinary was going on. On the enemy's right I saw that a cross fire had been commenced, and that troops in the same dress had turned the extremity of their line and were advancing rapidly. I immediately informed the adjutant, who said that perhaps it was a mutiny in the French army, and that we had better form our companies close so as to be ready to march to any point. At this instant an aide-de-camp came galloping down our rear, and calling out, 'The day is our own—the Prussians have arrived.' All eyes were now turned to the right to look for the signal to charge which was to be given by the Duke of Wellington. Nothing could stop our men, and it was only by force that the non-commissioned officers could keep them from dashing into the French lines. No language can express how the British army felt at this time ; their joy was truly ecstatic.

By this time the aide-de-camp had returned to the Duke who was standing in the stirrups with his hat elevated above his head. Every eye was fixed upon him, and all were waiting with impatience to make a finish of such a hard day's work. At last he gave three waves with his hat and the loud three cheers that followed the signal were the heartiest that had been given that day. On seeing this, we leapt over the hedge that had been such a protection to us during the engagement and in a few minutes we were among the French lines. Nothing was used now but the bayonet, for, after the volley we gave them, we set off at full speed, and did not take time to load. All was now destruction and confusion.

The French at length ran off throwing away knapsacks, firelocks, and every thing that was cumbersome, or that could impede their flight.   One division at the farm house of La Belle Alliance made an attempt to stand, and came to the charge.   When the three Highland regiments saw the resistance offered by this column, we rushed upon it like a legion of demons.   Such was our excited and infuriated state of mind at the time, and being flushed with thought of victory we speedily put an end to their resistance.   The Prussians were now among us—the one nation cheering on the other, while the bands were playing their national anthems.

It was now dark, and we were ordered to halt for the night, while the Prussians marched past us.   The place where we bivouacked was immediately at the end of the house where Bonaparte had stood all day, which was by this time filled with the wounded.   As we had not got any water during the day numbers of us went in search of it.   After looking about for some time, we at length discovered a draw-well and accordingly supplied ourselves.   The next morning I looked into the well and discovered that it was full of dead bodies ; but as we were not aware of this circumstance when we drank the water we never felt any bad effects from using it.

In fact, we were not in a condition to quarrel about the quality of the liquid we got as a cup of water of almost any kind was considered a boon by our unfortunate wounded comrades, who were suffering that insatiable and dreadful thirst which is experienced by men in their situation.   The night was now far advanced and as we could not see what was going on at a distance we lay down to repose ourselves, cherishing the fond hope that as we had now vanquished the enemy, we would be permitted to sleep in peace.

When morning came, I arose and went out to view the field on which so many brave soldiers had perished.   The scene which then met my eyes was horrible in the extreme. The number of the dead was far greater than I had ever seen on any former battle field.   The bodies were not scattered over the ground but were lying in heaps—men and horses mixed promiscuously together.   It might truly have been called the 'crowning carnage,' for death had indeed been here and had left visible evidences of his grim presence in the misery and devastation that surrounded us.   I turned away with disgust from this heart-melting spectacle, and had scarcely arrived at my quarters when every person that could be spared was sent out to carry the wounded to the roadside, or any other convenient place where the waggons could be brought to convey them to the hospital.

We had not proceeded far in this humane duty when we were ordered to make ready and at seven o'clock marched to the right to get on to the great road that leads to Paris. At any other time we would have hailed the order with joy but a very different feeling now pervaded our minds. When we thought that we were called to leave the place where so many of our brave companions were lying, without either seeing the dead interred or the wounded taken proper care of, our hearts were filled with grief and vexation. Numbers who had fought by our side on the preceding day were now stretched lifeless on the open field; and we were not permitted to ive them the common rites and see them decently interred in the field where they had spent their heart's blood. I confess my feelings overcame me; I wept bitterly and wished I had not been a witness of such a scene.

The following is a list of the killed and wounded belonging to the 92nd, on the 16th and 18th days of June 1815, at Quatre Bras and Waterloo :—

June 16th, at Quatre Bras—1 colonel, 2 captains, 14 lieutenants, 2 ensigns, 3 sergeants, and 61 rank and file.

June 18th, at Waterloo—1 major, 4 captains, 4 ensigns, 1 surgeon, 10 sergeants, and 298 rank and file. Total of killed and wounded on both days, 402.

Having at last got on the great road to Paris, we had not marched many miles from the field when we took some prisoners from whom we learned that Napoleon had set off for Paris. There was not an inhabitant to be seen, all having fled to the woods. We halted near a small village for the night, when the Duke of Wellington in person came up and thanked us for the manner in which we had conducted ourselves during the engagement, and lavished the highest eulogiums upon us for our exertions to uphold the reputation of the British army. But he had one fault to find with the 92nd, and that was for being so forward in crossing the hedge in the early part of the action. He said, as it turned out all was well; but had it happened otherwise it might have ruined all his plans, and caused the destruction of the whole left wing of the army; and he urged upon us to pay attention to the words of command that might be issued next day. He then galloped off to pay his respects to the other regiments who had been similarly engaged.

After remaining in Paris for some time, Sergeant Robertson adds, 'medals were awarded to us but some disagreeable feeling was likely to arise, when we heard that there was to be a difference in the material of which they were to be made. We were told that officers were to receive gold medals, while those for the privates were to be composed of brass, which partiality nearly caused a mutiny. At length, when the Duke of Wellington learned the dissatisfaction that prevailed, he ordered that they should be all alike, that as we had all shared equally of the dangers of the day we should all partake alike of its glories.'

Sergeant Robertson remained with his regiment after his return to Scotland until 1818 when he says that owing to a disappointment in his promotion he applied for his discharge, which, after some delay, was at last granted.

VIII

LIFE GUARDSMAN SHAW

A HERO OF WATERLOO
BY THE LATE E. BRUCE LOW

A HERO OF WATERLOO

From documents in the possession of a near relative, it appears that the father of the famous Life Guardsman was William Shaw who came from Wolsey near Colchurch, Rugeley, Staffordshire. His mother was a daughter of John Dewse of Hutton, Wandesley, Yorkshire. William Shaw became a large farmer at Wollaton, Nottinghamshire where he died in 1825. Our informant has in his possession a cigarcase which was found in John Shaw's haversack when his body was taken up from the field of Waterloo.

Life Guardsman Shaw was looked upon by the citizens of London and of his native county of Nottingham as the embodiment of courage, coolness, and bull-dog tenacity. 'Old Shaw the Life Guardsman!' says Dickens in *Bleak House*, 'Why he's a model of the whole British army in himself. Ladies and gentlemen, I'd give a fifty-pound note to be such a figure of a man.' Shaw had come to London from Cossall, his native village, a short time before entering the army; and in an age when pugilism was patronised by all classes, his feats in the prize-ring brought him to the notice of princes and peers, and rendered him the hero of the whole sporting fraternity. In 1807 when he had reached the age of eighteen years he was cordially received into the ranks of the Second Life Guards, where pugilism was then much cultivated. He is described as remarkably large-limbed for his age, and of great muscular strength; he possessed a fair education and held a good character, and it was not long before he was promoted to the rank of corporal, which in the Guards, as is well known, corresponds to that of sergeant in line regiments.

Numerous incidents in his career at this period are still remembered in the ranks. At the beginning of the nineteenth century it was usual for the lower orders to cast vulgar abuse upon private soldiers, and on one occasion Shaw was followed and insulted by a number of strongly built roughs. Determined to put an end to the continuance of this practice towards himself and his fellows, Shaw resolved to tackle the crowd, and soon sent three of their number sprawling into the gutter ; but on recovering themselves they again set upon the Life Guardsman. In a few minutes he had dealt out such a lesson to them that the whole crowd was put to flight. He had not again to face such an encounter.

After this Colonel Barton took him in hand and introduced him to the Fives Court, which was regarded as the Carlton Club of pugilism in London. At his appearance in this new arena he was described as follows : 'His height, weight, length, and breadth were of so valuable a nature that, united with a heart that knew no fear, they rendered him a truly formidable antagonist.' The Cockney public, as well as the army officers, took him up, and he soon justified their faith by fighting some of the celebrated pugilists of the day, including Molyneaux and Colonel Barclay of Ury.

It was at this time that he was selected by the well-known artist Haydon to sit as his model for some of his famous paintings. In height he was over six feet, with a fair complexion, grey eyes, light hair, and a round visage, and was so magnificently developed as to be universally admired.

His last prize-ring encounter took place on Hounslow Heath on 8th April 1815, when enormous crowds turned out at early morning to visit the scene of the fight. Shaw had boldly challenged all England for the championship. Three other competitors entered the ring in succession. These were Harmer, Skelton, and Painter. The first two fought twenty-eight rounds before Harmer was declared victor ; and finally Shaw found his antagonist in Painter. Of the latter it is related that he had distinguished himself in numerous encounters previously, and had beaten men apparently twice his strength, and, like Shaw, had tackled and overthrown a crowd of bullies who had insulted him at Manchester.

In this encounter with Painter, however, Shaw soon gained the upper hand ; and it is reported that although Painter delivered some terrific blows, Shaw seemed to be able to do what he liked with him, and ultimately, after half-an-hour's fight, completely overcame his opponent. This victory left Shaw virtually champion of England. Less than a month before this, Napoleon Bonaparte had returned to France from

Elba, and Wellington had hurried from the Peace Conference at Vienna, with full powers as Commander-in-Chief of the Allied Army to oppose any movement which 'the little Caporal' might make towards the Rhine or the Belgian capital.

Shaw had henceforth to face the sterner work of the battlefield; for, although his admirers offered to buy him out of the army when the order for foreign service was received, he refused.

If Shaw was the hero of London sportsmen before the war, he became the idol of the whole nation after Waterloo.

After a short period spent in cantonments with the 1st Cavalry Brigade, under Lord Edward Somerset, Shaw's regiment received orders to march to Quatre Bras on the morning of the 16th of June, the day when Napoleon was defeating the Prussian army at Ligny, while Ney was endeavouring to gain a similar victory over the hastily formed advance guard of the British army. Wellington had prophesied, after an inspection of the dispositions of the Prussian army, that it 'would receive a most d—d licking,' and this was amply fulfilled, with the result that the victorious British wing of the allied army was compelled to carry out a parallel retreat, so as to protect the Prussian flank and at the same time cover Brussels.

On the 17th Shaw's brigade saw some fighting with the French cavalry in the neighbourhood of Genappe, when the Guards overthrew the lighter French lancers. Thereafter the retreat was completed without molestation, and the brigade took up a position on the high ground through which the main road to Brussels ran. A corresponding parallel high ridge was soon occupied by the French army. The country has been too often described to necessitate other details being given here; but the reader may be reminded that on the extreme right of the British position lay the château of Hougoumont, in the centre the farmhouse of La Haye Sainte, and on the extreme left the village of Papellotte. The Horse Guards were drawn up on the slope in the rear of La Haye Sainte, and here some of the fiercest fighting of the day took place.

As is well known, the soldiers spent the night of the 17th and the morning of the 18th in the greatest discomfort, after their long march from Quatre Bras in the sweltering heat of midsummer. A downpour of rain continued throughout the night in tropical torrents, while the lightning played around them.   The men were without protection, and lay upon the muddy ground, rising next morning thoroughly stiff and chilled.   Shaw's regiment was composed of tall, muscular men, about six feet in height, and the powerful black horses which they rode exceeded sixteen hands high.   Every man wore a brass helmet with a blue-and-red crest and a scarlet-and-white plume on the left of it.   Unlike the French cavalry, they had discarded the cuirass.   Their dress was a double-breasted red coat, with blue trousers, and they wore a sash of scarlet round the waist.   Their arms were carbines, pistols, and long swords.   The 2nd Life Guards were commanded by the Honourable Lieutenant-Colonel E. P. Lygon, son of Earl Beauchamp.

At eleven o'clock, when the first cannon-shot was fired, Corporal Shaw was engaged with some of his comrades at a distant part of the field foraging for supplies ; but he sharply called together his men, and had joined his regiment before the first cavalry charge was made.

The advance of Prince Jerome's corps on Hougoumont took place about one o'clock ; and, while the attention of the British army was directed to that quarter, Bonaparte delivered his first grand attack upon the centre and left of the allied position.   The French force employed was of overwhelming strength, and succeeded in producing a panic among the Dutch-Belgian troops who were stationed slightly in advance of the cross-road which marked the crown of the ridge behind which the allied army lay.   The attacking infantry force was composed of four divisions from D'Erlon's infantry, Roussell's cavalry division, a division of light cavalry, chasseurs, and lancers, and seventy-four guns.   The advance of the French infantry compelled the British battalions to deploy into line ; and so soon as this was effected, Roussell's cavalry charged among the allied regiments and cut into a number of them, with the result that the moment appeared so critical that Lord Uxbridge, in command of the British cavalry, was compelled to take immediate action.   He ordered the Union Brigade on the left to support Picton's troops, who were being threatened by three French divisions, and he himself determined to lead Lord Edward Somerset's brigade of Guards simultaneously upon the fourth of the infantry divisions, which had reached the British line on the west of La Haye Sainte, and, if possible, to overthrow at the same time the cuirassiers and carbineers composing Roussell's cavalry division.

In the British advance the First Life Guards rode on the right, the Second Life Guards on the left, and the Dragoon Guards in the Centre. Corporal Shaw was in the centre of the left squadron of the Second Guards. Opposed to them was a line of cuirassiers. Both forces were riding at full speed, and neither attempted to draw rein or to avoid the combat. It was remarked that in consequence of the British swords being shorter than those of the cuirassiers, the Guardsmen were forced to wedge themselves in between the files of the enemy before they could strike effectively. This they were able to do exactly as in the Heavy Brigade charges at Balaclava, by superiority of weight and strength. Lord Edward Somerset compared the ringing of the British sword upon the French armour to 'the hammering of so many tinkers at work,' and the noise of the charge was soon mingled with the groans and shouts of the combatants. It was not long, however, before the masses of Frenchmen in the scrimmage were borne down and forced across the ridge by the red-coated Guardsmen. All along the flanks and rear the cuirassiers began to gallop wildly from the field, while the main body was pressed down the ascent to the plain beyond La Haye Sainte. The Second Life Guards rode obliquely through the cuirassiers, who had been checked by the unexpected obstacle of a hidden hollow way (the *chimen creux* of Victor Hugo) cut in the ridge where the cross or *verd cocou* road left the main Brussels road. The Frenchmen sought to regain the high ground, but were pursued by the Life Guards, who came upon them at full speed and compelled a number of the French cavalry to return and seek concealment in the hollow way, in the hope of escaping to the main road. The Second Life Guards, however, pursued them so hotly as to be themselves thrown into confusion by the broken nature of the ground.

It was when the combatants reached La Haye Sainte that Corporal Shaw distinguished himself in a desperate hand-to-hand contest on the level ground adjoining the farmhouse.

Siborne, the official historian of the Waterloo campaign, tells us that Shaw alone slew nine of the cuirassiers in this charge, and there are preserved a number of detailed accounts of his prowess, given by eye-witnesses. On one occasion, mentioned by Sir Evelyn Wood, he was seen to ride straight at a cuirassier who had taken up a position at the junction of the two roads. The Frenchman with his long sword thrust strongly at Shaw below the belt, but his thrust was swiftly parried, and the Life Guardsman's sabre crashed through the Frenchman's helmet, splitting his skull to the chin. In the words of the eye-witness, his face 'fell off like a bit of apple.' At one point two of Shaw's comrades, Dakin and Hodgin, saw him attack the standard-bearer of the cuirassiers, and after a short encounter slay him. When, however, he was about to seize the eagle, he was surrounded by an over-whelming number of the enemy, and lost sight of the trophy in the mêlée.

Captain Gronow, in his well-known *Reminiscences*, tells how, at a later stage of this first charge, Shaw again dis-tinguished himself by saving the life of an officer of the First Life Guards.

Having overthrown Roussell's cavalry division, the Guardsmen of the different regiments followed in pursuit, and the British corps had become intermingled. Many of them, in their ardour, had reached the summit of the position occupied by the French, when Napoleon ordered several regiments of cuirassiers and Polish lancers to intercept their retreat by taking possession of the low ground lying between the two opposing armies. Captain Kelly of the First Guards had, with a few men of his regiment, reached the Grand Battery collected by Napoleon in support of his attack, when he noticed the swift approach of the fresh cavalry, and, rallying his men, determined to cut his way back to the British lines. At this moment Corporal Shaw hastened to the assistance of Captain Kelly, and the two riders, riding side by side, headed the returning troopers, and, in the words of a spectator, 'cut down their antagonists as if the latter had been poppies.'

In the retreat Shaw was now opposed by a giant cuirassier in armour. In order to successfully defend himself, he selected the vulnerable part of his opponent, and, parrying his lunges, slew him with a thrust in the neck.

When the remains of the regiment reassembled on the ridges, the heavy losses they had sustained became apparent. Shaw found that the two files which in the morning had stood on each side of him had been slain. He was himself wounded, but refused to leave the ranks.

For two hours afterwards the Guards remained in position inactive under a heavy cannonade. In his official dispatch, Marshal Blücher declares that the decisive moment in the battle occurred at half-past four ; and Baron Von Muffling, the Prussian Commissioner on Lord Wellington's staff, states emphatically in his *History* of the campaign that up to that moment the battle had been 'bloody enough, but in no wise dangerous for the British army.' He adds, 'There was absolutely nothing to fear,' and then goes on to state that 'the position was really more favourable than would appear to Wellington, and that 'from that moment the battle was considered as gained' (p. 28). The Prussian troops which had been promised to Wellington for the morning of the 18th now showed themselves, so that by half-past four (Blücher's 'decisive moment') two brigades of Bülow's corps had appeared before Planchenoit ; but, although Sir Evelyn Wood points out that it was after five o'clock before the Prussian cavalry approached the British left wing, Wellington never considered it necessary to call up his reserve of eighteen thousand men stationed between Tubige and Hal, eight miles off.

Wellington's understanding with Blücher had been for the assistance of only one corps and from a greater distance. It cannot be admitted that the arrival of this force saved the British army from destruction (as recently claimed by the German Emperor in direct contradiction of the Prussian officers who were engaged in the struggle), and the later events of the day confirm this, for the British had repulsed and driven off the Old Guard and the whole French divisions of the left wing by eight o'clock, while the Prussians were still engaged on their first point of attack at Planchenoit.

It is true that the German Legion, who occupied La Haye Sainte (and to whose bravery the British writers have done honour) lost the position assigned to them, which had to be retaken by a British line regiment. Unfortunately, also, the King's German Legion, being ordered to deploy by the Prince of Orange, had its flag captured by the French Chasseurs of the Guard, and it was not recovered ; but that no reflection can rest upon the British troops in this connection is proved by Houssaye, the latest French writer. There is something grim and sardonic in the fact that the Kaiser should tell the soldiers at Hanover that their countrymen saved the British army from destruction, when we remember that it was the cavalry of Hanover (the Duke of Cumberland's Hussars) which turned tail and fled in disorder to Brussels when ordered by Wellington to move forward to support the British line.

NEY'S TERRIBLE ATTACKS

After four o'clock Napoleon, noticing the advance of the Prussian troops, charged Ney with the duty of making a second attack upon the allied position, while he himself directed operations upon his right for the defence of Planchenoit against the new assailants. The French cavalry, led by Ney, approached the British position in three great lines, forty-three squadrons in all (four thousand five hundred horsemen), and soon reached the crest of the ridge where the British batteries lay. There, however, they were met by a tremendous fire, which caused tremendous losses ; but the cuirassiers rode gallantly forward to the charge, shouting, '*Vive l'Empereur !*' and '*Victoire !*' They were received at thirty paces with a withering fire from the squares, and were broken up into a disorganised mass, which swept round the squares without charging home. Lord Edward Somerset used this opportune moment for making another advance with the Guards brigade, who, after a very slight resistance from the French cavalry, drove them in confusion into the hollow between the armies, whence after a time they renewed the attack, only, however, to be foiled again. In this way the French cavalry became thoroughly exhausted. Supports were sent for, which were seen moving forward with great apparent determination. Again the diminished squadrons of British cavalry fell upon the advancing troops and sent them headlong to the rear.

Undismayed by these successive defeats, Ney sent for further reinforcements, and obtained thirty-seven squadrons of fresh horsemen, drawn from Kellerman's corps and the heavy cavalry of the Imperial Guards, and then advanced at the head of eighty squadrons to a final attack upon the British right. The reader must be referred to the brilliant pages of Siborne's *History* and Sir Evelyn Wood's *Cavalry in the Waterloo Campaign* for details of these successive attacks. Victor Hugo says : 'There were a dozen assaults. Ney had four horses killed under him. Half the cuirassiers fell on the plateau. The conflict lasted two hours.' It ended in the total rout of the Frenchmen. The British squares stood fast, though decimated. Ney, perspiring, his eyes aflame, foaming at the mouth, with uniform unbuttoned, and one of his epaulets cut off, saw the broken regiments returning in complete disorganisation to the French lines.

DEATH OF SIR WM. PONSONBY AT WATERLOO

Facing page 176

In these encounters Shaw and his comrades had taken a
glorious part, and many are the thrilling accounts left to us
of the deeds of the troopers in his brigade. We must, however, restrict ourselves to the narrative of Shaw's last charge.
He had distinguished himself throughout the day, and now,
when the British cavalry swept forward and rode through the
remains of the French squadrons, Shaw still bore a prominent
part, till in the last mêlée on the level ground to the east of
La Haye Sainte he found himself cut off from his companions
and surrounded by overwhelming numbers of the foe. The
contest was a long one, and it was only when his sword had
been broken in his hand that Shaw's defence was overcome.
Hurling the hilt of his weapon among the enemy, he tore
off his helmet and struck out right and left with it ; but the
swords of the cuirassiers ultimately cut him down, and he was
left for dead on the ground. Victor Hugo tells us that as
Shaw lay on the ground a French drummer-boy gave him
the *coup de grâce*. That night a comrade, wounded like himself, had taken refuge near one of the houses which line the
Charleroi road, and there he found Shaw.

After being rendered unconscious by the many wounds
which he had received, he had crept in pain from the
open ground to the protection of the farm-buildings which we
know as La Belle Alliance. He, we are told, 'was almost
cut to pieces and scarcely able to move.' On recognising
the other as a comrade, Shaw was only able to whisper,
' My dear fellow, I am done for,' and then fell back from
sheer exhaustion. When morning broke his companion
found him lying dead, with his face resting on his hand, and
having the appearance of having passed away while in a state
of insensibility. His death was occasioned rather by the loss
of blood from a variety of wounds than from the magnitude
of any one. So was ended the career of the best swordsman
in the British army, after he had given splendid evidence of
his heroism and skill, the memory of which still lives in the
ranks of his regiment. The visitor to Waterloo will
experience little difficulty in discovering the small stretch of
level ground where Shaw was overwhelmed by the superior
number of the enemy.

The buildings of La Belle Alliance remain, after the lapse
of nearly a century, in a state of wonderful preservation ; the
only evidence of the titanic struggle being the cannon-ball
which rests embedded in the brick wall above the doorway,

M

where it is discernible with difficulty, the proprietor having recently painted over the building, and having thus almost obliterated this interesting relic. It may well be that the cheers which were raised on all sides when Lord Wellington met Marshal Blücher on this spot at the close of the day may have served to attract the wounded Guardsman towards them, and roused him to make the final and supreme effort to reach the shelter of the building where he died. Long ere this Wellington had ridden off to the village of Waterloo to pen his famous despatch, written while his heart throbbed with emotion at the loss of so many of his veteran comrades in arms, and Blücher had started in pursuit of Napoleon and his retreating legions, now fast becoming a disorganised rabble. As darkness fell over the stricken field, the remnants of the two brigades of British heavy cavalry were drawn up within a stone's-throw of our dying trooper, at the spot where the Prussians entered on the pursuit.

Of the seven magnificent regiments, the Guards and the Union Brigade, numbering nineteen hundred swords, only fifty files remained.

It is satisfactory to know that a suitable memorial has within recent times been erected in honour of John Shaw at his native village of Cossall, Nottinghamshire. When Thomas Wheately of the Guards who was also a native of Cossall, died in June 1875, his countrymen remembered that Shaw had fought side by side with him at Waterloo, and that no memorial existed to the hero who had so long retained their admiration, and no time was lost in repairing the oversight.

> And can the brave whose blood had bought
> This mighty triumph be forgot ?
> No ! He who battled there and fell
> Needs not the line of cumbrous swell.
> This epitaph enough shall tell :
> He died at Waterloo.

IX

WITH NAPOLEON AT WATERLOO

DIARY OF NAPOLEON'S EQUERRY FROM
A MS. FORMERLY IN THE COLLECTION
OF SIR THOMAS PHILLIPS

LORD HILL AND THE 13TH REGIMENT.   WATERLOO

Facing page 181

JOURNAL OF NAPOLEON'S EQUERRY AT WATERLOO

THE MORNING OF WATERLOO

THE following is a translation of the Journal of Napoleon's Equerry (Jardin Ainé) referred to in the introduction to this volume. Napoleon's valet Coustans mentions Jardin and tells the story that Napoleon on the day of Waterloo called for his horse and, Jardin being absent for the moment, a groom saddled one but used the wrong bridle so that the horse became restive and threw Bonaparte who fell heavily to the ground. Jardin rushed up in alarm and his master in a towering rage struck him across the face with his riding whip. The Equerry was insulted at this abominable treatment and M. de Coulaincourt, the Chief Equerry, went to the Emperor and expostulated with him. Napoleon then apologised and presented Jardin with a sum of three thousand francs.

Napoleon, says Jardin, left the Elyssee at four o'clock on the morning of 12th June * to join the army, passing by Laon, Avesnes, Beaumont, Charleroi and Fleurus, where the first battle between the French and Prussians was fought. Having reached Laon at six o'clock in the evening he mounted his horse and made a tour of the town and the defences : at eight o'clock he returned to the house of the Prefecture where he lodged ; at four o'clock on the morning of the 13th he again set out for Avesnes, where were his general headquarters. He remained there on the 13th and on the 14th he proceeded on horseback at 10 a.m. to Beaumont where he slept : he rose very early and walked upon the balcony, taking note continually of the weather and conversing with his brother Jerome. † On the 15th

---

* Napoleon's Secretary Fleury says three o'clock (*Memoirs*, p. 148.)
† This fact is noted by Gleig, *Waterloo*, p. 54

he climbed the hill Charleroi, after having driven back the
enemy who only surrendered it towards three o'clock in the
afternoon.   There he made the whole army march past him
in column.   At seven in the evening he proceeded to the
outposts, returning at ten o'clock to sleep at a citizen's house
in the Place de Promenade at Charleroi. *   During the
night various officers of the staff kept coming and going to
give Napoleon accounts of the movements made by the
different army corps.   From their investigations they reported to him that General Bourmont had joined the
enemy.   Napoleon considered it necessary to make fresh
plans, being pretty sure that this General from his treachery
would give the enemy an exact account of the position of
the French army.   Napoleon, therefore, left Charleroi at
ten a.m. on the 16th and visited one or two places where he
found strong columns of the enemy's army.   He continued his observations until a sufficient force had arrived
to enable him to commence the battle.   Towards three in
the afternoon † the firing began with much fury and lasted
until nine o'clock in the evening when the Prussians were
completely defeated.   Napoleon spent the evening on the
battlefield, until eleven o'clock, when he was assured on all
sides that the position had been taken.   He passed through
the ranks in returning to a village (Ligny) towards Fleurus
where he slept.   There several of the brave men who had
accompanied him from the Isle of Elba, said to him, 'Sire,
your majesty has here, far from Elba, the brave men of
Elba.'   He replied 'I rely wholly upon you and the
courage of the brave army.'   On his return in the evening,
an infantry Colonel who had just had his arm carried
away said to the Emperor, 'Sire, I have one arm less, the
other remains at the service of your Majesty.'   The Emperor
stopped and asked him what regiment he commanded, he
replied, 'The first Grenadier regiment of your Guard.'   He
was carried to the village with Napoleon's orders that the
greatest care must be taken of him.

On the 17th June, Napoleon left the village where he
had slept, and visited the battlefield of the evening before as
he always did on the day after a battle.   He went very
quickly up the hill to Genappes where he remained making

* Gleig, p. 59.
† Fleury, p. 163.

observations on the movements of his advance guard ; the
cavalry attached to which several times charged the British
cavalry as it passed out of the town.   At this time a violent storm
threw into confusion the whole French army which, owing to
their many days of rapid marching, lack of provisions, and
want of rest was in a most pitiable state.   At last the courage
of the French overcame the horrible weather.   The troops
struggled on with unparalleled valour ; in the evening
Napoleon visited the outposts in spite of the heavy rain and
did his utmost to encourage the men.   At seven o'clock, he
took out his watch and said that the troops had need of rest,
that they should take up their positions, and that the next
day early, they would be under arms.

At this moment shouts were heard from the British army,
Napoleon asked what these could be.   Marshal Soult (then
Chief of the Staff) replied ' It is certainly Wellington passing
through the ranks that is the cause of the shouting.'   At
seven o'clock, Napoleon said he wished to bivouac ; it was
pointed out to him that he was in a ploughed field and in
mud up to the knees, he replied to the Marshal ' Any kind
of shelter will suit me for the night.'   He retraced his steps
and came near the village of Genappes where confusion was
at its height owing to the passing of the whole of the Imperial
Guard which was hastening to seek shelter from the bad
weather.   Napoleon went into a kind of Inn out of which the
troops, who had installed themselves in it, were turned, and
here he fixed his General Headquarters, because he did not
wish to go to the town of Genappes, which was only a league
distant, saying that during the night he would here receive
more readily reports from the army.   At the same time
everyone had found the best available quarters in which to
pass the night.   Generals Corbineau, La Bedoyere, Flahaut,
Aides-de-camp de-service on Napoleon's staff, spent the night
in riding between the various army corps and returning to him
to give an exact account of the movements which were taking
place.

On the 18th Napoleon having left the bivouac, that is to
say the village Caillou on horseback, at palf-past nine in the
morning came to take up his stand half a league in advance
upon a hill where he could discern the movements of the
British army.   There he dismounted, and with his fieldglass
endeavoured to discover all the movements in the enemy's
line.   The chief of the staff suggested that they should begin

the attack ; he replied that they must wait, but the enemy commenced his attack at eleven o'clock and the cannonading began on all sides ; at two o'clock nothing was yet decided ; the fighting was desperate.   Napoleon rode through the lines and gave orders to make certain that every detail was executed with promptitude ; he returned often to the spot where in the morning he had started, there he dismounted and, seating himself in a chair which was brought to him, he placed his head between his hands and rested his elbows on his knees.   He remained thus absorbed sometimes for half-an-hour, and then rising up suddenly would peer through his glasses on all sides to see what was happening.   At three o'clock an Aide-de-camp from the right wing came to tell him that they were repulsed and that the artillery was insufficient.   Napoleon immediately called General Drouet in order to direct him to hasten to reinforce this army corps which was suffering so heavily, but one saw on Napoleon's face a look of disquietude instead of the joy which it had shown on the great day of Fleurus.   The whole morning he showed extreme depression; however, everything was going on as well as could be expected with the French, in spite of the uncertainty of the battle, when at 6 o'clock in the evening an officer of the mounted Chasseurs à Cheval of the Guard came to Napoleon, raised his hand to his shako and said 'Sire, I have the honour to announce to your majesty that the battle is won.'

'Let us go forward,' Napoleon replied, 'We must do better still.   Courage mes braves : Let us advance !'   Having said this he rode off at a gallop close to the ranks encouraging the soldiers, who did not keep their position long, for a hail of artillery falling on their left ruined all.   In addition to this, the strong line of British cavalry made a great onslaught on the squares of the guard and put all to rout.

It was at this moment that the Duke of Wellington sent to summon the Guard to surrender.   General Kembraune replied that the Guard knew how to fight, to die, but not to surrender.   Our right was crushed by the corps of Bülow who with his artillery had not appeared during the day but who now sought to cut off all retreat.

Napoleon towards eight o'clock in the evening, seeing that his army was almost beaten, commenced to despair of the success which two hours before he believed to be assured. He remained on the battlefield until half-past nine when it

was absolutely necessary to leave.   Assured of a good guide,
we passed to the right of Genappes and through the fields ;
we marched all the night without knowing too well where we
were going until morning.   Towards four o'clock in the
morning we came to Charleroi where Napoleon, owing to the
onrush of the army in beating a retreat, had much difficulty
in proceeding.   At last after he had left the town, he found
in a little meadow on the right a small bivouac fire made by
some soldiers.   He stopped by it to warm himself and said
to General Corbineau 'He bien Monsieur, we have done a
fine thing.'   General Corbineau saluted him and replied 'Sire,
it is the utter ruin of France.'   Napoleon turned round,
shrugged his shoulders and remained absorbed for some
moments.   He was at this time extremely pale and haggard
and much changed.   He took a small glass of wine and a
morsel of bread which one of his equerries had in his pocket,
and some moments later mounted, asking if the horse galloped
well.   He went as far as Philipeville where he arrived at
mid-day and took some wine to revive himself.   He again
set out at two o'clock in a mail carriage * towards Paris
where he arrived on the 21st at 7 a.m. at the Elyssee † whence
he departed on the 12th inst., in the same month.

Certified correct by me,
JARDIN AINE
Equerry to the Emperor Napoleon.

* Fleury says, 'Une chaise de poste à moitié brisée,' p. 198.
† Fleury, p. 210.

X

LAST MOMENTS AT WATERLOO

JOURNAL OF NAPOLEON'S AIDE-DE-CAMP

THE DEFENCE OF HOUGOUMONT

Facing page 188

JOURNAL OF NAPOLEON'S AIDE-DE-CAMP

ADVANCE OF THE OLD GUARD

THE following further details of the last terrible moments at Waterloo are given by another of Napoleon's Aid-de-camp.*

From two o'clock until a quarter before seven, Buonaparte commanded all the operations and movements from a position where he remained without any danger whatever to his own person ; he was a distance of at least a cannon shot and a half from the enemy ; nothing in short, could reach him. When he was at length convinced that the corps d'armée which he had so long and so obstinately taken for that of Marshal Grouchy, was in reality a Prussian corps, he seemed to think that affairs were desperate, and that he had no other resource than to make a great effort with the reserve of his Guard composed of fifteen thousand men. This he accordingly prepared to do and he assumed an appearance of resolution which re-animated a little those who surrounded him. He advanced saying, 'Let every one follow me (Tout le monde en arrière)' which clearly signified that he wished to be in front. In fact he made this movement at first and headed, for about ten minutes, the formidable column which remained to him as his forlorn hope ; but when he arrived within two hundred toises (1200 ft.) from three solid squares of Allied troops which occupied a ridge, with a formidable artillery— 'and which ridge it was necessary to carry'—he suddenly stopped under the broken ground of a sand-pit or ravine and a little on one side out of the direction of the cannon balls.

This fine and terrible column which he had for sometime headed, found him here as it passed and defiled before him in order to advance, taking a demi-tour to the bottom of the hillock and directly in front of the enemy's squares. These

* My recollection is that there is no name on this MS. I understood that Mr Low was fully satisfied of its authenticity. Ed.

Buonaparte himself could not see from the lateral point which he occupied, although it is very true that he was close enough to the enemy's batteries.   As the corps passed him, he smiled, and addressed to them expressions of confidence and encouragement.

The march of these old warriors was very firm and there was something solemn in it.   Their appearance was very fierce.   A kind of savage silence reigned among them : There was in their looks a mixture of surprise and discontent occasioned by their unexpected meeting with Buonaparte who as they thought, was at their head.   In proportion as they ranged up the eminence and darted forward on the squares which occupied its summit the artillery vomited death upon them, and killed them in batches.

This part of the scene came directly under Buonaparte's eye, without his being able to see what passed on the height itself as he still kept himself, as it were, enveloped in the corner of the ravine.   It was then precisely a quarter of an hour from seven o'clock and it was at this very moment that the decisive crisis of the battle commenced.

Buonaparte had then six persons close to him : these were, his brother Jerome, Generals Bertrand, Drouot, Bernard, Colbert, and Labedoyere.   At every step which he took, or seemed to take to put his own person in front Generals Bertrand and Drouot threw themselves before his horse's head, and exclaimed in a pathetic accent :—'Ah ! Sire, what are you going to do ?   Consider that the safety of France and of the army depends entirely upon you ; all is lost if any accident happen to you.'   Buonaparte yielded to their entreaties with a real or apparent effort by which he seemed to gain control over himself.   But one thing appeared very singular, namely that the two men who knew so well how to moderate his ardour and to restrain him, were the only persons whom he never sent out to reconnoitre the state of the battle, though he sent the others twenty times into the midst of the fire, to carry orders, or bring him information. One of them having told him that the Duke of Wellington had been for a long time in front and at the head of one of his squares, he made a sort of grimace which showed that this part of the narrative vexed him much.

Jerome having thought proper to take aside and whisper with one of his brother Aide-de-camps, to whom he spoke his mind very freely, Buonaparte sent him (Jerome) several times into the middle of the fire, as if to get rid of such an importunate critic.

Jerome, in fact, took it greatly to heart that his brother did not profit by this occasion to die in a glorious manner, and I distinctly heard him say to General Bertrand ' Can it be possible that he will not seek death here ? Never will he find a more glorious grave ! '

At nightfall Buonaparte disappeared from us under pretext of going himself to ascertain the state of things and to put himself at the head of the Guards to animate them. Before I conclude, there is a peculiarity which deserves to be noticed namely that, before effecting his personal retreat, in order to get rid of impertinent witnesses he directed those around him to carry different orders all at the same time, and to bring information the result of which could not concern him in the least.

GALLANTRY OF THE BRUNSWICKERS.   WATERLOO

XI

THE NEW LEGEND OF WATERLOO

BY THE LATE EDWARD BRUCE LOW

THE NEW LEGEND OF WATERLOO

The French, though fewer in number, (than the Allied and Prussian armies) would have won the victory but for the obstinate and un-conquerable bravery of the British troops which alone prevented them.—
NAPOLEON, *Correspondence*, xxxi. 240.

It is becoming daily more apparent that a determined effort is being made in certain quarters on the Continent to write on new lines the history of Waterloo. Since the Emperor William delivered his famous address to his recruits at Hanover, and informed them that their ancestors had, with the assistance of Blucher and the Prussian army, 'saved the British under Wellington from destruction' other new versions varying widely from the accepted accounts of eye-witnesses, have appeared. The allegation of the Kaiser that the Hanoverians rescued the British army from destruction is itself a startling departure from ascertained fact.

All British writers have gladly recognised the services rendered by the Prussian troops ; but it cannot be forgotten that the only Hanoverian cavalry regiment present on the field —namely, the Duke of Cumberland's Hanoverian Hussars, commanded by Colonel Hake, when summoned by Wellington's staff to take up a position during the battle in support of the first line, refused to advance, and ultimately turned tail and rode from the field in the wildest panic without drawing rein till Brussels was reached. They carried with them consternation and the unfounded report—readily, however, accepted by the Kaiser and the cult of the New Legend—that the British army which was at that moment engaged in actually driving the French Imperial Guard before them from the field, were about to be routed.

The result of the distinguished services rendered by these gallant allies, to whom we are now to believe the victory was due, is best judged by the reward meted out to them by their contemporaries rather than by the romancists of a later century.   Colonel Hake was promptly cashiered by a court-martial, and his conquering troopers were dispersed among the other cavalry regiments of the allies, so that the very name of this redoubtable corps was erased in ignominy from the army roll.

It may also be recalled that ten thousand men had deserted the Prussian colours after the defeat at Ligny two days before ; in addition many prisoners and guns had been taken from the Prussians in that fight and later in the retreat. There is, indeed, something sardonic in the claim now put forward by the Kaiser that these Hanoverian swashbucklers had secured the hard-fought victory for Wellington.

On the other hand, and in vivid contrast to the treatment meted out to the Hanoverians by the German Emperor, is the revised version of the share in the battle taken by the single regiment of Scottish cavalry engaged at Waterloo. Eye-witnesses of all nations have hitherto agreed that the Scots Greys, when they fell upon and dispersed the dense masses of D'Erlon's corps and captured the Imperial Eagle of the French Invincibles, had earned for themselves and the whole British army immortal renown, and had, even amid the strain of the pitched battle, drawn from Napoleon himself the involuntary encomium, 'These terrible grey horses, how they fight !'

The visionaries who seek to propagate the New Legend now tell us that Bonaparte's eulogium had no reference to the Scottish dragoons, but was in reality intended to apply to a hitherto overlooked, but magnificent regiment of French cavalry mounted on superb grey horses.   The awed astonishment of the Hanoverian soldiers at the Kaiser's apocryphal description of their disgraced ancestors would probably only be surpassed by that of Napoleon himself if he could hear of the existence of this reserve of cavalry which he had been unable to conjure up at the critical moment of the battle ! Fortunately, the belief in the valour of the Scots troopers is founded upon such a sure basis of testimony that it would be beyond the power of even the Kaiser and his *entourage* of *claqueurs* to secure evidence in support of this story of the phantom regiment of the revised version.

Again, if there is one phase of the battle which has become settled in the minds of students of the history of the campaign, it is the fact that both at Quatre Bras and Waterloo the Dutch-Belgian brigades (commanded by Perponcher,

Bylandt, and Tripp) gave way before the onslaught of the French. Now, however, there has been published 'for the use of schools' a work dedicated with due solemnity to the Prince Albert of Belgium, entitled *Waterloo Illustrated*, and having for its principal object 'to remove from history the legend that the Belgians took flight at Waterloo.' The incident of Bylandt's collapse and panic-stricken retreat is recorded in almost every history of the engagement; but we are now told that the Belgian Division of Chassé defeated the Imperial Guard of France! It is not denied that one brigade misbehaved grossly, but we are to believe that the other (Dittmer's) actually repulsed and pursued the Old Guard. Eye-witnesses, however, are agreed that this heroic brigade advanced exactly twenty minutes after the Guard had been dispersed, and fully ten minutes after the British cavalry had swept past the Belgians in the final pursuit.

The Kaiser having sounded the first note, which is intended to produce discord in the universal recognition of Wellington's victory as having been gained by dint of the bravery of the British troops under his command, all the minor participants have now begun to regard themselves as equally, if not more justly, entitled to the laurels won on that day.

The Kaiser, as essential for the purposes of the New Legend no doubt, was compelled to overlook the facts that (1) the Hanoverians and King George's German legion, to whom he referred as combining with the Prussians to rescue the British army, were themselves part of Wellington's army, mercenaries in British pay, serving our and their King George III; and (2) that Prussia herself owed her ability to fight for continued existence as a state to the enormous subsidies, amounting to many millions sterling, provided by the British Government to enable the conquered Prussians to continue their struggle against the French during the long period of the Napoleonic wars. Eleven millions were granted by Britain as subsidies for the allies in 1815 alone, out of ninety millions granted by Parliament that year for this campaign.

Lest the New Legend should assume larger proportions, and appear to be based upon fact, it is well to remember that the battle of the 18th June would not have taken place at or near Waterloo but for the fact that Blücher had in writing (see his despatch of 17th June, 9.30 A.M.) given his under-taking to move at least two of his corps by dawn of day across the short ten miles which separated the Prussian army from their allies.

How came it, then, that the Prussian staff, in giving effect to that promise, caused repeated and needless delays by selecting, as Wellington said, 'the stoutest man in the Prussian army' to carry the despatches to Wellington, and by ordering the most distant of the four corps, worn out by its rapid march after the Prussian defeat at Ligny, to lead the way to the support of Wellington?

Again, it may be asked, why was it necessary that the army corps of Pirch should be called upon to cross the line of march of Ziethen's corps, involving the complete cessation of the Prussian movement in support?

No reason has ever been given for these extraordinary tactics; but it may be fully explained when one remembers the words of Müffling, the Prussian attaché on Wellington's staff: 'It was no secret to Europe that old Blücher, who had passed his seventieth year, knew nothing whatever of the conduct of a war. When it was seen that General Gneisenau really commanded the Prussian army and Blücher merely acted as an example of the bravest in battle, the discontent of the four (Prussian) generals became louder.' All of the Prussian corps commanders but Blücher were jealous of Wellington. Müffling again says 'I know General Gneisenau's distrust of Wellington, and I was apprehensive that this might influence the impending arrangements.' These officers were apparently prepared to allow the British army to be driven back if thereby the victory could be claimed by them.

The ultimate result of all this was that the Prussians did not 'fall upon the right wing of the enemy,' as was promised by Blücher, 'at the first attack of Napoleon' upon the British lines. Their failure to do so had led Wellington to despatch officers in search of the Prussians in the early morning of the 18th.

It was only after the engagement had lasted five hours that the Prussian strength was applied, and then it came not as Wellington expected, as a reinforcement on the left flank of the British army, but at Planchenoit many miles distant and almost in the rear of the French army, where for some hours its usefulness was lost. In the attack on Planchenoit they were absolutely unsuccessful and the place *was not captured till after the general advance of the British line.*

The first Prussians to arrive from Planchenoit found the gallant 52nd piling arms at Rosomme, beyond La Belle Alliance, Napoleon's own headquarters, after our men had pursued the French Guard a distance of two miles.

Houssaye, the latest French historian, in his work, ' 1815-Waterloo,' tells us, after an exhaustive examination of all the evidence, that ' the defeat and retreat of the French army was marked by three very distinct movements, of which the first and third were due to the British troops alone.   The defeat of the French Guard occasioned the yielding of more than two-thirds of the French army.   Later on, the approach of the Prussians provoked the disorder on the extreme French right ; finally the general forward march of Wellington hastened the disaster to the French left ; and, he concludes, it is *false* to say, with the Prussian Müffling, that Wellington only hurled his troops against the French to appear as if he were winning the victory without the help of the Prussians.   Had Wellington at eight o'clock remained in his position, without advancing, the Prussians under Zeithen would very probably have sustained a check.'

Müffling himself admits that General Zeithen's advance-guard suddenly turned round and disappeared in retreat from the heights on the British left just as the French Guards advanced against our right centre.   It was only with difficulty and on Müffling himself assuring Von Zeithen that the British army was holding its ground and that *the Prussians were in safety* to continue their advance, that he could be induced to again face the enemy.   Müffling proceeds : ' By this retrograde movement of General Von Zeithen the battle might have been lost.'

Further he might have added that even when at the close of the day they advanced to co-operate with Wellington's left wing, the Prussians almost created a disaster for, (in his report dated 19th June) Prince Bernard of Saxe Weimar, who commanded the left wing of the Anglo-Belgian army, has placed it on record that the Prussians opened fire with their artillery upon the allies, whom they mistook for the French army, and drove the Nassau troops, with heavy loss, from the outlying villages for a distance of over half a mile.   Captain Seymour (*Waterloo Letters*) tells us of the Prussian batteries taking up position between the first and second British lines and causing heavy loss.

This incident goes far to confirm the account given by

General Mercer (vol. i. p. 328) in his 'Journals,' when he describes the serious injury done to his battery and to the infantry squares around him by the fierce artillery fire opened upon them by the enfilading Prussian battery which suddenly appeared on his left and was only silenced when he retaliated by opening fire with his heavy guns.

Such was the extraordinary mode adopted by the Prussian army of 'rescuing the British from destruction'!

The actual share of the honours due to Von Zeithen's junction with the British left may be judged from the fact that only one brigade of Von Zeithen's force was engaged in the fighting, and not a single officer was killed (Rose 298). Yet it is claimed by the modern German legendaries that Zeithen's advance decided the fate of the day! Napoleon himself declared that 'at the time of the defeat of the French Guard by the British the Prussians were checked, and if the Old Guard had succeeded the day would have been won.' Müffling, a Prussian eye-witness, admitted that 'the battle could have afforded no favourable result to the enemy even if the Prussians had never come up.'

The truth of the whole matter seems, as already indicated, to lie in the fact that it was only after receiving Blücher's undertaking to fall upon the French at the first attack by Napoleon that Wellington agreed to hold the position of Waterloo, instead of retiring upon his reserve of eighteen thousand men. These he had stationed seven miles off, at Hal, to which place two brigades were actually despatched on the morning of the 18th (Gurwood, *Wellingon's Despatches*, vol. xli., p. 477). By thus retiring Wellington's army would have occupied a much stronger position in the immediate neighbourhood of Brussels, where he could have been joined by the re-formed force of Blücher on the following day.

That Wellington maintained the fight for nine hours *after* 'the first attack' was due entirely to the unflinching valour of the troops under his command. It is quite certain that had he retired, as he was entitled to do, on discovering that the Prussians had failed to fulfil their engagement by joining him at the first attack, the whole army of Blücher must have been destroyed, as it would have been caught between two fires while scattered in straggling lines among the narrow defilés of the Dyle and Lasne, and incapable of resistance. Grouchy, with thirty-three thousand men, was pounding away in their rear after defeating the Prussians at Wavre; and Napoleon, relieved of all opposition from the British army, would have been free to strike home with an overwhelming force of seventy thousand men and two hundred and fifty guns. The conclusion which an impartial writer must draw from these facts is that so far from the Hanoverians and Prussians having, in the Kaiser's words, 'rescued the British army from destruction at Waterloo,' it was solely due to the unflinching tenacity of Wellington and his indomitable squares of infantry that the Prussian army was saved. Saved and that from a fate compared with which the *débâcle* of Sedan would have faded into insignificance ; for the moral effect of the surrender of the Prussian army would certainly have decided the fate of Europe, and would have placed Napoleon in a position to dictate his own terms to the allies.

XII

A BRITISH PRISONER IN FRANCE

HIS SUFFERINGS AND HIS ADVENTURES FROM THE DIARY OF SERGEANT NICOL

CHAPTER I

IN THE SIERRAS

THE account of Nicol's later adventures in the distant mountain districts of the Peninsula as a prisoner, though of great interest and value as a picture of that troubled time, is somewhat apart from the great arena in which the fate of Europe was being so desperately fought out, it is therefore here given after the account of the more stirring events of the Waterloo Campaign.

At Madrid, continues Nicol writing in November 1809, it will be remembered after the battle of Solanese we had good accommodation, each patient having a bed and blanket and good provisions, ¾ lb. of white bread, ¼ lb. of beef with soup, and ½ a pint of wine twice a day. We rejoiced to find such good rations after keeping Lent so long. We found here some of the first parties sent from Talavera looking clean and well. On the 18th all that had no open wounds were examined by a French doctor in order to be forwarded to France, and about 200 were picked out and sent to the Retiro, a place in the east part of the city, nigh the palace.

This place was enclosed with stockades, and the French were busy erecting batteries making it into a fortification, as it stands on a commanding situation ; all houses in the way were taken down, and parties of the inhabitants were daily at work upon the batteries, redoubts, etc. We prisoners were lodged in the Riding School, a shocking dirty place to put either man or beast into, and the fever soon broke out amongst us. In front of us was the Grand Square or Parade, where guards and all duties were mounted, and where King Joseph and some of the French Marshals usually attended.

A party of Spaniards taken prisoners only a few leagues from the city was brought here ; a sergeant-major and an intelligent lad of about sixteen assured us we would be relieved in three or four days, as some large Spanish armies were advancing on the city. This we believed, as the French seemed in a bustle. On the 22nd I and some others having the fever were sent in two carts back to the hospital. The inhabitants were exceedingly kind to the British wounded while passing through the streets, giving them money, shirts, and shoes, unperceived by the French.

On the 28th, before daylight, a heavy cannonading began on the east of the city. This made us think the Spanish armies were attacking the French and that we would all be speedily relieved as we knew there were not many French troops in town; but to our mortification we found it to be the celebration of the fact that King Joseph and the French had now been a year in possession of Madrid. Some of the inhabitants thought it was a trick to see if any of them would turn out and the French dragoons were ready to fall upon them. On 4th December arrived sixty wagons loaded with Spanish soldiers wounded at the battle of Ocana where the French destroyed the army that was to take Madrid, and thousands of prisoners were marched past the hospital on their way to France, very miserable looking soldiers indeed. All hopes of our being relieved were now sunk in despair,— until a general exchange or the end of the war.

I continued very bad and there was no man in the fever ward I had ever seen before, and the Spanish orderly men would rather play cards than give assistance to anybody. One night I crawled out of my bed to a window where stood a large earthen jar with water. I brought it to one side to get some, when down it came upon me on the floor, and there I lay on the bricks in a fine cold bath until the orderly man came. He with many damns and curses lifted me up and heaved me into bed, making my bones crack again—all for a thing I could not help. For ten days after I was unable to move about, then I was removed out of the fever ward, a place where I expected death and prayed to God fervently to receive my soul, for I had no desire or inclination to live. But it pleased the Lord to prolong my days when numbers were cut off around me.

Christmas Day was ushered in with the ringing of bells from all the churches in the city, and I believe no town in Europe has so many places of worship as Madrid. I now began to walk about and had plenty of room for exercise in the galleries and passages of this large building, which is for

South America what our East India house in London is for
India. It was called by the French the Military Hospital of
St Francis, and no place in Madrid could have better accommodation for the sick, with a fine free air. I soon recovered
strength, and was often sent out into the town ; this was by
the favour of a Spanish orderly man named Antonio, for
whom I sold tobacco. By this I made a little money to help
me on my journey to France.

The fine weather set in on Tuesday 20th February 1810,
and thirty-seven British cripples were to have carts and join
some French officers and 200 Spanish prisoners. This day I
had a fine view of Madrid. We having only a French grenadier
sergeant in charge of us, and being in number thirty-seven,
and all cripples, halted where we thought proper, and
examined any curiosities.

We passed through many fine streets and squares, and
saw many tradesmen working in the streets in front of their
shops. We were stopped by an old Scotch lady opposite her
house ; she gave us each a glass of wine and a piece of bread
and about 2½d. in money ; the French sergeant got a double
allowance. Passed through the Plaza Major, one of the
finest squares I saw in the city ; it has many fine buildings,
generally of brick, with the under stories strongly stanchioned
with iron bars, which gives them the appearance of prisons.
This is also a public market place. Our sergeant gave us
leave to see a Spanish execution, and he drove the Spaniards
out of the way with many hard names to let his British
friends have a front view. The man was on the scaffold
with some friars about him in a praying posture. He was
then seated on a stool with a post behind him, when his neck
was squeezed with a cord to the post until he was choked.

On the east side of the town we passed along some fine
walks shaded with trees and some fountains of water repre-
senting Neptune in his chariot drawn by horses with streams
of water issuing from their mouths ; in other parts of the
walks were figures of men, women, fishes, etc., all spouting
water. Passed in front of the Palace, two stories high on a
rising ground, and entered the Retiro now a complete French
garrison. We were put into a room where I had a very
dirty billet.

On the 21st we were put into bullock carts and bade adieu
to Madrid with all its fine steeples and churches and fountains,
and above all, its kind inhabitants, who I believe used the

British wounded as well as they durst for fear of the French. We were escorted by about 200 French, a skeleton regiment going to France to be filled up. A major commanded who had lost all his baggage at Oporto when the British entered. He did all he could to make us comfortable. I being the best at speaking French of our party, he and I kept up conversation, so as to be understood, in French, Spanish, and English all mixed together.

We crossed the river Manzanares which half winds round the city, and halted at Las Rozas, where we were crammed into stables, the town being full of troops. Indeed every village had French in it and some of the houses were fortified as barracks, for they were obliged to protect the roads to keep open communication with France, and could only move from place to place in large bodies, for fear of the Spaniards attacking them, which they often did. Between all the contending parties the country was in a very unsettled state.

On the 22nd we saw the Escurial, a stately palace at the foot of the hills about half a league from us to the left of the road ; the sun shining bright upon it at the time gave it a grand appearance. There is a large extent of deer parks surrounded with high walls on the plain.

We began to ascend the mountains the Sierra de Guadarrama, which were covered with trees, and I saw the bones of many Spaniards belonging to former parties of prisoners who had been shot by the French—for those sick or lame who were unable to keep up were instantly shot without being given an opportuniry of offering up a prayer for their souls. Many of their bodies were picked bare by the wolves and birds, eagles, etc., which inhabit these mountains. We were obliged to walk here as the bullocks had enough to do, in pulling up the empty carts, to keep pace with the party. The French kept us as close together as they could ; notwithstanding this some of the Spaniards at one of the zigzag turns of the road made a rush into the wood and got clear off. The French halted the party and kept firing after them but to no end ; they then beat unmercifully with the butts of their firelocks some of those who remained. To this bad usage the Spaniards patiently submitted ; but no wonder that retaliation came upon the French in their own evil day.

We reached the top and had a splendid view of the plain

WELLINGTON ORDERING THE GUARDS TO CHARGE.   WATERLOO

Facing page 208

country on both sides of the mountains. The French had a battery and some works in the principal passes, with men in huts—a very cold position, as the snow lay not far from them. Halted at about eleven o'clock at night at a small village called Ortar, and got a snug room to ourselves.

On the 23rd we passed a royal palace at the foot of this great range of mountains, called Ildefonso. We halted while the French officers went to it (it lay a little to the left, off the road) and got breakfast. Came to Segovia, a fine town surrounded by a wall with turrets in the Moorish style, with a castle, etc. It lies between two valleys with streams of water. A brigade of Germans in the French service was doing duty here. There is an ancient aqueduct here said to have been built by the Romans which conducts water over the river Frio and a deep valley into the town. The arches are exceedingly high, built without lime or cement. The inhabitants were kind to us : we were quartered in a convent. Many of our Spaniards got into hospital here. 24th to Santa Maria. This village was palisadoed, and we entered by a drawbridge into the French barracks ; most of their stations were done in the same manner. Here some Spanish officers joined our party.

Since we passed the mountains that divide the Old and New Castiles the country is of a wild nature, bare and un-cultivated. 25th, to Baladosphe, a village. 26th, to Baldeer. Here lay a Dutch regiment which had been charged at Talavera by the 23rd Dragoons : they showed us many of the appointments of that regiment. 27th, passed a long sandy plain among fir trees ; crossed a stone bridge over the Douro, which river has here a very different appearance. The French have some very strong works here to defend the passage of the river. There had been a large village here but it is now burnt down and in ruins. We met two regiments of Dutch on the road some of their men hailed us in good English.

There was also a regiment of Polish Lancers, formidable looking men, the first I had seen, but I met many afterwards.

We arrived at Valladolid, which stands in the midst of a fertile plain and is watered by two small rivers. The first thing that presented itself to us at the gate was the body of a Spaniard nailed high up on the wall in the same manner and attitude in which he was taken, with his guns beside him. I was told he had been a chief of brigands and had

o

murdered some French soldiers in a cruel manner. The
Spanish officers sighed and hung their heads as they passed.
A guard of French cavalry turned out as we passed on to
the market place where stood the French park of artillery—
some very heavy battering cannon and mortars—drawn up
in three lines. This place is called El Campo and is surrounded by a number of convents many of them converted
into barracks for the French, as a division of their army
lay here at this time. We passed another fine square with
good buildings having piazzas all round and many good
shops. The houses are more regularly built here than in
Madrid being about four stories high with iron balconies
gilded, which look well when the sun shines on them. There
is a large cathedral, a university, and many churches with
hospitals. In the streets are many fountains and fine gardens
within the wall. This is the best looking city I have seen
in Spain and the inhabitants look very respectable in a time
like this when the country is in such a state of confusion.

We were quartered in an old convent on the south side
of the city, facing the open country. Our rations here were
scanty, but we had liberty to purchase. Bread was our only
demand ; it was for sale for about 3d. for a 4lb loaf of the
finest flour. We got wine clear as distilled water very cheap.
The army of Portugal consisting of about thirty thousand
men were drawn up on the plain, to be reviewed by Marshal
Massena and General Jounot. We had a fine view of them
from the roof of the convent, where we were permitted to
go by the French commandant, who pointed out to us the
Generals and the movements of the army. He was an old
wounded veteran and was rejoiced to see them, exclaiming
' Bon ! ' or ' Bravo ! ' at every change of position. While
here three men of a party of British which had arrived before
us were shot while attempting to escape.

We remained at Valladolid until 22nd March when at
daybreak a party of us of twenty men and six women, British,
and about a hundred Spanish were turned out without rations
and delivered over to a captain who was to escort them. He
was told to shoot any man that fell behind or that attempted
to escape. But the captain was a humane man and got the
British into artillery waggons ; we went six leagues this day.

CHAPTER II

LE AMOR DE DIEU

BEING very hungry and seeing a French soldier with more bread than he could make use of I asked him to sell me some. This he would not do but gave me a large piece for 'L'amor de Dieu.' This was the first charity I received in my life and from an enemy too. The good man certainly thought I had need of it and he was right. I thought much of his kindness especially as he had carried the bread so many miles on his back. Halted at Bertavilla where we were lodged in a chapel ; here we got plenty of bread and soup. 23rd, met some heavy cannon and ordnance stores with an escort of French cavalry. Halted at Pallanzuela which lies low between two rivers ; here we were joined by a party of the Guards (British wounded) who had been detained all winter at Palencia where they were fed by the inhabitants like fighting cocks. When they began to make their escape the French hurried them off.

24th, to Mazula. This day we were put in alarm by a body of Spaniards who came down the hill on our left and showed as if they meant to attack the party. The French drums beat to arms, the advance and rear guards closed ; a guard was left with the prisoners with orders to fire if any one offered to move, and a party was sent forward to bring the Spaniards to action, but they scampered up the sides of the hills. 25th, to Pamplige. We were now getting into a better cultivated country, villages more plentiful and good roads.

26th, reached Burgos, the most thriving town I have seen in Spain. But for the presence of the French troops who had raised some works and fortified the Castle, which commands the town, there was no sign of war here. We crossed the bridge over the river ; a guard of gendarmes was stationed here, and I saw some Mamelukes riding after some of the French generals as orderlies, but they were not to be compared with the fine looking fellows I saw in Egypt. Here also I saw many British soldiers who had volunteered into the

French service. We had a fine clean room in the centre of the city and were allowed port liberty. There is a large cathedral with a fine spire of curious workmanship. The streets are broad, and level by the river side ; there are many good shops and everyone seemed to be employed.

We halted here on the 27th, and some gentlemen of the town came among us and gave us money telling us it was raised by the inhabitants for the British wounded. On the 28th we were put into bullock carts and got on a good road planted with trees on each side many of them being cherry trees in full blossom. An Irish captain had charge of us. He told us his name was Hussey from Sligo. He said he had been out with the ' Boys ' in the United Cause and his heart warmed to see us ; he gave us a dollar to buy wine, and said he liked the French service very well.

We came to Birbeisca which lies in a hollow ; a brook runs through the centre of it ; the 3rd French regiment was doing duty here. 29th to Miranda de Elbro having a castle on the hill and many additional works made lately by the French to guard the pass where the road passes through this range of hills. Some friars brought us a large mess of boiled beans which went down very sweetly. 30th to Vittoria a fine town enclosed by a kind of wall ; houses much scattered, gardens inside the walls. The Irish brigade in the French service were on duty here ; they came among us looking for volunteers but got none. 31st halted ; being Sunday some of our women went begging to the chapel doors and got much money and were soon the worse of liquor and kept rioting and disturbing the party and fighting with their husbands, etc. It is a great pity such vagabonds should be allowed to go abroad with the army.

On the 1st April we first got an escort of gendarmes which was always continued afterwards. Crossed the river Zadona and began to ascend the Pyrenees through a fine fertile country ; the sides of the hills covered with wood. This day was very wet and some of our Spaniards got clear off and were not missed until night. We passed through many villages ; everything seemed here to be in a state of prosperity.

Halted all night at Salvatierra a fine village. 2nd to Villafranca. This day we passed on our right some very high mountains capped with snow ; rain on the hills and the sun very hot in the valleys. On the 3rd, we came to Tolosa, a large town. We passed by a stately bridge over a brawling river that comes down from the mountains. In the main street there are boards shelving from each side to throw the

WELLINGTON LEADS ON THE 52ND AND 95TH REGIMENTS. WATERLOO

Facing page 213

rain into the centre. On the sides you can walk dry. The crowd that had collected and the French guards kept us poor prisoners right in the middle where the rain poured on us from neck to heel. I always rejoiced to see our faithful allies the Spaniards do a clean thing. Between twenty and thirty of them made their escape, some into shops, others mixed with the crowd. The French cursed them but being wet and tired gave themselves no further trouble. We were quartered in a chapel. The French had their barracks fortified. 4th, halted; many troops passed here on their way into Spain. 5th, to Audoin. Passed many fine villages; ironworks, water mills, etc., seemed all busy. A battalion of French marines lay here and came to see if any of us would enter the service.

Some American captains whose vessels lay at Sebastian gave us sixpence each: this was very good of Jonathan. 6th, saw St Sebastian off the road to our left; it has a fortified appearance from the heights. Saw some British gunbrigs cruising out at sea, we rejoiced to see salt water and British war vessels again. As this was the boundary between Spain and France the French escort had some brandy shouting out 'Vive l'Empereur! Vive la France!' They then handed round the bottle to the British, who emptied it without a 'Vive' but we felt happy at being on French soil without knowing the reason of our being so.

Came to St Jean de Luz the first town in France. The inhabitants were very kind to us and many young women came among us selling brandy. I got more cheerful here than I had been for ten months before and sold my blanket which I had carried until it was becoming a nuisance; these Frenchwomen were disposed to buy any article we had to dispose of. 7th, to Bayonne a regularly fortified town with a deep river and many ships. We were lodged in the citadel, a very strong place and had the liberty of the courtyard. Here was a gang of convicts in chains with a shot or two dragging after them. These men are made to work on the batteries etc., for a number of years according to the nature of their offences.

On the walls of the fencing were cut in stone the names of some British sailors taken in 1756 and 1760. The Spaniards got money, bread, and beef from Prince Ferdinand but no rations for the British; we were obliged to our faithful allies who gave us a share of their mess. 8th, halted. A man came from the town to see how many were of us; I made out a list of our names and regiments: we got shirts, shoes and trousers; some of our party had much need of them.

CHAPTER III

THE ROAD TO BRIANCON

ON the 9th we marched through the town. Most of the houses look very old and stand with their gables to the streets. Crossed the river by a drawbridge and parted with the Spaniards, who went another road. We expected to embark in boats for Bordeaux but in this we were disappointed. We were marched off by a gendarme who let us walk as we pleased to a village called Parade. 10th, got into transport carts—to Orthes, and were put into the Nun's hospital, where those Sisters of Charity attended us and gave us the best of rations, wine, etc. 11th, halted.

12th, to Lescar Hospital. Here we found about seventy or eighty British who had been here for two months. About half of these marched, leaving the remainder and sixty Spaniards, who were in a most filthy state with the itch. Their skin was black, rising in scales like that of a fish ; I pitied the poor fellows they were very loathsome to look upon. We had good clean bedding and our rations were good but scanty—I wrote a letter to the commissary at Pau, who sent us an order to march after being here for a month.

Thursday, 10th May, we came into Pau, and were met by the Commandant, a very pleasant old gentleman. He told us it was for our good he had kept us in hospital for he was certain we were better there than in our depôt ; this we afterwards found to be true. He conducted us to the promenade and served us with shirts and shoes, and told us to take care of them, for it would be a long time before we would get any more. We got five sous and $1\frac{1}{2}$ lb. of ration bread every day on the march afterwards. Marched to Tarbes ; it was late before we got in. This is a fine large town. Halted here on the 11th, had a good room and full

liberty.   The Freemasons among us got five francs apiece and
in every town where there was a lodge relief was given more
or less : a fine thing to be a Mason in France !   12th, got
transport waggons to Rabastens ; 13th, Miranda ; 14th, halt ;
15th at Auch, halted in the Grand Square.   The inhabitants
used us very kindly and gave us bread, money, and wine
until half of the party was speaking loud.   This is a beautiful
tract of country, well cultivated.   Nature is bountiful in her
productions here.   We passed through to Toulouse which is
an ancient city the capital of a fertile province.   The soil is
very rich and I have seen fields with heavy crops of wheat
among rows of large fruit trees and vines at the same time,
warped along from tree to tree ; this had a beautiful
appearance.   Here is the river Garonne which is navigable
to Bordeaux, and a canal connects the town with the
Mediterranean.   We crossed the river by a stone bridge ;
there are some fine level streets and some good buildings in
and about the principal square.   Provisions of all kinds are very
cheap ; wine is sold for three or four sous a bottle, and brandy
for twelve sous.   We were quartered in the jail and used but
indifferently, for in most of the large towns prisoners of war
were strictly looked after.   A gentleman waited upon us and
told us an exchange of prisoners was going on between the
two countries, and that a Mr MacKenzie had come from
England to make arrangements.   This put us in agitation lest
we should not arrive at our depôt in time.   The gentleman
left us some money.   We went on to Villefranche : and
marched on a long causeway for about six post leagues.
     On the 21st we came to Castelnaudary and were put into
another dirty jail.   It being dark they sold us soup made of
snails, and good well seasoned soup it was.   Some of our
people made a row about it ; the French folk just laughed at
us.   I thought it was composed of livers or lights, and lay
down and slept.   At this place there is a trade in silk, and
here begins the rearing of silkworms, with paper windows,
and mulberry trees whose leaves are stripped to feed the
silkworms.   On the 22nd we reached Carcassonne, an ancient
walled town.   A regiment of Spaniards was doing duty here
and seemed very happy in the French service.   There is an
old town and a new separated by the river.   23rd Leanill.
Narbonne, a large fortified town in a deep valley among hills
has a very ancient appearance : the Grand Canal comes
through here—many boats passing and repassing.   25th, to

Beziers, a large walled town. In the centre of the principal square is a statue of a Captain Peire who defended the city against the British in days of yore. Monsieur pointed this out to our party in a very gasconading manner. This town stands in a well cultivated country, the vineyards on the slopes of the rising ground. We could see the Mediterranean with its gentle waves within a couple of miles of us. On the 26th we halted, some nuns or Sisters of Charity came among us, an elderly lady said prayers and gave us bread and wine.

On the 27th we were joined by some Spanish officers three of whom, a colonel and two captains, were in chains having attempted to escape. Seven British and some sailors who had deserted from the French fleet at Toulon also joined us. These sailors got us all into trouble. As we were passing a wood in sight of the sea, the French tars with a knowing wink and a nod to the British jerked up their trousers sailor fashion and started off. The gendarmes raised a hue and cry and one raised his carbine to fire when out fell the flint. At this we burst into a roar of laughter. The gendarme then turned on us and punished some of us with the butt of his carbine, but the sailors got clear off. We came to Meze, a town by the seaside : here the gendarmes got us closely locked up. 28th we were badly used by that wicked gendarme ; he made one of our party march all day with thumbscrews on for shaking his fist at him, yet I had some sympathy for the gendarme, for I knew myself what it was to lose prisoners. Saw some of our cruizers off the coast, and no doubt we wished ourselves on board. To Poussan ; 29th Montpellier. I can say little about this city for I did not see much of it. The air is said to be purer and less scorching than in the surrounding country. It stands on the slope of a hill where you have the great plain between you and the Pyrenees and the Mediterranean, as far as the eye can reach. There are some good stone buildings broad streets and walks shaded with trees, with statues and fountains. Distance from the sea five miles. But for all the fine balmy air of this place it was ordered that we should have none of it at this time, for our officious gendarme reported us as being the occasion of his losing the sailors, and we were locked up in a dungeon in the citadel outside the town until the 31st, when we were glad to see daylight again. Crossed a beautiful country to Lunel.

On 1st June we reached Nimes, an ancient city. On

entering there is a Roman amphitheatre which has stood the test of time with little damage. There are three or four rows of arches one above another, some at the bottom are converted into shops ; also a large acqueduct called Pont de Font, consisting of three rows of arches said to be above 100 feet high across the river ; a citadel with bastions to keep the inhabitants in order, they being chiefly Protestants : the chief trade here is in silk stockings. At St Esprit we crossed the rapid river Rhone over a stone bridge of thirty arches. We passed through a pleasant country, the Rhone to our left and the roadsides planted with mulberry, cherry and chestnut trees. A regiment of Portuguese was doing duty at Montetimait. We reached Valence, formerly a walled town. There was a large depot for Spaniards at this place. They were allowed to work about the country. We had the liberty of the town. The Spanish officers treated us as well as we could expect, considering their means. On the 9th we arrived at Tain, where we were quartered in a hospital for lunatics. 10th St Marcellin Italian regiment was doing duty here. The chief business in this town is the rearing of silkworms, and the houses have a nasty close smell with them ; all the houses about this quarter have paper windows, which give them a disreputable appearance. On the 11th to Grenoble, capital of the Province of Dauphiny, situated at the entrance of the mountains, a fortified place. Many troops were in the town and we saw some of the Spaniards who had marched on the road with us doing duty in the French service. Provisions are very cheap here. There are some excellent stone buildings and a large square with a fountain throwing water many feet high. Over the archway of the main gate are the words, in large letters, PORT DE FRANCE, and over the doors of many houses in the principal streets were the words 'Liberte et Egalite.' We were quartered in barracks in the citadel. Halted here on 12th and 13th. On the 14th we entered the mountains ; the valleys are well cultivated and the corn harvest was almost over ; came to Sombero. On the 16th at St Bonnet, all villages beside a brawling stream rushing down from among the hills. 17th to Gap. Here our women six in number, were sent back to go to England, they carried a letter from every man in the party. This is a fine little town to be in this part of the country, 18th, met a large party of British who had volunteered out of the depôt into the Irish brigade in the French service. Halted at a village,

Savines. 19th, Embrun, a fortified town. 20th, Largentiere :
here the Germans left us to go to Mont Dauphine, a strong fort
in one of the passes leading into Italy, a depôt for all
foreigners taken under the British flag. 21st, met some
officers of the Maltese regiment who had been taken in Italy.
They gave us each fifteen sous—a very handsome present in
these times of poverty—and charged us not to volunteer into
the French service, as we would all be exchanged in a few
weeks. This was hope for us. We travelled along a very
wild road this day, with streams of water rushing down the
hills. Reached Briancon.

CHAPTER IV

THE TERRIBLE CONDITION OF MANY PRISONERS

WE were taken into the Governor's office to give our descriptions, our names, the regiments or ships we belonged to, when and where taken, father's and mother's names, when and where born, etc. On coming out we were beset with those harpies of the Irish Brigade, Captain Reilly and Sergeant-Major Dwyer, offering us brandy and telling us all the evils of a French prison ; they got three of our party to join them.

Briancon is the last town in France on the principal road to Italy. It lies in one of the passes among the mountains and is very strong both by nature and art. It is surrounded by a single wall. The streets are narrow and steep ; the best buildings are the barracks and stores and a church with two steeples. It lies under the Grand Fort or Citadel called les Trois Tetes from which it is separated by a small river called Durance (well named, thought I) over which is a lofty bridge.* This bridge, it is said, is the highest in Europe above the sea level : there is a brass plate on it with an inscription stating that it was built in the time of Louis the 14th. The road goes zigzag up the hill, where is a natural crop of lavender in full bloom as far as we could see.

We crossed three drawbridges and entered the garrison ; the line walls were mounted with cannon and there are many outworks. On the shoulder of another hill stands a fort which commands this, and a third higher up, commands it in turn : at this place is the reservoir which supplies all the forts with good water and plenty of it. High above all this is a mortar battery. The place is said to be impregnable, but I think might be starved out very easily. Mount Genevre

* The Bridge consists of a single arch of 128 feet span and is 180 feet above the ravine below. Briancon is the most elevated town in France, if not in Europe, being 4285 feet above sea level.

stands near, and although this was the longest day in June, is capped with snow.

As we entered the grand square we saw above 1000 of our countrymen in a miserable condition, one half of them being nearly naked, with pieces of old blanket round them.   A cold shudder came over me as I looked at them.   Their condition was a disgrace to the French nation for there was abundance of clothing in the stores and since the month of March above 900 suits had been given to men who had entered the French service, which should have been served out to those prisoners who had been longest in garrison ; and if a man entered prison to-day and volunteered to-morrow he got a new suit of prison clothing away with him.

There are good bomb proof barracks all round the square, which were used for the accommodation of prisoners.   There we were taken and put into messes or sections 33 men in each, one man having charge ; three of these sections formed a company, or un cent, one man taking charge of the whole : he was called chief of a division and made out all returns for provisions, mess utensils, all sick reports, etc., and required to be a man that could speak French if possible.   I got charge of a company and had many civilities shown me and was allowed more liberty than I would have had otherwise.   Each gendarme had charge of five companies and all reports from them were made to the Marechal des Logis, who communicated with the Commandant.

Our provisions were scanty, consisting of 12 oz. of bread and 6 oz. of beef, with a very small allowance of rice or callarances, which were barely sufficient to support nature ; we were allowed one sou and a half per day from the French, paid monthly and two sous per day from Lloyd's Committee. What bedding we had was rotten and full of vermin, from which we could not keep ourselves free.   There was a market in the garrison where bread was to be got for three sous per lb., beef for six sous and wine for seven sous the bottle, brandy thirty-two sous.   The people in the little villages in the valleys brought milk, meal, potatoes, etc., for sale, but money was very scarce.

We received a letter from Lord Beverley, with the welcome present of a franc a man : he resided as a prisoner at Moulins ; he told us to be of good cheer as the exchange was going on.

On the 6th August there were eight men belonging to the

FRENCH RIDE UP TO THE MOUTH OF OUR GUNS AT WATERLOO

Facing page 220

92nd regiment in this depot, John MacDonald and Alexander
MacKinlay volunteered into the French service.   I went to see
if it was true and was nigh hooked myself.   Captain Reilly
said it was a glorious thing to serve an Emperor and offered
to make me sergeant at once, never to be reduced without an
order from the Emperor himself. ' Look at me,' said he ; ' I
enlisted a private soldier and see what I am now : an officer
seldom springs from the ranks in the British service.'   I
acknowledged the justness of his observation, but it had no
effect on me I told him I was quite content to serve a King.
The Captain did not trouble me again, but he certainly did not
forget me for I often got a bottle of wine and a loaf of white
bread more than the prison regulations warranted, which I
have no doubt were sent by his order.   I shook hands with
MacDonald and had a glass of brandy with him ; when I
turned to go away he cried bitterly.   He was made Corporal
and in a few days marched for Landau, the headquarters of his
regiment.   Poor John was a good soldier but had his full
share of bad luck.   This left only six of the 92nd : James
Sangster, James Gardner, John Semple, John Chambers, John
Orr, and myself.

Letters concerning the exchange of prisoners were coming to
the garrison from so many trustworthy gentlemen that nothing
was talked of but Home Sweet Home.   We were inspected
by the General of the district, who seemed to take compassion
on our ragged condition, he told us we would be provided
with clothing before we went to England.   The French are
the best of promisers and seldom give you poor encouragement.

On the 24th of October, a letter arrived from Mr Anthony
Aufrere, telling us that Mr MacKenzie the agent who had
come from England to arrange about the exchange of prisoners
had left the country without coming to any agreement.   This
was a grievous disappointment to us all.   Some men cried
like children, and others did not open their mouths to speak
for days.   I wrote to the Honourable Colonel Gordon at
Lyons ; he sent the men of our regiment three francs each :
I also wrote to Sir John Hope, Colonel of our regiment.

A large party of the Rifle Brigade taken in a skirmish at
Almeida arrived here, also a party of the 2nd battalion 4th
regiment which had been shipwrecked in Cadiz Bay.

CHAPTER V

THE STRANGE HEADQUARTERS OF THE NINETY-SECOND

On the 5th November the snow, which we had seen at a distance began to come down and fell three feet the first night and continued until it was nine feet deep. This made us sit round the stoves; a kind of sulphury coal dust got among the hills was brought to us, this when slaked with water and wrought into balls made a strong fire. At length we got clothing served out, this made us look more respectable and our condition mended every day after this. About this time a body of men formed themselves into a banditti, stealing bread, money and everything they could lay their hands on; by dint of severe punishments we got them into order and kept them so. On 25th December, Christmas Day, a great many had something extra to eat and drink.

January 5th, 1811, Saturday, a dreadful cold day with wind and snow and pieces of ice flying about. We had to go to the town every fourth day for bread. This chanced to be one of the days for this duty and some men did not get the better of it for a long time. Our windows which were only oiled paper, were battered in by the storm. We made roads through the snow, and when the weather cleared up got out again, after being closely confined for a long time; few people but those who have felt it can imagine what a winter is in the Alps. Our chief amusements were playing cards, dominoes, etc., and mending our clothes. On 16th January I wrote to Archibald Campbell, Esquire, No 8 Hans Court, London, our prize agent, for the first payment of our Denmark prize money.

An unlucky thing happened to me at this time : the best shirt I had was either stolen or blown over the line walls. I believe it was the former, for I had washed it that morning and was very particular in securing it. This was a great loss to me.

About the end of March we got rid of the snow after a long winter and I began my walks in the square from six to eight every morning weather permitting, then went in, took a little breakfast, and read or wrote till dinner was ready, then kept talking or hearing stories, news, etc., until afternoon when I walked for an hour in the square before we were locked up, which was always about sunset. This I carried on day after day.

Friday the 24th of May was a bright day for the six men of the 92nd regiment. We received our Danish prize money in answer to the letter I wrote to Mr Campbell, amounting to 53 francs 10 sous each. This put us on a respectable footing; no doubt some of it was spent foolishly in drink, but much good was done also. Alexander Beattie of our regiment arrived; he had been detained in some hospital in the country since the retreat to Corunna. June 22nd, my 33rd birthday, was kept with great glee by the men of the regiment for the service I had done them in getting money.

On the 2nd October I received an answer to the letter I sent to Sir John Hope; it came from Alexander Bruce our army agent, with our pay from the date of my letter, at 3d per day, and we received 49 francs in a lump, and it was sent every month afterwards. This was an exceeding good change for the better, and we now enjoyed every comfort rational men could expect to be prisoners of war.

A party of the 89th regiment arrived. They had been taken at Malaga with their colonel, Lord Blaney, who did much good to the prisoners, in regulating the pay; he sent clothing for each man. This banished poverty, rags, and vermin from the depot. The charitable money was all given to the merchant seamen which bettered their condition also. All the waste ground about the garrison was converted into gardens and patches were sold or let out to the prisoners by the Marechal des Logis. I paid 60 sous for a piece and erected a kind of house with stones. This was called the headquarters of the 92nd regiment. And there I sat many an hour writing this narrative; at other times digging and planting or watering, but I never had a crop that came to maturity. So my French Lairdship brought me little profit but it was an employment to me and I had the pleasure of having a place to myself.

On 3rd October arrived a large party taken in June of the Guards, 42nd, 71st, 79th, 85th regiments and Johnston Caird of our regiment. From him we learned all the particulars of the army and of our own regiment, and all the news of the Walcheren expedition.

We passed this winter in a more agreeable manner than we did last. Christmas was kept in grand style, big loaves, sirloins of beef and plenty of wine and brandy etc. The jollification was kept up by some as long as they could raise the wind, and the new year came in with a great number of blue eyes and broken noses, and credit and money being gone things were at a dead stand until a fresh supply arrived.

One of the 71st regiment, Michael Floyd, brought between fifty and sixty doubloons into the garrison. Some plunder he had got his fingers over. He took the fever and was removed to the hospital, where the men in the ward with him, thinking he was going to make his exit took the money and divided it. But he recovered and an uproar was made about the Spanish gold. The men were put into close confinement and the money was delivered to the French authorities ; they were afterwards sent to Gap and tried for robbery but were acquitted. What with law expenses and one thing and another Floyd did not get back half of his money.

This spring the crew of the *Alacrity* gunbrig taken off the isle of Corsica was brought in here : each man received ten sous a day from the French for relieving some French prisoners confined by the Spaniards on a desolate island in the Mediterranean.

There came in about 200 soldiers, British, taken near Burgos, most of them belonging to the 3rd Buffs, 66th and 48th regiments. By what these men told us we thought the French were losing ground in Spain.

All the shoemakers and tailors were taken to Grenoble during the summer to work for the French.

On the 25th October there came in about 200 condemned prisoners from Bitch, many officers among them, who had been trying to escape and had been guilty of other misdemeanours. They were closely confined having only two hours' liberty in the square every fourth day. They caused much trouble in the garrison and abridged our liberty much. A committee consisting of two French and two British was formed to do justice between man and man, concerning our rations and other affairs of the prison, the market, etc. Mr

THE GENERAL ADVANCE WATERLOO AT THE CLOSE OF THE ACTION

Facing page 225

Nisbet the carpenter of the *Proserpine* frigate and Sergeant Lyle of the 21st regiment were chosen.

Christmas day and New Year's Day passed over much the same as the last, a battle royal was carried on until the French soldiers had to charge some of them into the barracks and all of us were locked up.

On Sunday 17th May 1812 I joined a society of Methodists who had hired a barrack room for a place of worship and prayer meeting. I continued with them until the breaking up of the depot, and received much edification : there might be about a hundred of us. In June we got new beds and blankets, things we had much need of. I was placed in a small barrack room with sixteen men and was very comfortable. There came in a party of the *Venerable*, 74, and some Royal Marine Artillery taken at Bilbao in Spain.

On the 25th November our regiment was put on the strength of Lord Blaney's Committee for pay, after our having received from an agent £8 3s. 9d. being 3d. per day for 655 days and we received clothing from the committee for 1813. About this time a pawnbroking company was formed and at Christmas many of our men had stripped themselves of every article of clothing they had and sold their pay for a month to come, at a discount. Orders came for 600 of the oldest prisoners to march ; this caused a consternation and very long faces were made by the per cent gentlemen who had bought the payments beforehand.

On 27th January 1812, 200 marched for Arras ; 200 next day for Valenciennes ; James Sangster of our regiment marched with this division ; 1st February, 200 for Givet ; Alexander Beattie, 92nd went with this party. This gave us more room in the garrison.

We had much finer weather this winter than last. A new society called the Crusaders was formed among us by Sergeant-major Goldsmith, 23rd dragoons : a great many of the young men in the depôt joined it.

On the 11th April I obtained liberty from Colonel D'Avrill, commandant of the garrison, to go into the country. With six others I went about from village to village eating white bread and drinking wine, for six days when our money was spent and we returned to the depôt. A few days after this liberty was stopped because a party on leave had attempted to escape and were captured in Italy, not far from Turin, about 14 leagues from here. The Commandant said 'You British

P

cry for liberty, but when you get it you do not know how to use it.' We all know the truth of this. And the Commandant was kind to us always as far as was consistent with the prison regulations.

On 24th May, an atrocious act was committed by one of the gendarmes, Perrier Houssier, when going his rounds. Some of our men were playing cards and had a light burning; without giving warning he fired through the door upon them and killed George Nail of the Rifles and broke the arm of Charles Reid, 3rd Guards. The Commandant declared his disapprobation of the cruel deed and caused a court to be held, half French, half British. The gendarme was sent to Grenoble to be tried by court-martial. He was condemned to slavery and our man was interred outside the walls very decently; prayers were read by Sergeant-major Goldsmith, 23rd Light Dragoons.

On 11th July there was a heavy fall of snow: this we were told was frequently the case after a mild winter. There came in a young lad of our regiment Alexander Murray who enlisted at Aberdeen only about seven months ago: he has certainly made the Grand Tour in extraordinary quick time.

The French kept all news from us as far as they could, concerning any defeat their armies had sustained. But it was impossible to hide altogether that they were nearly driven out of Spain and that things were not going on well in the north. 2nd November there fell 4 feet of snow, it then cleared up into frost.

16th November (1812), we heard of the burning of Moscow and what great things the French had done in destroying the Russian armies. But on the 29th another tale was to be told: that the Austrians were entering Italy with a large army, and that the prisoners of war were to be sent off and the garrison to be put into a state of defence.

CHAPTER VI

THE JOURNEY THROUGH FRANCE

I MARCHED on Wednesday the 8th December 1813, after being
three years and five months a prisoner among the high Alps in
this garrison : this is the longest time I have been in one place
since I became a soldier. And no prisoner in France could
have enjoyed better health than I did, or been more miserable
when I entered it or more comfortable when I left it.

Some were sorry to have to march at this time of the year,
and no doubt since we received a regular supply of money
from Britain we were more comfortable here than we would
have been with our regiments. For myself I was better
prepared for the march now than at any time since I was
a prisoner, for I was strong and in good health, had two good
suits of clothing, and ten dollars in my purse, which proved
ten good friends to me during the winter.

The town and garrison were all in a bustle. Some of the
merchants in town had trusted goods to a large amount to
some of our people who acted as retailers for them, and got
themselves swindled out of large sums of money. We were
paid up to the 24th January 1814, by Lord Blaney's
Committee. There were about 2,300 prisoners in the depôt,
and we were to march in five divisions.

We trudged along through the snow, every one with
a light heart and a merry countenance, the inhabitants coming
and shaking hands with us ; they were sorry to part with
us and no doubt we had spent much money among them.
When far down the road I took a long look back at the
garrison and thought it a dismal abode in the centre of the
mountains among so much snow.

Some of our men got drunk on the road with brandy
and one Cochrane of the 42nd regiment died through it and
through being exposed to the cold. Came to St Crespin and

were lodged in stables; the inhabitants brought us boiled
beef, soups of all kinds, etc., wine for the ready penny, but
all had to pay toll to the French guard before entering.   9th
to Embrun.   I bought a good blanket from one of our men
for 26 sous; he thought it too heavy to carry but he repented
doing so before he got out from the mountains.   10th to the
village of Chorges.   11th Gap: we were inspected by the
General of the Department.   12th, St Bonnet: a great fall
of snow during the night; had to get guides to keep us on
the road for fear of falling into the valley below, about half
a mile down the side of a hill, in some places nearly perpendicular, to a place called Corff.   13th, to La Mure.   The
country is getting more level and the air is warmer, not so
much snow lying.   We were lodged in the theatre and had
plenty of clean straw.   14th, a very wet dirty day; to Vif.
With some others I went to an auberge and got lodgings for
the night.   We had supper and bed very comfortable.   But
this was a serious pull on my pocket, 5 francs each.   After
this, when I had to provide lodging as I sometimes had, I
made a bargain with mine host before I took possession.

15th, Grenoble; we halted here on the 16th and 17th, were
lodged in the barracks, but had the liberty of the town, which
was not to the profit of some.   18th: we were now in a level
country and a warmer climate: good roads.   Came to
Moirans.   19th to La Cote St Andre.   We were lodged nigh
the church and could observe the good agreement between
the Catholics and Protestants, one party having the use of
the church in the forenoon and the other in the afternoon;
they seemed to be on the best of terms with each other, a
thing that is very rare.   20th to Bourgoin.   21st the shortest
day but the longest march: seven country leagues or twenty-
eight miles or more, into Lyons a large and populous city
in a fine country and climate, well built, with broad level
streets, squares, etc.   Its lies in the cleft of two fine rivers.
We crossed the river Rhone by a long stone bridge, well
lighted with swinging lamps in the centre, which is the usual
way of lighting streets in the principal towns of France.   We
arrived in front of the Hotel de Ville in the centre of the
grand square and parted with the good old captain who had
escorted us from Briancon and who had done all in his
power to make us comfortable.   We were closely confined in
a large prison.   22nd, halted: we were visited by Colonel
Hall of the 9th regiment, who paid us up till the 31st

January 1814 : this was the last money I received in the country.

On the 23rd we marched through the north-west part of the city ; there are some fine streets by the side of the river on the quays, the houses ranging from five to six stories high. Crossed the Soane by a new stone bridge ; many boats were passing up and down the rivers laden with the produce of the country. Saw the statue of a man standing on a rock ; he had been a deliverer of the city in some war of ancient times. There was a great appearance of trade in Lyons and everybody seemed to be employed. We had a wet morning and a dirty road. Many fine villages and chateaux lined the banks of the Soane, which we kept on our left most of the way to Villefranche : here we were at liberty to go where we pleased. Many of us got supper and a bed for 11 sous, but many never joined again. 24th, to Macon, a fine large town and a depôt for Spanish officers, who were very inquisitive about the armies in Spain, but we had no news to give them of a later date than they had themselves. 25th, Christmas Day : many of our party got drunk and spent their all and the French commissary cheated us out of two days' pay ; met a great many Spaniards changing their depôt.

Came to Tournus, an ancient town in a fine country. It was very late before we got in after a long day's march and my wounded leg began to fail me and swelled much, owing to the long marches we were making every day. 26th to Chalons-sur-Soane, a fine town, good buildings and level streets, a market-place, and many boats on the river. I saw some corn mills here, built like large boats and anchored in the centre of the river : the millers do not require to draw water for their mills at this place. We crossed the Soane over a stone bridge into Isle St Laurens. There is a depôt for conscripts here, and about 500 Spanish officers were in it. The Central Canal connects the rivers Soane and Loire at this place, which gives communication between the Atlantic and the Mediterranean. 27th, halted. 28th, to Beaune. We met many wounded French and Austrians : this let us know the fighting was not far off : 29th, to Dijon, the capital of the province of Burgundy. It seems to be well fortified with a ditch and line walls. In an open space in the shape of a horse shoe, stands the old palace, a noble building now getting out of repair ; there are some fine churches and convents.

Into one of these large buildings we were bundled among 2000 Austrians newly taken, and more arriving hourly. The nuns came among the wounded men and dressed their wounds. We were shifted to another part of the building and allowed port liberty. I took a walk round the ramparts, and a fine promenade they are for the citizens, with a full view of the country and the mountains of Switzerland. The town was full of troops and all seemed to be in a bustle, and waggons full of wounded French soldiers were arriving at intervals ; we could hear guns firing at a great distance and were told it was at Besancon. 30th, halted : It appeared to me that the men and women in the province of Burgundy were stouter and taller than I had seen anywhere else in France. The women at this time wore an odd kind of head-dress, a fine lace cap and a small black hat about the size of a tea saucer placed on one side of the head, tied under the chin with a black ribband. 31st to Dijon, where we got billets.

CHAPTER VII

THE RASCALLY GOVERNOR OF MAUBEUGE

SATURDAY, 1st January 1814, to Langres, a fortified town; it stands high and commands a view of the level country to a great distance. 2nd, to Chaumont which stands on a height and was seen long before we came to it; it is a depôt for Spanish prisoners. 3rd, to Degary, a village; met a division of prisoners from Givet. 4th, to Joinville. This day I met forty-seven men of our regiment lately taken in the Pyrenees, got all the news from them that time would allow, as they were moving in another direction. 5th, to St Dizier: met a division of Spaniards on the march. 6th, to Vitry, an ancient town; many of the houses have their gables to the streets. We were crammed into stables by the side of the river Marne. This day we passed four regiments of cavalry of the Imperial Guard, fine looking men, mounted on the best horses I have seen in the country. But we got the worst usage from them of any troops since we were prisoners. The roads were dirty and in passing they caused their horses to prance and bespatter us with mud, and we were in danger of being ridden over, while the troopers laid on us with their scabbards, cursing and calling us all the bad names they could think of. No doubt the men were grieved at being taken out of their comfortable quarters in Paris, for they did not seem to be troops that had seen much service, but we certainly expected better treatment from the Imperial Guard. Little did they think that in a few days afterwards many of them would be in the same condition as ourselves. A fine train of artillery accompanied them.

7th, to Chalons-sur-Marne, a clean town in a level unenclosed country; it is surrounded by a wall and a ditch. Got a gentleman's house to ourselves, with plenty of clean straw; good bread was sold in the marketplace, 6 lb. for five sous. 8th, to Petit Logas, I was billeted on a farmer who

used me very well.   As we advanced to the north we felt the
weather colder.   9th, to the city of Rheims, which is walled
in and has a deep ditch round it.   There is a large cathedral
with lofty spires, seen at a distance from the city.   In it the
kings of France were crowned.   The buildings appear to be
very old.   At this time the town was full of French soldiers.
We got some of our men into hospital here ; they had been
badly for many days and been conveyed in carts, but none
of the towns we passed through would receive them.
10th, a heavy fall of snow during the night.   This was a
very cold day, wind north, in our faces.   Passed more
cavalry on the road who were more civil than the Imperial
Guard.

Came to Craonne, which was full of troops ; I was billeted
in the country about a league from the town.   11th, to Laon.
This town stands on a commanding height, and has a great
appearance at a distance as you advance to it on a stone causeway with trees on each side of the road.   It is strong by
nature and art, and could easily be defended by a few brave
men against a greatly superior force.   There is a depot for
artillery here and this day about forty or fifty pieces were
taken off to the army, escorted by some troops of cavalry.
There is also a large cathedral.   12, halted : a cold frosty
day.   We were lodged in a church.

As some of a former division here had run off on the road
to Dunkirk, and others had escaped into the Netherlands, the
country was alarmed and we were escorted by a strong guard
to Vervins, a long march and were put into close confinement at
the end of it.   14th, to Avesnes : all these towns on the
frontier are more or less fortified.

15th, came to the strong fortress of Maubeuge on the
river Sambre which was to be our depot.   We crossed three
drawbridges, as many line walls mounted with cannon, and
ditches filled with water.   Hundreds of people were working,
putting the garrison into a state to be able to stand a siege,
and as the authorities did not expect prisoners at this time we
were lodged in good barracks, but no firing or utensils were
given out and no rations but bread.   An old blanket was
served out to every three men, and every way was taken to
annoy us.   Great stores of flour and all other kinds of
provisions were brought in from the country.   These articles
were very cheap in the market and we could get a hatful of
potatoes, apples or onions for one sou, and good beer or

porter for four sous the quart, but money was very scarce among us.

For the first few days we had the liberty of the town, but when it was rumoured that a Prussian army was advancing the Governor ordered us to be put in divisions and work on the batteries.   This we at once refused to do and some rash words spoken by some of our people enraged the Governor. It was given out that we were going to seize the town as some of our folk had been seen about the arsenal.   The drums beat the alarm ; the troops assembled under arms on the ramparts, and the National Guards in the streets, while a regiment of Lancers drew up in front of our barracks.   We were all turned out and beaten and abused, and many a thump and blow was given us and many a ' diable ' and 'sacre foutras Anglais ' were bestowed on us.   At last they drove us into the bombproofs under the ramparts and pointed two field-pieces to the only entrance, and here we were kept under ground for forty-eight hours, and for all this no reason was assigned : if the enemy had been within cannon shot we would have thought it all right.   We got no provisions and water was scantily supplied through the stockade, a large gate. Many were very badly off but my comrade and I had just got a four lb. loaf at the time the scuffle commenced.   We got out on the 21st January, on condition that we were to make a palisade in front of our barracks and confine ourselves within it.   We were now ready to promise anything or do anything to get out to the light of day once more and so we began the work.   On the 24th an order arrived for all the prisoners to march.   Next morning at daybreak we marched in a close body amounting to 1800 men ; we were strongly guarded.   Snow and strong frost.   Came after dark to Landrecies, a strongly fortified place.   The French soldiers entered the garrison and we were quartered in some villages on the road to Cateau without any one being left to look after us.   On this long march my wounded leg began to fail and I was very lame for some days, yet I was contented and happy that I had made my escape from that rascally Governor of Maubeuge.

On the 26th we marched through the plains of Cateau to Cambray, a pretty large city with good streets and a large square ; it is strongly fortified with a fort and citadel and other works and the country can be laid under water by the river Scheldt.   In the citadel had been about 3000 British prisoners ; they had been marched off a few days before we arrived, and the French were busy mounting cannon there. Every one seemed in a bustle and so many troops were marching in and out that we could not get bread until the evening of the next day. Many went without it, and some of the party began to steal bread, and got themselves and others beaten and abused by the French soldiers. We got off at last and had to march on the 27th, 10 leagues to Peronne, a small strong town on the river Somme in the late province of Picardy. We got billets and were supplied with food by the inhabitants, and but for their kindness many of our party would have starved.

As we were too many to subsist together we separated into three divisions without the knowledge of the French ; one took the road to Paris, and another made for the coast. I remained with the centre division. 28th, very bad road to Montdidier. 29th, Bolea, a little village. I was billeted on a fine motherly woman, who dried and mended my clothes. Poor woman, she had two sons in the grande armee who were I have no doubt, in a worse condition than I was. 30th, to Beauvais, a fine large town surrounded with hills on a small river. It has been a place of strength in days of yore and has some good buildings and streets, an ancient cathedral and a large marketplace. We were billeted in the country and were well used. 31st, halted and were mustered by the commissary ; found our party numbered between six or seven hundred. We got bread and two francs each and were glad to get this trifle ; it was a relief to many and was the means of keeping some from doing mischief among the country people, for some lawless gangs were making their appearance, although many desperadoes had left in the two divisions that went off without routes.

CHAPTER VIII

THROUGH NORMANDY

1st February, marched to Gisons, an ancient town in Normandy. 2nd, Vernon ; crossed the river Seine over a long stone bridge ; many boats were passing up and down the river. As this town was crowded with troops we were billeted in the country. 3rd, to Paucy. This day we went by a cross country road where, from some high grounds near, we had a view of Paris, with its domes and spires. It was about twelve o'clock and the sun was shining brilliantly upon them. We could trace the river Seine in all its turnings and windings up to the city. With some others I stood for more than an hour looking at a place we might not have an opportunity of seeing again. Others would not stir off the road to have a peep, but jogged on like donkeys, growling out, John Bull fashion, 'D—— Paris and everything in it.'

4th, crossed the country to Evereux. All was in a bustle here : troops on the move, driving shot and shell ; roads much cut up. 5th, passed a palace outside the town near the river, fine trees, ponds of water with fish swimming about : this place I was told formerly belonged to the Duke of Orleans. We crossed the country by a very dirty road ; it rained all day ; I was billeted at a village called Britty on a poor widow who, I believe, treated me better than she could well afford. 6th, to Cochen, a short march, the day being wet. 7th, to Verneuil, an ancient walled town ; it being full of troops we were sent to the country. I was billeted on a jolly blacksmith who used me well. Observing a hole in my shoe he said he would mend it if I took it off. I did so, when for my comfort he spit upon it saying it was bon pour la marche demain for a prisoner of war, many a French soldier had not a shoe to his foot. 8th, on this day's march our party seized a waggon load of bread belonging to a party of

Spaniards.   They gave battle for it but were not able to with-
stand us.   Some of our men had formed themselves into
gangs, and let nothing pass them that could be lifted and we
all got into trouble and disgrace through them.   When we
arrived at Montagne the Spaniards reported our party to the
prefect of the department who called us a lawless banditti.
He stopped our bread and money, called out the National
Guard and gendarmes, and drove us all out of the town.   I
saw about fifty wolves' heads piled up at the gate of the Hotel
de Ville all lately taken in time of snow.   Wolves are plentful
in this wooded country.   9th, reached Bellesme.

10th February to Bonnetable, where I was billeted in a
gentleman's house.   When I told him I came from Edinburgh,
he took me into a room to see his mother, a venerable looking
old lady.   When she learned where I came from she clapped
her hands and called the household to see a man from the
town where all the women went barefoot, for she had been
there long ago when she was a little girl in the time of Prince
Charlie.   I was well entertained in this house.

Some villains of our party got us into trouble again by
plundering ; they were found out and lodged in jail to the
good of us all.

11th to Le Mars where we halted on the 12th.   This is a
well built town with a cathedral and large square.   There were
about 700 British prisoners here from Givet.   I envied them :
they seemed very comfortable while we were doomed to
wander about like vagabonds without a place of rest.   13th,
marched on good roads with trees on each side, to Ecmoy
where I had a good billet on a miller.   Many of the
inhabitants here live in caves hewn out of the solid rock.   The
weather had now changed for the better, warm, with sunshine.
14th, to Chateau du Loire very like an English town, with
flying signs etc. : it is on the main road from Paris to
Bordeaux.

On the 15th we reached Tours, where we thought our
journey was to end and that we were to get into a depot at
last.   But no : this town was full of prisoners of all nations.
We were joined by many of the men who left us at Peronne.
We halted at some stables by the side of the river Loire at
the end of a stone bridge by which you cross into the town
which is large and well built, with broad level streets and a
good looking cathedral.   It stands on a plain in an elbow of
the river, which is very broad here.   We were waited upon by

some of the committee for relieving British prisoners ; they said their funds were done, but gave us six sous per man. A great number of young soldiers passed us in waggons on their way to Paris singing 'Vive, vive, Napolean le Grand.' 16th halted. Although we had heard much of this Tours in Touraine, here we were not to remain, but were ordered to make for Rennes, the capital of Brittany.

We marched on the 17th, in company with Russians, Spaniards, etc. The road was quite covered with us until we came back to Chateau du Loire. I went to my old billet and was made welcome. The French seemed much more kind to the British than to any other prisoners travelling the country, bad as we might be at times. 18th, we left the main road and parted with our faithful allies. Came to Le Lude. 19th, to La Fleche. Here is a grand Military College and Hospital.

The people hereabout do not seem over attached to the present Government and some brigands had donned the White Cockade and taken a party escorting ammunition. They offered some of our men money to join them. I did not see any of them myself, or I should have gone with them if they would have accepted my company for I was weary of this vagrant life. 20th, to Sable. 21st, Melay, fine country billets. 23rd, Laval on the Mayenne a stirring town in the weaving business. It has two old castles. The inhabitants provided shoes for such of our men as were barefoot and were very kind to us. 24th, to Vitre, an ancient walled-in town ; here we were all put into close confinement on account of some bad behaviour on the road.

We reached Rennes on the 25th and found our depot ready for us. It was an old nunnery and a very convenient place it was to be a prison. We were allowed at first to be out all day until many of our men were seen begging in the streets. These miscreants had their prison allowance and had no need except for drink. This caused the liberty to be withdrawn, with the consent of the chiefs of division and all decent men. A great number of prisoners were marched into this province ; many of them were sent to Brest, but the British were never sent near the seaside. At this time the Austrian, Russian, Prussian, Spanish and British prisoners were said to be above 55,000 in this province alone. Yet provisions were plentiful and cheap, two lbs. of bread for three sous, beef five sous per lb., cider three sous per bottle ; but money was very scarce.

The inhabitants were very charitable to many of our men and their goodness was often abused. Some men were taken about the coast trying to make their escape to England and were brought back ; this caused us to be more strictly looked after.

Rennes is a fine large town well built, with good broad streets, squares, etc. Our prison was on the north side of the town on the river Vilaine. About this time our rations were served out very irregularly and we began to suspect all was not right, and some of the military gentlemen looked rather dejected. We wrote to Lord Blaney for money, and signed for a month's pay we never received, for at this critical time any of the gentlemen of the committee who had money would not advance it.

On the 4th April, we were told by some gentlemen of the town, who communicated with us privately, that Paris was taken. On the 8th, one of our men belonging to the 51st regiment, got drunk, and while attempting to climb over the wall was shot through the body by one of the sentinels ; he expired on the spot.

CHAPTER IX

THE WHITE COCKADE !

On the 10th of April, Easter Sunday, an express came in, there was a great bustle in the town and about twelve gentlemen came opposite our prison, donned the White Cockade, pulled out white handkerchiefs and gave three cheers, which we answered by giving three times three. Our guard was immediately doubled ; the military was called out and paraded the streets, and some gentlemen were stabbed and abused by the soldiers. From our top windows we could see what was going on on this side of the town. The quarters of the Commander-in-chief and Prefect of the Department were surrounded by the inhabitants clamouring for information. They were dismissed until 4 o'clock at which time the white flag was hoisted on the steeple of the townhouse amid shouts of ' Vive le Roi ! Vive Louis 18 ! ' while our convent was not a minute behind. We hoisted a white sheet on a pole on the highest part of the building and three hearty cheers were given, while joy beamed on every man's face. The French soldiers were much dismayed. This great change was done in an orderly manner, all things considered.

The gentlemen of the town mounted all the guards and took possession of the Place des armes. The soldiers were ordered to their barracks, except those that chose to hoist the White Cockade, which were very few indeed. Many of them went off and disbanded themselves. The cavalry and artillery took up a position on the other side of the river, opposite the town, and refused to submit until the Royalists sent them word that if they did not go to their barracks, or offered to fire a gun or cross the river, they would arm the British prisoners who would not be slow to attack them. This threat had the desired effect for during the night they withdrew to their former barracks.

In the evening some of our sailors climbed up the steeple of the townhouse and brought down the Imperial eagle, then cut down the Tree of Liberty that stood in the centre of the principal square (and a fine tree it was and had grown well since first planted) and burnt them there. The Royalists were in great triumph and kept patrolling the streets all night, and the military kept strong guard on their own barracks.

On the 11th, the Conscript Act and Les Droits Reunis were abolished by proclamation and beat of drum and all Imperial eagles and other coats of arms belonging to the old Government took flight. Twenty-one guns were fired when the proclamation of the Provisional Government was read. All the officers, civil and military attended, but I could see all this went down ill with the most of them.

We had now liberty to go anywhere we chose during the day, and in general we got home before dark by a kind of natural instinct. On the 14th, orders were posted up printed in English and French stating that as the two countries were now at peace we were to behave to the inhabitants the same as if they were British, and any man guilty of crime was to be lodged in jail and sent prisoner to England ; and as we were now at liberty we were to show ourselves worthy of it and behave like freemen ; and we were to leave our prison and be billeted in the town. Signed by Count Conclaux, commanding for the French, and by Sir William Codrington, baronet, for the British. We gave three cheers on leaving the old convent, where we had been very well treated, but prisoners are never content. Routes were made out for the prisoners of different nations to leave. Three sous a league were given and a good many of the British, after getting their route and their money kept hanging about the town getting their names put down for other divisions, etc. About 1,200 British, lately taken, were encamped outside the town on the Champ de Mars. In this party was Sergeant-major Duncan MacPherson, who had been wounded. I spent a very pleasant day with him. He marched for Morlaix : this and St Malo were where the British were to be embarked. I convoyed him on the road and assisted him with meat and money for which he promised great returns when we got to the regiment. I spent a few days very pleasantly and took long walks into the country. The military and the Royalists became more reconciled to each other and things began to have a more smooth appearance.

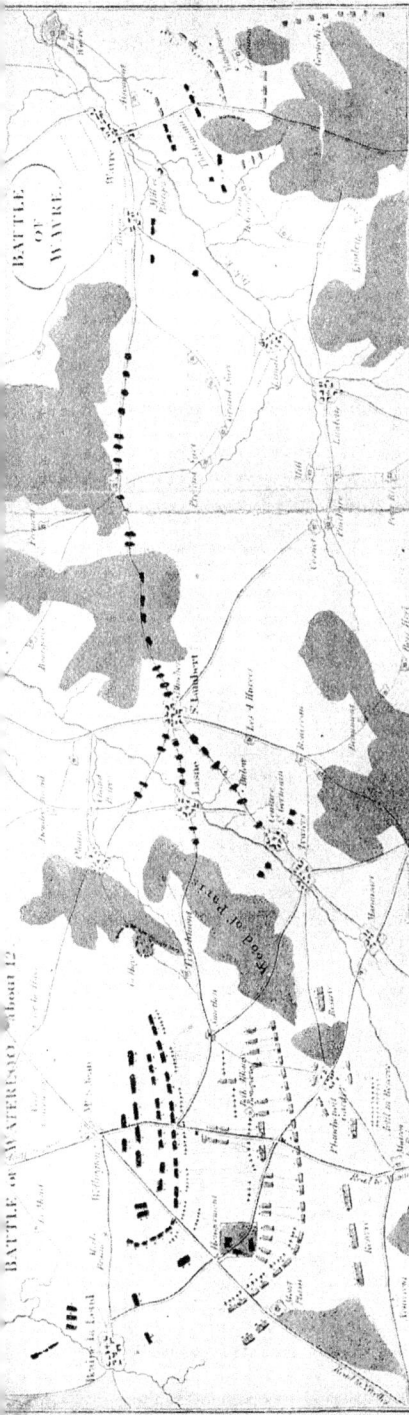

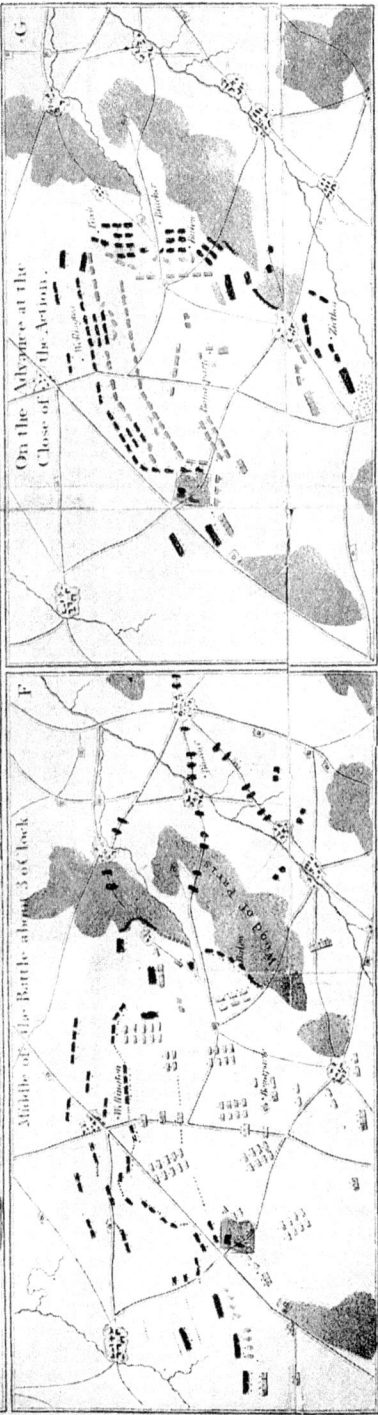

WATERLOO AT 12 O'CLOCK, 3 O'CLOCK, AND AT THE CLOSE OF THE ACTION

On the 27th April I marched with 200 men ; we had a route, but I believe many came with us without one. Came to Ida. 28th, to St Pierre, and never men marched with lighter hearts some laughing and others singing, and 'The Soldier's Return' was often sung with full chorus. 29th, St Maloes, and was very glad to see the salt water again. I had not seen it since I lost sight of the Mediterranean, 31st May 1810. We marched to Fort Servan and got our names entered into the Commandant's books for embarkation. About 1,500 men were in the fort waiting for a passage. 150, the first on the books, went off in the evening in a French gun-brig, and some of our people made interest to get their passage in trading vessels. We looked out with great anxiety for vessels to take us away every tide. The barracks being choke full I sold my old friend my blanket and got a bed in town. Our rations here were one and a half pound of bread, one pound of beef and a pint of cider daily.

This place is strong by nature and art, being a rocky entrance into the bay, in which are several small islands mounted with heavy cannon. The town is surrounded by high walls and batteries and the sea nearly surrounds it at high water. A causeway defended by a strong castle connects it with the town of St Servan. There are some good buildings and shops and a fine quay for the shipping, and ships that have been lying idle for many years are being fitted out with all expedition. Some British vessels have come to this port already with goods and this place bids fair to be a brisk trading town. The dockyard for the navy, victualling offices, etc., are at St Servan ; and a line of battleship and two frigates ready for sea are lying in an arm of the sea in rear of the town, where they have had a long rest.

On Tuesday, the 3rd of May long looked for came at last. Five French gun-brigs arrived crowded with French from Plymouth. When they landed some of them got into a rage, showing us the bad loaves of bread they had got served out to them in England, and it was very abominable stuff. I had no way of parrying this, but by shaking my empty haversack and telling them I was leaving France with no bread at all. On this, a huge grenadier pushed his loaf to my face and said 'Pauvre diable, take that and carry it back to England ; I got it there yesterday.' I took it from his hand but did not eat it, as I never saw a worse compound. While I examined it I certainly thought many a man's case

Q

was worse than our own, and on summing up the matter I found I had little reason to complain of my treatment while a prisoner of war.

On the 4th we got on board and sailed. The wind set against us and all things went wrong with the French sailors ; they brought the vessel to anchor off the Isle of Sark while the other brigs went off for England. Our tars offered the captain to take the vessel into Plymouth but of course this offer was rejected. 5th, got up anchor and made into Jersey. The seamen were taken on board the guardship and the soldiers landed at the pier where General Don and a brigade major received us. Many soldiers gathered round us asking questions about friends and comrades. Captain Corby of the 15th regiment with some noncommissioned officers took charge of this division, and we marched three miles to Groveville barracks on a fine sandy beach not far from Elizabeth Castle. Here we had an opportunity of bathing. We were inspected by a general doctor to see that we were clear and clean of scurvy and itch and other evils that come from France, and the whole party was reported free of any disease whatever. It seemed wonderful to some of the officers that so many men left to the bent of their own inclinations should be so free of disease. But it may be easily explained. Those men, being in the habit of marching every day in their divisions for months together, were more afraid of losing their party than if they had been with their regiments ; while those who had been irregular in any way were not able to be among the first to reach the coast. And strange to many officers as it may appear I have seen nearly 1000 men marching in France under charge of only two gendarmes and no more disorder among those men for weeks together, than I have seen in a regiment marching in Britain under the command of above 100 officers and non-commissioned officers, and these men generally in billets.

We received 1s 1d per day of pay, and got a shirt, shoes and a pair of stockings each. Bread sold at 4d per 1lb here ; how different in France !

This island is strongly fortified all round the coast and the garrison consists of, General Don, Commander-in-chief, Major-General Horton, the 15th and 18th regiments at St Helier ; a veteran battalion in the fort, 2nd battalion 6th and 2nd battalion 66th. The able bodied men in the island form a militia and are drilled every Sunday.

On the 19th we marched at two o'clock in the morning for St Helier. I thought myself lucky in getting on board the gunbrig *Intelligent*, but when we got to sea a French war vessel came bump upon us. This put us all into confusion. The French folks being so long out of practice do not know how to manage their ships. We were obliged to bear off for Guernsey and anchored off the town of St Pierre and reported our case to the Admiral. We asked to be put on board another vessel, but this was refused, so we set about putting things to rights and sailed on the 21st and anchored in Plymouth roads on the 22nd when the King's sailors went on board the *Salvador del Mundo* guardship, formerly a Spanish 4-decker. The merchant sailors were sent into Plymouth, where they got £2 each to take them home, and the soldiers were landed at Mount Wise, and right happy were we all in getting our feet on British ground again. We waited on the Green until the arrival of the Fort-major and other officers, when our names and regiments were taken down; we were marched to the district paymaster's office at Stonehouse, who gave us clothing to the value of 31s. 6d. and we got our pay daily. We were formed into companies of sixty men each with officers and sergeants. Our division was commanded by Major T. Craigie of the Perth Militia, which regiment was doing duty at the Dockyard. All the Germans and Maltese embarked for their own countries; the lame were sent to Chelsea where if I had been a friend to myself I should have gone. We got billets about four o'clock in the afternoon, and I was more tired hanging about this day than if I had marched thirty miles. I was quartered near that infernal den called Castle Ray where every other door is a public house, full of sailors and soldiers, fiddlers and pipers, etc., so that the whole street stank of gin, tobacco, and red herrings.

I visited all the principal works about Plymouth, the Docks, Naval Hospital, Marine Barracks, etc. Nearly all the duty here is done by Militia regiments. All men landed with us whose regiments were in the district, which were the 11th, 20th, and 28th, joined them.

A riot broke out in the town concerning the bakers and millers mixing a white kind of pulverised clay among the flour and selling it to the public. The Mayor seized a ship-load of this stuff in the harbour consigned to some wealthy individuals of the town who had been carrying on this diabolical traffic for a long period. Some of them were lodged in the castle, the jail not being considered a safe place to keep them from the fury of the people.

The French prisoners were all cleared out from this, and the last division came from Dartmoor. On seeing us they exclaimed against our country. But we easily convinced them that we had greater reason to complain for most of us came home in rags, while they were leaving Britain with new clothing and many of them with large sums of money.

I went to a fair at New Passage to see the Cornwall men wrestle with the Devonshire men for purses of money. Many a severe fall was given and some had to be carried out of the ring. Many coaches and gentlemen were here and I believe above half the women of both counties. The Cornishmen carried the day.

The subsequent history of Daniel Nicol may be related in a few words. Having served continuously from 1794 to 1814, he, on the return of Napoleon from Elba, at once volunteered for service and joined a veteran battalion, until on the return of the troops from France, he was again discharged but was offered the rank of sergeant in his old regiment, then lying at Cork. This, however, he declined.

Exceptional interest attends the closing years of Nicol's life. In 1819 he was engaged by Robert Cadell, of the firm of Archibald Constable and Co., the publishers of Sir Walter Scott's novels, in whose publishing-house, he notes, on account of the extraordinary demand for Scott's writings, the work was often very heavy. When misfortune overtook the concern in January 1826, his services were retained by the trustees, and Mr Cadell invited him to remain, as, if he commenced business on his own account, he intended to engage him. Accordingly, in October of that year, when the stock was purchased by Cadell and Co., Nicol was at once employed. He continued in the same service till Mr Cadell's death in 1849, and his trustees subsequently employed him, till in May 1851 the business was purchased by Messrs Adam and Charles Black, to whom the rights of the publication of Scott's novels were transferred. In October 1851, however, Nicol died from inflammation of the lungs at the age of seventy-three, having spent twenty-two years in the army and thirty years in the service of Mr Cadell's firm.

INDEX

INDEX

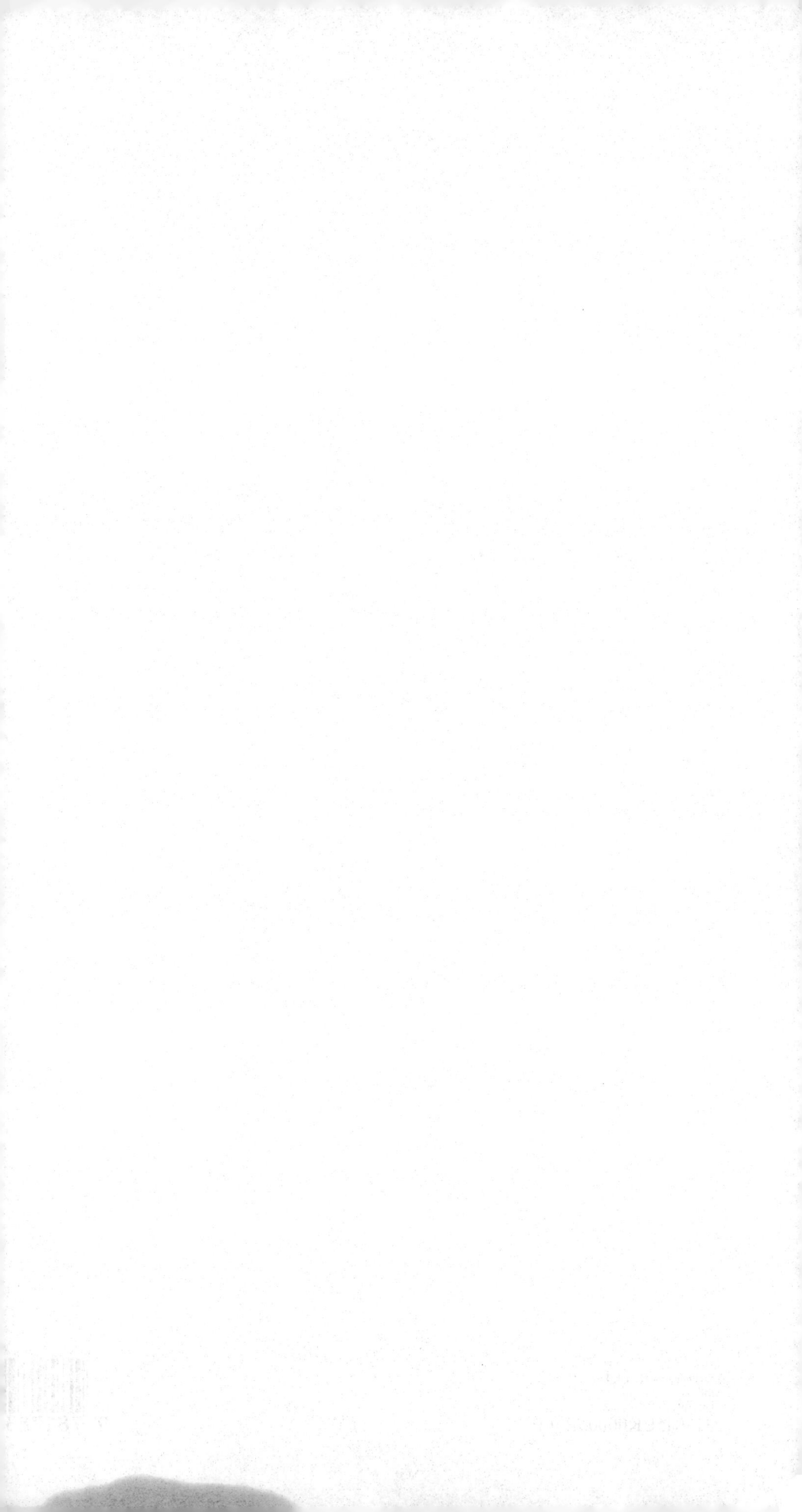

Lightning Source UK Ltd.
Milton Keynes UK
UKOW05f2251290118
317045UK00001B/9/P